SO YOU WANT TO BE IN PICTURES?

A Christian Resource

for 'Making It' in

Hollywood

TED BAEHR

BROADMAN
&HOLMAN
PUBLISHERS

NASHVILLE, TENNESSEE

0-8054-3192-6

Published by Broadman & Holman Publishers,

Nashville, Tennessee

Published in association with the literary agency of Alive Communications,
Inc., 7680 Goddard Street, Suite 200, Colorado Springs, CO 80920.

Dewey Decimal Classification: 791.4

Subject Heading: MASS MEDIA—VOCATIONAL GUIDANCE \
HOLLYWOOD (CA) \ OCCUPATIONS—HOLLYWOOD (CA)

SPECIAL BONUS FOR BOOK OWNERS: For more interviews, articles, features, and updated information, go to http://www.movieguide.org, click on the link
for "So You Want to Be in Pictures," and log in with the password "massmedia."

Unless otherwise noted, all Scripture quotations have been taken from the
Holman Christian Standard Bible, © 2000 by Holman Bible Publishers. Other versions
cited are NIV, the Holy Bible, New International Version, © 1973, 1978, 1984 by
International Bible Society; GNB, Good News Bible: The Bible in Today's English
Version, © American Bible Society 1966, 1971, 1976, used by permission; NKJV, New
King James Version, copyright © 1979, 1980, 1982, Thomas Nelson, Inc., Publishers;
AMP, The Amplified Bible, Old Testament, copyright © 1962, 1964 by Zondervan
Publishing House, used by permission, and the New Testament © The Lockman
Foundation 1954, 1958, 1987, used by permission; and KJV, King James Version.

1 2 3 4 5 6 7 8 9 10 09 08 07 06 05

Do your best to present yourself to God as one approved, a workman who does not need to be ashamed and who correctly handles the word of truth.

2 Timothy 2:15 NIV

Father in heaven,
Thank you for giving us good news to proclaim—the news of new life available to each of us through your Son, Jesus Christ. Thank you for your Holy Spirit, our Teacher. Bless all who read this book. Grant us, as your people, the ability to communicate your truth more effectively to the world through all the media. Help us to reveal your Word to those in need. Help us to lift up your holy name, Jesus, through the power of your Holy Spirit. Amen.

Dedication

With love and great thanksgiving, this book is dedicated to:

My Lord and Savior, Jesus Christ,

And my wonderful wife, Lili, and faithful children, Peirce, Jim, Robby, and Evy.

Also, I want to thank:

Sandra Bell

Penelope Foster

Rick Garside

Len Goss

Beverly Hartz

Carol Jubinski

Claude Lawrence

Chip MacGregor

Ron Maxwell

Korey Pollard

Lisa Rice

David Shepherd

Joel T. Smith

Tom Snyder

Eddie Turner

And all our contributors, directors, supporters, and friends.

Table of Contents

PREFACE

● ● ● ● ● ● ●

Stories and Parables

Jesus told the crowds all these things in parables, and He would not speak anything to them without a parable, so that what was spoken through the prophet might be fulfilled:

I will open My mouth in parables;

I will declare things kept secret

from the foundation of the world.

—Matthew 13:34–35

One day more than seventy years ago, two literary giants in England stood talking about language, stories, and religion.

In the middle of the conversation, the taller gentleman blurted to his slightly balding companion, "Here's my point: Just as a word is an invention about an object or an idea, so a story can be an invention about truth."

"I've loved stories since I was a boy," the other man admitted. "Especially stories about heroism and sacrifice, death and resurrection. But when it comes to Christianity, well, that's another matter. I simply don't understand how the life and death of Someone Else (whoever he was) two thousand years ago can help me here and now."

The first man earnestly replied, "But don't you see, Jack? The Christian story is the greatest story of all. It's the *real* story, the *historical event* that fulfills the tales and shows us what they mean."

About a week later, Jack—also known as C. S. Lewis, the author of the classic books *Mere Christianity* and The Chronicles of Narnia series among many other works—announced his conversion to Christianity to a friend. Lewis attributed much of his decision to his conversation with J. R. R. Tolkien.[1]

Of course Tolkien is the author of one of the greatest books of the twentieth century, *The Lord of the Rings,* which has been transformed into a magnificent movie trilogy by director Peter Jackson. Although Tolkien, a Roman Catholic, didn't always see eye to eye with Lewis, who was more inclined toward Protestantism, they both understood the truth of the ultimate story.

Storytelling and Mythmaking

As Tolkien and Lewis said so long ago, stories matter deeply. They connect us to our personal history and to the history of all time and culture. Human beings are meaning-seekers and meaning-makers. We strive to connect ourselves to our experiences and to the experiences of others. We are addicted to those "aha" moments in our lives when we see meaning, purpose, and significance.

Stories help us do this. They bring us laughter, tears, and joy. They stimulate our minds and stir our imaginations. Stories help us escape our daily lives for a while and visit different times, places, and people. They can arouse our compassion and empathy, spur us toward truth and love, or sometimes even incite us toward hatred or violence.

Different kinds of stories satisfy different needs. For example, a comedy evokes a different response from us than a tragedy. A hard news story on page 1 affects us differently than a human interest story in the magazine section or a celebrity profile next to the movie or television listings. While different kinds of stories satisfy different needs, many stories share common themes, settings, character types, situations, and other recurrent archetypal patterns. They may even possess a timeless universal quality.

Many stories focus on one individual, a heroic figure who overcomes many trials and tribulations to defeat evil or to attain a valuable goal. We identify with such heroes because we recognize that we are each on our own journey or quest. How a hero's journey informs and illuminates our own journey is significant. We look for answers in stories.

However, every story has a worldview, a way of viewing reality, truth, the universe, the human condition, and the supernatural world. Looking carefully at a story, we can examine the motifs, meanings, values, and principles it suggests. For example, a story can have a redemptive Christian worldview that shows people their need for salvation through a personal faith in the gospel of Jesus Christ, or it can have a secular, humanist worldview that explicitly or implicitly attacks Christianity. By examining a story's worldview, we can determine the cultural ideals and the moral, philosophical, social, psychological, spiritual, and aesthetic messages the story conveys, as well as determine the emotions the story evokes.

Movies and television programs are the storytelling media of our age!

So You Want to Be in Pictures?

Whether or not you want to be in pictures or just watch them or even just complain about them, almost everyone is interested in the mass media of entertainment. *So You Want to Be in Pictures?* tells you what you need to know about telling stories through the mass media of entertainment, how to use your faith to change the culture of Hollywood and the mass media of entertainment, and how to make a creative contribution to the whole world. This book will show you how to develop your screenwriting, acting, directing, producing, behind-the-scenes interests, and critical skills to make Hollywood and the world better places for our children and grandchildren.

In the original draft of *So You Want to Be in Pictures?* most of the chapters contained articles by some of the best and brightest in the entertainment industry who shared their secrets of how to make a great blockbuster movie or hit television program. The contributors list is impressive, covering stellar people who are highly successful: series creators, writers, directors, producers, animators, studio executives, actors, and a television network owner. Each contributor addresses an important part of the entertainment industry, including development, agency, writing, finance, production, and distribution. Each contributor shares his or her keys and secrets to success. When appropriate the contributor shares his or her faith and spiritual insights from a Christian perspective.

So that this valuable information is not lost, we are publishing these important articles in *MOVIEGUIDE®* and then in a special section in the members-only area of the www.movieguide.org Web site. If you contact us with proof of purchase of this book, you will receive one month of access to the Web site.

The contributors you will read about in *MOVIEGUIDE®* include:

- Donzaleigh Abernathy, actress in *Gods and Generals, Stranger in My House, Camp Nowhere,* and many other movies and television programs
- Pat Boone, star, celebrity, and singer
- Morgan Brittany, star of many movies and television programs, including *Dallas, The Saint,* and *Melrose Place*
- Stephen Collins, star of many movies and television programs, including *7th Heaven, Star Trek: The Motion Picture,* and *All the President's Men*
- Richard Cook, chairman of Walt Disney Pictures
- Peter Engel, producer of *Last Comic Standing; All about Us; Malibu, CA; City Guys; USA High; Hang Time,* and the famous *Saved by the Bell*
- Bill Ewing, former executive vice president of Columbia Pictures
- Bill Fay, executive producer of many movies, including *Independence Day* and *The Patriot*
- Penelope Foster, coproducer of many movies, including *Operation Dumbo Drop, Free Willy,* and *Rosewood*
- Don Hahn, producer of many movies, including *The Lion King, Beauty and the Beast,* and *The Hunchback of Notre Dame*
- Brenda Hampton, writer of many television programs, including *Love Boat, Safe Harbor,* and *7th Heaven* (creator and executive producer)
- Bruce Johnson, president of Porchlight Entertainment
- Dave, Gary, and Joan Johnson, writers and producers of many television programs, including *Against the Grain, Doc,* and *Sue Thomas: F. B. Eye*

- Al Kasha, Academy Award-winning songwriter and composer for many movies and television programs, including *The Poseidon Adventure, The Towering Inferno,* and *Rugrats Go Wild!*
- Paul Lauer, director of Icon Pictures marketing for *The Passion of the Christ*
- Ron Maxwell, writer and director of many movies, including *Parent Trap II, Little Darlings, Gettysburg,* and *Gods and Generals*
- Brad Moore, president of Hallmark Hall of Fame
- Jim Muro, director of photography and cinematographer for many movies and television programs, including *Open Range* and *Crash*
- Dan Nichols, producer of many movies, including *Raiders of the Lost Ark* and *Always*
- Bud Paxson, owner of PaxTV
- John Ratzenberger, a voice in every Pixar movie, star of the hit TV show *Cheers,* and producer of *Made in America*
- Barry Reardon, former president of distribution for Warner Bros.
- Phil Roman, executive producer of *Garfield, Tom and Jerry,* and *The Simpsons*
- Jane Russell, movie star
- Linda Seger, script doctor and author of many books, including *How to Make a Good Script Great, Creating Unforgettable Characters, The Art of Adaptation, From Script to Screen,* and *Advanced Screenwriting*
- Clifton Taulbert, novelist, producer, and screenwriter for *Once upon a Time When We Were Colored*
- Bob Tessier, theatrical film buyer for Regal Theaters
- Andrew Stanton, scriptwriter for *Toy Story, Toy Story 2, A Bug's Life, Monster's, Inc.,* and *Finding Nemo,* which he also directed and produced
- Chuck Viane, president of Walt Disney Company's Buena Vista Film Distribution Group
- Randall Wallace, the writer of many movies, including *Braveheart, Pearl Harbor,* and *We Were Soldiers,* which he also directed and produced

- Frank Yablans, former president of Paramount Pictures

These renowned contributors have many Christian virtues in common:

1. The common factor among these Hollywood believers is their incredible humility. They deflect praise, giving God the glory and their teammates the honor.

2. Most of these are nonjudgmental, careful-to-be-wise Christians walking a fine line of wisdom about sharing their faith without being too preachy. Many mentioned the fact that they do not like heavy-handed preachiness in a movie; but rather they value stories, parables, and allegories as the way to inspire the heart.

3. Most are clear about being believers. They are the real deal, set against a dark, New Age background.

4. Several spoke about the "opposites" in the Bible: the last shall be first; you have to go down to go up (humbled to be exalted); make less of yourself and exalt Jesus, who will draw all men unto himself.

5. Many of those on the business end of things talked about the value of the team, while the writers were dramatic and inspirational, including quotes and parables.

6. These people are at all different levels of spiritual growth and development—some deep and poetic, some scriptural and matter-of-fact, others staying in the more shallow waters of the faith, happy to be camping on the level of salvation. Don't judge these leaders on their spirituality or expect things of them that only the Holy Spirit can accomplish, which he often does over the course of time.

7. These are people, real people! We caught them running children to school in carpools, talking to their mothers on the other lines, gardening, and cleaning house. Some were on the set on location, doing impressive things with expensive equipment, but they were vulnerable, down-to-earth folks, for the most part.

So You Want to Be in Pictures? will help you answer:

- How do you communicate through the mass media of entertainment?

- What do you want to communicate?
- Why do you want to communicate?
- To whom do you want to communicate?
- What are your gifts and talents?
- Who is your audience?
- What are you communicating?
- What medium should you use?
- How do you develop an idea?
- How do you write a script?
- How do you find an agent?
- How do you find financing?
- How do you get distribution?
- What do you want to know about production?
- What about television?
- What about movies?
- What does God want you to communicate?

So You Want to Be in Pictures? shows you how to go from treatment to theatrical release so you can get the word/gospel out through the mass media of entertainment. Every chapter also includes valuable information about the key principles of communicating through movies and television programs from a Christian perspective. This book also deals with the opportunities as well as the trials and tribulations Christians face in the mass media, and how to develop your craft to be more than conquerors in the entertainment industry. Moreover, this book helps you understand the entertainment industry and helps you and others with stars in their eyes not stoop to conquer.

In this regard, our article with Pat Boone provides some timely cautions. Please read it in *MOVIEGUIDE®* or on www.movieguide.org.

So, What's It All About?

The primary teachers of our children are the mass media of entertainment. The average child sees forty thousand hours of media by the age of seventeen, compared to eleven thousand hours in school, two thousand with parents, and eight hundred hours in church if they go for an hour every Sunday.

As a result, our children have lost contact with the values and faith of their forefathers. The number of children familiar with the Bible has gone from 70 percent in 1950 to 4 percent in 2001. Without moral guidelines, children are facing an epidemic proportion of sexually transmitted diseases and other physical and psychological problems.

Therefore, it is critical that people of faith and values become the best communicators through the mass media of entertainment. The New Testament uses five Greek words that we translate as "preaching" in English. The most common word is *kerysso,* which Jesus uses 63 percent of the time. It means to go into the marketplace to proclaim or herald the good news of the gospel. *So You Want to Be in Pictures?* intends to help you do just what Jesus commanded—herald his good news in movies and television.

CHAPTER 1

There's No Business like Show Business

A growing number of Christians these days have stars in their eyes either because they spend too much time watching the current crop of celebrities on television or on the silver screen or because they have visions of receiving their own star on Hollywood Boulevard for producing some great movie or television program that will communicate the truth. Thirty years ago there was a suspicion of the entertainment industry in the church, now there is a keen interest in the mass media of entertainment. A surprising number of people in my audiences come up to me after my lectures or sermons to tell me that they want to make movies or they have a family member who has gone to Hollywood to seek fame and fortune.

The church has discovered Hollywood. Perhaps, more importantly, Hollywood has discovered the church. As a result, the major movie studios today hire Christian publicists to market movies to the 135 million to 165 million people who go to church every week. They write Bible study materials to complement a particular movie for church use. Considering that the average movie audience per week is only 17 million to 29 million, the church is the largest demographic group in the United States and has the potential to make a film a blockbuster, earning more than $100 million (i.e., *The Lord of the Rings* and *The Passion of the Christ*). Of course, not all the movies being marketed to the church are theologically or morally sound, but at least

1

the church is being sought after, and many good movies deserve the support of the Christian marketplace. When Hollywood markets a movie, it is up to the church to be discerning and make wise decisions by choosing the good and rejecting the bad.

The purpose of this chapter is to explore how the church and culture, especially as reflected in the mass media of entertainment, have historically interacted with each other and how we as Christians can use our gifts and talents to communicate effectively to God's glory through this powerful medium.

The Church and Culture

Over the past 20 years we have seen the nation's theological views slowly become less aligned with the Bible. Americans still revere the Bible and like to think of themselves as Bible-believing people, but the evidence suggests otherwise. Christians have increasingly been adopting spiritual views that come from Islam, Wicca, secular humanism, the Eastern religions and other sources. Because we remain a largely Bible-illiterate society, few are alarmed or even aware of the slide toward syncretism—a belief system that blindly combines beliefs from many different faith perspectives. (George Barna, Barna Research Group, "Americans Draw Theological Beliefs from Diverse Points of View," The Barna Update, 8 October 2002)

In the past the church shaped Western civilization, otherwise known as Christendom, with an aim to heal the sick, feed the hungry, clothe the poor, and create art to worship a just and loving Creator who gave form and function to reality. Now our culture is shaped by the mass media of entertainment. The results are confusion at best and the vilest paganism at worst.

The Barna survey quoted above also shows that a shockingly large number of Americans believe that when Jesus Christ was on earth, he committed sins, which would mean that his death on the cross could not have been a sinless offering. Sadly, most of those who contend that Jesus sinned are under thirty-eight years of age, the generation impacted by the Supreme

Court's crazed, unconstitutional decision to remove prayer and faith from the public classroom.

If Jesus is no longer a sufficient sacrifice for our sins, then it is no wonder that almost half the population believes that deliverance from eternal condemnation for one's sins is earned rather than received as a free gift from God through Jesus' death and resurrection. Thus, half of all adults argue that anyone who "is generally good or does enough good things for others during their life will earn a place in Heaven."[1]

In reality, everyday human relationships illustrate the biblical truth that no one is righteous. Therefore, it is not surprising, though it is heartbreaking, that 40 percent of all adults, especially younger adults, hold the confused belief that "the Bible, the Koran and the Book of Mormon are all different expressions of the same spiritual truths."[2] Of course, if they bother to read these books, they will find that each claims a unique way of salvation that excludes every other way. A large majority of both adults and teenagers contend that there is no absolute moral truth and that truth is always relative to the individual and the circumstances. This relativism provides a valid, if heinous, argument for those who argue that nothing is wrong per se, including abortion, suicide, and euthanasia. The common rubric seems to be: "It's just a matter of opinion."

Nice Is Not Good Enough

This moral relativism may be the reason the antihero in movies has become so prominent that people are now actually considering the antihero as somehow "good." For instance, the protagonists in *Ocean's 11,* starring George Clooney, Brad Pitt, and the rest of the new rat pack are nice, but clearly they are not good. They lie, they cheat, and, of course, they steal. They are the heroes, and we are apparently supposed to root for them.

This theology of relativism is also creeping into the church. In the United States we are experiencing an unprecedented 22-percent decline of Christianity among children and teenagers (a personal observation by George Barna). Good News Publishers has noted that fifty years ago 70 percent of children had heard the gospel and were familiar with the Bible.

Today that number is just 4 percent. As in other countries where the church has collapsed, many in the believing evangelical church are grasping at straws and forming alliances with strange non-Christian bedfellows to try to slow the fall.

These nonbelievers are nice people who often preach a legalistic theology of works and even seem conservative. In a way these non-Christian, conservative leaders are unconsciously guarding the adversary's right flank, just as the anti-Christian liberal leaders were guarding the left flank in the era of the social gospel. Neither lawlessness nor legalism will cure our culture's ills.

As Paul writes in Ephesians 4:1–32, God does not want us to live as the godless pagans do, in the futility and darkness of their thinking. Instead, we must live a worthy life and gently, humbly, patiently, lovingly make every effort to keep the unity of the Holy Spirit through peace. There is to be only one faith, one Lord and one God, who has given each person his measure of divine grace as Jesus the Christ has apportioned it. Jesus prepares God's people for works of service "to build up the body of Christ, until we all reach unity in the faith and in the knowledge of God's Son, [growing] into a mature man with a stature measured by Christ's fullness. Then we will no longer be little children, tossed by the waves and blown around by every wind of teaching, by human cunning with cleverness in the techniques of deceit. But speaking the truth in love, let us grow in every way into Him who is the head—Christ. From Him the whole body, fitted and knit together by every supporting ligament, promotes the growth of the body for building up itself in love by the proper working of each individual part" (Eph. 4:12–16).

It is not possible to do any of this if we listen to people, no matter how well intentioned and smart, who do not know Jesus Christ or who practice a theology of relativism. "Since you put away lying," Paul writes in Ephesians 4:25 and 5:1–2, "speak the truth, each one to his neighbor, because we are members of one another. . . . Therefore, be imitators of God, as dearly loved children. And walk in love, as the Messiah also loved us and gave Himself for us, a sacrificial and fragrant offering to God." Furthermore, Paul writes in Ephesians 5:6–10, "Let no one deceive you with empty arguments, for because of these things God's wrath is coming on the disobedient. Therefore, do not become their partners. For you were once darkness, but now [you are] light in the Lord. Walk as children of light—for the fruit of the light [results] in all goodness, righteousness, and truth—discerning what is pleasing to the Lord."

Are There Limits to Tolerance?

It is understandable why the mass media place a premium on tolerance, given the increasingly diverse culture in which we live. While some of this tolerance is aimed at diluting the influence of Christians in our culture, most is born out of trying to reach the entire demographic range in the United States.

However, in stark contrast to the media's obeisance to tolerance, the late intellectual and humorist Steve Allen spoke on this important topic at the National Religious Broadcasters meeting at my invitation. Since his wife was a committed Christian, Steve decided to tackle this difficult topic, even though he himself claimed to be an atheist who read the Bible every day.

Steve waxed eloquent on the subject of tolerance and explained why intolerance was sometimes the only option. He asked the audience, if you were a Jew and came upon a burning bush where it was clear that God himself was speaking to you, and the event was so frightening that you fell on your face before him, and God told you he is a jealous God who would have no other gods before him and told you exactly what judgment you faced if you refused to obey him, what would you do? Steve concluded that you would obey the awesome Almighty Creator God whom you just met in person, and you would forever after be intolerant of other gods. In other words, the divine distinctives of Judaism, as well as Christianity, often compel intolerance if you believe that your faith comes directly from the Almighty.

Yes, intolerance to relativism is appropriate. It is not just a matter of opinion. There is an absolute truth that sets us free.

Seek Wisdom, Knowledge, and Understanding

The church needs to be discerning in order to prevent Hollywood's manipulation. In this regard the church has always had five different perspectives toward culture, with one or another perspective in the ascendancy. Each of these perspectives can be proof-texted with the appropriate Bible verses that support a particular position, but none of them can be shown to be the correct reading to the exclusion of the others. So none of them is creedal or a measure of orthodoxy.

Yale theologian H. Richard Niebuhr first distinguished between the five approaches Christians have historically taken with regard to their world in his book *Christ and Culture*.[3] His distinctions have been modified and clarified for the purposes of this book.

The first position could be called "retreat from culture," though Niebuhr calls it "Christ against Culture." The Mennonite and Amish communities are the obvious examples of this tradition, and the monastic tradition in the church. While there are rich traditions of service within these groups, the world is viewed as a place from which to escape into communities of "separated brethren." The Schleitheim Confession of the Anabaptists (1527) argued: "Since all who do not walk in the obedience of faith are a great abomination before God, it is not possible for anything to grow or issue from them except abominable things. God further admonishes us to withdraw from Babylon and the earthly Egypt that we may not be partakers of the pain and suffering which the Lord will bring upon them."

The second perspective, which Niebuhr calls "The Christ of Culture," tends to equate creation and redemption and can be seen in those groups that identify Christ with utopian socialism as well as those who identify Christ with American culture. Those who follow this tradition hail Jesus as the Messiah of their society, the fulfiller of its hopes and aspirations, the perfecter of its true faith, the source of its holiest spirit. For these people there is hardly any difference between Christ and the culture. These adherents view Christ as the moral example who points us to a perfect society.

The third approach, which Niebuhr calls "Christ above Culture," is occupied by the centrists who live within the world though they are not of the world. These centrists refuse to take either the position of the anti-cultural radicals or of the accommodators of Christ to culture.

The fourth tradition is "Christ and Culture in Paradox," which refuses either to reject culture or to confuse culture with Christianity. They see these as two different realms, not two antagonistic realms. In creation God gives us work, service, pleasure, government, and family. In redemption he gives us the church, the Word, and the sacraments. The Christian who follows the "Christ and Culture in Paradox" tradition participates in culture but not as a means of grace. Rather, it is an aspect of being human, not merely of being Christian.

The final category is "Christ the Transformer of Culture," which emphasizes God's lordship over all of creation and all aspects of life. Niebuhr appeals to John's Gospel as an example of this approach. Here Christ is "the Word made flesh," not only the priest of redemption but also the king of creation. This tradition, which is represented by Augustine and Calvin, takes the world seriously and contends that Christians have the potential not only to exercise leadership in the culture but to present the gospel as well. God loves the world, not just individuals in it (Rom. 8:20–23). Those of the "Christ Transforming Culture" tradition would view culture as a distinct, though related, part of Christ's universal reign. While creating a movie, building a house, and raising a family may not be the redemptive activities of the kingdom of God, they are important activities to which Christians realize a call because they are commanded by the universal Lord in the "cultural mandate" of the early chapters of Genesis. Though human activity can never bring salvation, the activity of Christian men and women does bring a certain transforming element as they live out their callings in distinction and honor, serving both to attract non-Christians to the gospel and to bring civil righteousness, justice, and compassion to bear on human relationships.

The church has historically moved through a cycle from one point of view to another. During the middle of the twentieth century, the church retreated from culture. Then the church took up the battle cry of cultural warfare to resist the moral decay in our society. Now the church is beginning to move out as ambassadors for Jesus Christ to redeem the culture.

Whatever cultural position you, your local church, or your denomination adopts, we are called to develop the discernment to know right from wrong, the wisdom to choose the right, the knowledge to pursue the right, and the understanding to persevere.

"For God has not given us a spirit of fearfulness, but one of power, love, and sound judgment" (2 Tim. 1:7).

Can Entertainment Be Holy?

The church has had a love/hate relationship with art, music, and drama for centuries. Although modern drama as we know it was invented by the church in the Middle Ages to help the illiterate populace understand the gospel, the mystery or miracle plays, as these Christian dramas were known, quickly became suspect, especially in the eyes of clergy who felt that these dramas were overshadowing their sermons. Therefore, Pope Innocent III outlawed drama, and the dramatists whose creative abilities and desires were a gift from God went into the alleys and the beer halls to exercise their God-given gifts in not-so-God-ordained ways.

A similar scenario has happened many times throughout history. Respected Roman Catholic theologian and scholar Michael Jones blames the growth of Protestantism on the willingness of the Protestants to use the newfangled printing press to print Bibles while the Catholic Church rejected the new technology of communication in the fifteenth century. Centuries later, at the beginning of the use of moving pictures, a Catholic cardinal in Paris was shocked by movies on the life and passion of Jesus Christ being shown in the Cathedral of Notre Dame and banned film from the church, thus turning the new medium over to the very people who were most opposed to the church. Edison tried to give the rights to the motion picture technology to his Christian denomination, but they rejected it. The first broadcast radio station was located in a church in Pittsburgh, but the rector of the church demanded that the younger associate have nothing to do with it and shut it down.

The other side of this love/hate relationship between the entertainment industry and the church is chronicled by Terry Lindvall, former distinguished chair of visual communication and professor of film at Regent University, in his book *The Silents of God*. This book begins with the historic Chautauqua Tabernacle's showing of a motion picture on June 22, 1900, and then moves on to discuss how many theatrical movies up to 1920 were shown in churches. This practice stopped when theater owners told the movie companies that they would not play their movies if they were also shown in churches. Covering the historical period from 1908 to 1925, this study showcases pamphlets, magazine articles from both religious and film periodicals, sermons, and other discourse that chronicle an early vision of church/photoplay cooperation and its subsequent dissolution with the advent of growing suspicion, Hollywood scandals, sabbatical reform movements, and alternative communication technologies. This collection of documents challenges the enduring fiction that the church was hostile to the moving picture at its inception; rather, the church sought to appropriate its potential for evangelism, education, social reform, and inspiration.

Proclaiming in the Marketplace

With regard to the love/hate relationship between the church and the new technologies of communication and art, there are five Greek words that are translated by the English word *preaching* in the New Testament. Sixty-three percent of the time, Jesus uses the Greek word *kerysso*, related to *kerygma*, which means "to proclaim or herald in the marketplace." The word *kerysso* was relevant to the people to whom Jesus was talking because they were familiar with the Roman heralds who ran into the marketplace every morning and shouted out the news of the emperor to the buyers and sellers.

Thus, Jesus Christ has always commanded his people to go into the marketplace of ideas to herald the good news. When Christians do so, as in the Protestant Reformation and the evangelization of South Korea, the church grows and prospers. When Christians fail to go into the marketplace, the church shrinks in size and suffers.

The Christian Worldview of Art and Communications

Several years ago I cochaired an art and communications committee of several prominent theologians for the Coalition on Revival to set forth *The Christian World View of Art and Communication*.[4] We had a belief in the need for Christians to move and have influence in the mass media of entertainment. Our dialogue produced a concrete vision of what was foundationally required to do that. The following are basic principles upon which a relationship between the arts and a Christian worldview is based:

1. "In the beginning God created" and "in the beginning was the Word." God is the Author of creation and communication. As the supreme Creator and Communicator, he is the Source of art and communication.

2. God has given all authority in heaven and on earth to his Son, Jesus Christ. Since Jesus Christ is entitled to have lordship over all areas of life, Christians must bring all art and communication under his authority.

3. Art and communication are part of God's created order. They cannot be labeled Christian or un-Christian. However, they can be used for good or evil.

4. Art and communication are neither synonymous nor mutually exclusive functions in God's economy. Communication is the act of sharing thoughts, ideas, information, and needs. The arts, whether or not they communicate, are expressions of God's creativity manifested through man.

5. Man, created in the image of God, has the capacity to create and communicate. Therefore, all artistic endeavor and communication involves more than technical skills. Their intended purpose is to glorify God. To accomplish this, all art and communication must be brought into captivity to the mind of Christ.

6. Christ is the standard of excellence. "Whatever you do, work at it with all your heart, as working for the Lord, not for men" (Col. 3:23 NIV). Within the framework of that excellence, art and communication should reflect the highest quality of creative work possible given the resources available. Since all abilities are God given, we can achieve excellence when we submit them

to the lordship of Jesus Christ and the guidance of God. This guidance comes from communication with God through prayer, study of his written Word, and other biblical disciplines vital to being a Christian.

7. Art and communication have a great influence on society in shaping man's view of reality. A career in these fields should be considered a worthy vocation. To achieve such a career, Christians should discern and develop their God-given talents.

8. It is legitimate for Christians to engage in art and communication without the need to include overt Christian symbolism or content. A Christian may participate in any area of art and communication as long as he submits himself to the lordship of Jesus Christ in accordance with his written Word, and acts in the conviction of faith, for "without faith it is impossible to please God" (Heb. 11:6).

Theology of Art

Up until the twentieth century, there was an active theology of art and beauty that placed God the Holy Spirit as the guiding influence in the arts and communication media. However, the reaction to modern secularism produced a retreat from culture within the church. The church is emerging from this retreat but in the process has regrettably lost many of its common symbols and modes of art and communication. Therefore, to a large degree, sacramental and incarnational modes of communication and art are often misunderstood by the contemporary church, which often simply proclaims the milk of the gospel as noted in Hebrews 5 and stops before getting to the meat of Hebrews 6. Some Christian colleges and schools have created either/or theories of art and communication and have neglected to note the both/and of the gospel, which involves Jesus Christ who was both God and man. These theories diminish the biblical view of art and communications.

Traditionally, there are four philosophies of art. Plato said that art represented the ideal. Aristotle reacted to Plato and considered art in a materialistic context as something that was: not useful (if it was useful, it was an artifact or craft), made by man, and contrary to nature. The Roman

Horace tried to syncretize the two Greek philosophers and defined art as something to delight and inform. The Bible emphasizes that art should concern the true, the good, and the beautiful.

As a result of the materialism of the modern culture that has followed the philosophies of four dead men (Marx, Darwin, Dewey, and Freud), the last fifty years have been primarily Aristotlean in that art has been too often defined as anything contrary to nature or pushing the envelope. In this view, if one movie features female nudity from the waist up, the next has to feature full frontal female nudity, and the next has to have frontal male nudity.

Hollywood's "Theology" of Art

In the last half-century, a new aristocracy has emerged, and the entertainer, whether an athlete, star, or news announcer, has become the new upper class. Not only do these Hollywood idols and their compatriots make incredible salaries (Michael Eisner earned more than $350 million in stock options one year; several Hollywood and sports stars earned more than $20 million; and the major television news anchors earned more than $5 million), but they also wield incredible power in every area of life by shaping the thoughts, dreams, and concerns of our culture. As actress Susan Sarandon has so aptly pointed out, movie stars are dangerous because "we are the keepers of the dreams."

The reason we have this new aristocracy is that we have become wealthy beyond our wildest expectations as a result of our American inheritance, and in the process we have turned away from the true joy of residing in God's grace in order to seek amusement in the world, the flesh, and the devil. In the process of our precipitous backsliding, a few in the entertainment industry have seized the opportunity of our addiction to pleasure to bamboozle a willing populace into misinterpreting the First Amendment to read that everything from pedophilia to pornography is "protected speech," except, of course, Christian speech. The reason these entertainment companies spend millions of dollars to stretch the notion of "protected speech" beyond any reasonable intent of the framers of the Constitution is to protect their profits from the sale of salacious pornography and extreme violence to vulnerable adolescents, children, and adults.

This new media aristocracy has developed its own form of noblesse oblige by selling us on the idea that the government should cover the cost of all social largess. They have reinterpreted sin to mean politically incorrect speech and have carefully removed any onus from the family-destroying sins of adultery and sodomy. As U.S. linguist and political analyst Noam Chomsky has said, "The United States is unusual among the industrial democracies in the rigidity of the system of ideological control—'indoctrination,' we might say—exercised through the mass media."[5]

The importance of this new elite demands the attention of the church. Please pray for the men who hold responsible positions of extreme national and international importance within the mass media of entertainment.

Jesus in the Movies

There is widespread confusion about what is a Christian movie. Since the beginning of the motion picture business, there have been Christians making movies about Jesus Christ, as well as the movie industry making movies with a Christian worldview and theology. In addition, Christians have made movies to disciple, instruct, and inform the church, including many missionaries who made movies to tell their mission stories to their supporters at home and abroad. Both the movies for the church and the movies for theatrical release are worthwhile, even though many people decry the movies for the church—which are usually produced on a small budget with limited resources—and bemoan the fact that Christians do not make Hollywood movies. However, many Christians do make Hollywood movies, some of the most successful movies and television programs, and you will hear from some of the best in these pages.

This two-tiered system in the church reflects the rest of the filmmaking community. Educational movies are not derided because they are not Hollywood big-budget, star-studded movies, nor are industrial or medical films. The educational community needs educational films, and the church needs discipling, training, and worship media, even though these movies and videos are not as expensive or slick as Hollywood movies.

Furthermore, from the beginning of the movie industry, before Mel Gibson's *The Passion of the Christ,* there were many movies featuring Jesus. Some outstanding movies about Jesus Christ are:

1897: *The Passion Play* was produced by American theatrical producers Marc Klaw and Abraham Erlanger in Horitz, Bohemia.

1898: *The Passion Play,* produced by R. G. Hollaman and A. G. Eaves, was photographed on the roof of a New York skyscraper. The length of the film is twenty-one hundred feet or about twenty minutes. A narrator takes the place of captions.

Oberammergau Passion Play was photographed by Mr. Hurd, Lumiere's American representative.

French Passion Play was produced for the Musee Eden.

1902–1906: *The Passion Play,* produced by Ferdinand Zecca, was two thousand feet in length. It uses panning shots, an innovation at the time.

Another *Passion Play,* produced by V. Jasset and Alice Guy, reproduced Golgotha at Fontainebleau and used a gramophone to help the actors convey their emotions. This may be the earliest use of an artificial aid.

1908: *The Life of Christ,* produced in color by Pathe in 1914, was expanded to seven reels. In 1921, a modern prologue was added.

Ben Hur was directed by Sidney Olcott and stars William S. Hart. Kalem was the production company.

1909: *The Kiss of Judas, The Birth of Jesus* was a French production, and *The Star of Bethlehem* was produced by Thomas A. Edison.

1911: *Though Your Sins Be as Scarlet,* a Vitagraph production, stars Charles Kent as Jesus Christ and Julia Swayne Gordon as Mary Magdalene.

Satan, or the Drama of Humanity is a four-part Italian spectacle from Ambrosio, directed by Luigi Maggi. The second episode features the life of Jesus Christ.

From the Manger to the Cross was the first major film depicting the life of Jesus from his infancy to his death on the cross. It was directed by Sidney Olcott for Kalem, the production company. The film was shot on location in Egypt and Palestine. *The Way of the Cross* was filmed on the actual Via Dolorosa in Jerusalem.

1916: In *Intolerance,* D. W. Griffith uses four stories to define intolerance: the Judean story, which presents a small portion of the life of Jesus of Nazareth and avoids the resurrection; the medieval story, which was a dramatization of the war between Catholics and Huguenots in sixteenth-century France; the fall of Babylon, which is a memorable epic of the ancient world; and the modern story, which is a dramatic conflict between capital and labor.

Christus was a large-scale production from the Italian Cines company, directed by Guilo Antomoro. Giovanni Pasquali plays Jesus.

Hollywood veteran Thomas Ince cast George Fisher in the role of Jesus Christ in *Civilization.* Ince employs allegory in this tale of the super-natural to show that all war is evil.

1923: *I.N.R.I.* tells about a convicted murderer who hears the life of Christ as told by the chaplain. The recounted scenes are enacted in the form of a passion play wherein Gregor Chmara plays Jesus Christ. As a result of hearing the story, the murderer repents.

1926: *Ben Hur* was directed by Fred Niblo for MGM (Metro-Goldwyn-Mayer).

1927: The famous H. B. Warner plays Jesus in Cecil B. DeMille's *King of Kings,* still the classic of all movies about Jesus Christ. Produced by Pathé Exchange, Inc., this was the most famous, the most discussed, and the cost-liest religious movie made up to that point and was used for many years by missionaries to evangelize.

1934: Written and directed by Julien Duvivier for Film Union, *Golgotha* was the first Passion to be made in sound. Robert le Vigan plays Jesus Christ, and the renowned Jean Gabin plays Pontius Pilate. Since it is a Passion, the movie covers only the events of Holy Week.

Oberammergau Passion Play was filmed again as a silent movie.

1951: *Quo Vadis* is one of those incredibly pro-Christian, biblical epics that it is hard to imagine Hollywood producing. Directed by Mervyn Le Roy for MGM, this exquisite movie clearly shows the redemptive power of the gospel of Jesus Christ transforming the evil world system of man.

1952: Robert S. Flaherty made the *St. Matthew Passion* based on the choral work by J. S. Bach.

1953: Directed by Henry Koster for 20th Century Fox, *The Robe* is utterly inspirational. Starring Richard Burton, Jean Simmons, and Victor Mature, this Hollywood classic is the story of a Roman slave, who turns to Christianity after embracing the robe of Christ. Burton plays Marcellus, a Roman centurion who won the robe of Christ on a roll of the dice after the crucifixion. Tormented by nightmares, he returns to Palestine to try to learn what he can about the man he killed. His slave Demetrius swoops up the robe and converts to Christianity. Mad emperor Caligula cannot abide Christians and demands that Burton secure the robe for him. When Burton does not give up the robe, he is sent to his death.

1959: *Ben-Hur* ranks among the most honored of films, taking eleven of twelve Academy Awards. The movie starts with the birth of Christ and the visit by the magi. Judah Ben-Hur of Judea (Charlton Heston) reunites with his friend Massala (Stephen Boyd), who becomes the Roman commander of Jerusalem. However, Massala asks Judah to betray his own people by informing on the dissenters. When Judah refuses, Massala finds a way to frame his friend and send Judah to the galleys of the Roman warships. He also sends Judah's mother and sister to a dark, cold cell. In battle Judah rescues the governor and becomes a Roman "favorite son." In time Judah becomes a skilled charioteer and defeats Massala in a daring chariot race. Judah then rescues his mother and sister who have become lepers and takes them to Christ. Though it is too late for them to meet Jesus, his shed blood heals them and regenerates Judah.

The Big Fisherman was directed by Frank Borzage for Centurion. This is a vast religious epic from Lloyd Douglas's novel about the life of St. Peter. Regrettably, Peter is trivialized, and the gospel is distorted. There is no crucifixion, and Jesus Christ is shown without an enemy in the world.

1961: *King of Kings* should not be confused with Cecil B. DeMille's impressive life of Jesus in the 1927 movie by the same title. Not only was this movie poorly edited, but it also treats the gospel as a revolutionary underground movement, with Barabbas and Judas working together to destroy Roman oppression and Jesus getting caught in the upheaval. Aside from the introduction of irrelevant battles, the movie lacks a clear emphasis on Jesus' divinity, omits miracles, and changes significant facts. Furthermore, Jeffrey Hunter does a poor job as Christ. However, the movie does portray an actual resurrection.

1964: Director Pier Paola Pasolini's *Gospel According to St. Matthew* adheres rigidly to the facts and the spirit of this one Gospel. Only at the crucifixion is the Virgin Mary allowed to be emotional, and the effect is shattering.

1965: *The Greatest Story Ever Told* is slightly overlong and crammed with stars but not as bad a movie as many critics claim. In spite of the involvement of the Protestant Film Office, the movie has some theological inaccuracies, including attempts to exonerate Judas, Judas falling into the sacrificial fire instead of hanging himself as the Bible tells us, and a weak ending, which has a conceptually resurrected Jesus appearing in the clouds in a vision that leans toward nominalism. These and other divergences from the Bible are so apparent that director George Stevens should clearly have stuck to the facts.

1973: *Jesus Christ, Superstar* presents a Jesus figure, using the musical idiom of the 1960s. It is interesting to note that it now appears very dated.

Godspell is a 1960s rock opera retelling of the story of Jesus in a New York setting. Directed by David Greene for Columbia Pictures, *Godspell* lost out at the box office to the overshadowing *Jesus Christ, Superstar.* Also based on a prior, successful theatrical musical, *Godspell* does not have the song recognition that *Jesus Christ, Superstar* does. Furthermore, the New York City setting provides a distracting backdrop to the movie's symbolic style. Even so, its cinematography is stunning.

1977: *Jesus of Nazareth* (TV) was directed by the renowned Franco Zeffirelli and produced by our friend and former history professor Vincenzo Labella for Sir Lew Grade and Radiotelevisione Italiana (RAI). This excellent television movie attempts historical accuracy. Many passages of the Bible are quoted verbatim, and the locations look authentic. Aside from Robert Powell as Jesus, Olivia Hussey as Mary, and Stacy Keach as Barabbas, many of the other characters are actually played by Semitic-looking actors. Of its six hours and twenty minutes, the first hour is devoted solely to the story of Jesus' birth, and twelve minutes is devoted to the Last Supper as well as twelve minutes to the crucifixion.

1979: The *Jesus* Film, released in 1979 by Warner Bros.; has been viewed by 3.3 billion people as of this writing thanks to the efforts of Campus Crusade for Christ; 108 million people have indicated they have placed their faith in Jesus Christ after seeing the film. The movie has been translated into 566 languages with 232 more in process. The audio/radio version is available in 54 languages, and another hundred languages will be added this year. Also, The *Jesus* Film has been reconfigured to reach different audiences (niche strategies).

1988: *Last Temptation of Christ* is the most blasphemous movie ever made. As if that was not bad enough, it is boring.

1996: *Matthew,* produced by Visual Entertainment, translates the Bible verbatim. The first in the Visual Bible series, *Matthew* is one of the best and clearest translations brought to life through the movie medium. Indeed, the words of Christ and every word by every character are lifted completely from the New International Version.

2003: *The Gospel of John,* a word-for-word movie taken from the Gospel of the same name, is one of the best movies ever made about the life of Jesus Christ.

2004: *The Passion of the Christ* is Mel Gibson's great masterpiece about the final hours of Jesus Christ's life on earth.

What Is a "Christian" Movie?

It would be a great breakthrough in contemporary communications if communicators would refrain from using the word *Christian* as an adjective and limit its use to the way the early church and the Romans used *Christian,* as a noun (Acts 11:26; 26:28; 1 Pet. 4:16). In the book of the Acts of the Apostles, a Christian is a person who confesses and follows Jesus Christ. Paul is a Christian who makes tents; however, the tents Paul makes are not Christian tents.

By restricting the use of *Christian*, we would no longer be confused by *Christian* art and media. Instead, we would have Christians who made a work of art or who communicated through a specific medium, such as television. The work of art, or the television program, that the Christian made may or may not communicate the gospel of Jesus Christ. If we evaluated the art as art, the television program as a program, and the tent as a tent (including any gospel messages woven into the fabric), then we would be delivered from worshipping the thing as a sacred object set apart by the use of *Christian* as an adjective.

Setting the art, music, book, or whatever apart by the adjectival use of *Christian* often allows several destructive attitudes to undermine the quality of a specific work of art or communication. Blinded by the word *Christian*, we often indulge sloppy or bad workmanship, thereby perpetuating inferior communication and art. Just as destructive to superior workmanship is the tendency of some artists and communicators to forsake excellence because they know that the adjective *Christian* pinned to their work will cover up a multitude of imperfections. Quality is also undermined by artists or communicators who decide not only to rest in the Lord but also to let the Lord do everything while they sleep or socialize. These individuals frequently fail to exercise their talents, learn their craft, or invest time and effort in the work he has given them to do. We are not saved by works (Eph. 2:9), but we are called to work with diligence and industry (Prov. 6:6; Rom. 12:11), knowing God will work in us, providing us with the strength to do his will (1 Pet. 4:11).

The adjectival use of the word *Christian* will clearly not be abandoned in the near future, by either pagans or Christians. However, as Christians, we must always do our best, evaluating our work honestly against the highest possible standards because we love God, trust God, and want all that we do to glorify God. Furthermore, we must help one another do our best by refusing to settle for anything less.

Once Upon a Time

Those who do not remember the past are condemned to relive it.
—George Santayana

Christians often forget that the church exerted a great influence on the entertainment industry from 1933 to 1966. For thirty-three years every script was read by representatives of the Roman Catholic Church, the Southern Baptist Convention, and the Protestant Film Office. Their job was to evaluate a movie in terms of the Motion Picture Code. If the film passed the Code, it received the Motion Picture Code Seal and was distributed. If it did not pass, the theaters would not screen it.

The Short Form of the Motion Picture Code provided:

The basic dignity and value of human life shall be respected and upheld. Restraint shall be exercised in portraying the taking of life.

Evil, sin, crime, and wrong-doing shall not be justified.

Detailed and protracted acts of brutality, cruelty, physical violence, torture, and abuse shall not be presented.

Indecent or undue exposure of the human body shall not be presented.

Illicit sex relationships shall not be justified. Intimate sex scenes violating common standards of decency shall not be portrayed. Restraint and care shall be exercised in presentations dealing with sex aberrations.

Obscene speech, gestures, or movements shall not be presented. Undue profanity shall not be presented.

Religion shall not be demeaned.

Words or symbols contemptuous of racial, religious, or national groups shall not be used so as to incite bigotry or hatred.

Excessive cruelty to animals shall not be portrayed, and animals shall not be treated inhumanely.

During the period of the Motion Picture Code, there was no explicit sex, violence, profanity, or blasphemy in movies. Also, films did not mock a minister of religion or a person's faith (the religious persecution in Germany prompted this wise counsel). For the most part movies and television programs communicated the true, the good, and the beautiful.

Then, in 1966, the churches voluntarily withdrew from the entertainment industry. Many of the media elite bemoaned the retreat of the churches. One prophesied, "If the salt is removed from the meat, then the meat will rot." Many studio executives felt that church involvement helped them to reach the large Christian audience in the United States and believed that Christians would avoid films that did not have the Motion Picture Code Seal.

Censorship or Patron Sovereignty?

Patron sovereignty has traditionally been commended by Hollywood as the right of movie patrons to determine what they want to see or avoid by their activity at the box office. When there was talk in the 1930s about government censorship, the movie industry requested patron sovereignty in the form of the Motion Picture Code. Throughout the life of the Code and its successor, the MPAA rating system, the entertainment industry has continued to express its preference for patron sovereignty rather than government intervention to curb tendencies in the industry toward obscenity and violence.

When the churches retreated, the Motion Picture Association of America instituted the rating system to take the place of the Code. However, this was like letting the fox guard the hen house, and the results were predictable.

Today, scripts are read by feminist, Marxist, and homosexual groups (such as GLAAD), but not by Christians. These groups award pictures and television programs that communicate their point of view and condemn movies and television programs that disagree with their point of view. For instance, one television network had to spend hundreds of thousands of dollars to reshoot and reedit a television movie so that it would not offend the Alliance of Gay and Lesbian Artists.

Whoever Controls the Media Controls the Culture

As a result of the influence of these antibiblical groups, movies and television programs have become purveyors of immorality, blasphemy, and rebellion and have influenced too many viewers to mimic the evil they see on the screen. Alan Alda noted in the movie *Sweet Liberty* that to capture an audience a movie must include the destruction of property (as in the car chase), rebellion against authority, and immoral sex. Of course, the audience he had in mind was the teenagers and young adults who flock to movies. This mirrors Karl Marx's four goals in his *Communist Manifesto:* abolish property, abolish the family, abolish the nation, and abolish religion and morality.

The destructive power of the mass media was highlighted by the 1988 television remake of the famous movie *Inherit the Wind,* which dramatically retold the story of the famous Scopes "monkey" trial. Although the Christians won the trial, they lost the battle in the media. William Jennings Bryan defeated Clarence Darrow in court, but he was defeated by the venomous anti-Christian reporting of H. L. Mencken. As in many cases since then, the Christians won the skirmish but lost the battle to the manipulators of the mass media.

Christians should never forget the lesson of the Scopes trial: it is futile to win the trial only to lose the battle to the power of the media. We need to claim God's victory and win the war by taking every thought captive for him.

To paraphrase John Locke, "Whoever controls the media controls the culture." In the Scopes trial, the press controlled the language and communicated a strong anti-Christian bias. Society adopted that bias and moved against the Christians even though the Christians had the law on their side. In the same manner, if those who control the language emphasize rape, pillage, and plunder, the culture will reflect those communications.

Like the Christians involved in the Scopes trial, we often forget that there is a war raging around us. This war is not taking place on the usual battlefield. It's being fought inside men's minds. It is a spiritual war for the souls of those who constitute our civilization, and it uses the most effective weapon ever conceived: communications.

Jesus was the master of communications. His parables are as pertinent today as they were two thousand years ago. He knew the power of communications and how ideas shape civilizations. His Word toppled one of the most powerful civilizations in history, the Roman Empire, and continues to transform the world today.

Though the tools of communications have changed, the words remain the same. The warfare of ideas and thoughts has exploded through the use of movies and television, revolutionizing our way of thinking. We are fighting against an enemy that is using every possible tactic to control our minds: materialism, secularism, humanism, Marxism—all the "isms" that conflict with Christianity.

Daily we are besieged with an onslaught of messages that tear us apart—if not from the morning newspaper, then from the nightly news, or from cable television movies portraying a life of drugs, illicit sex, and violence.

Ugly Americans

Already the United States is considered by many to be the most immoral country in the world. Movies are often reedited to include more sex and violence when released in the U.S. market. For instance, in Australia the movie *Return to Snowy River* had the hero and heroine getting married, whereas when it was released in the U.S., the hero and heroine went off to live with each other without marriage.

In January 2003, Boston University released a shocking study of the image of Americans held by teenagers around the world, entitled *The Next Generation's Image of Americans: Attitudes and Beliefs Held by Teen-Agers in Twelve Countries: A Preliminary Research Report* by Margaret H. DeFleur, Ph.D., and Melvin L. DeFleur, Ph.D., College of Communication, Boston University.

This study showed that young people around the world had a negative image of Americans and that this image was in part responsible for the outpouring of dislike for Americans underlying the bombing of the World Trade Center towers on September 11, 2001. The study concluded that the dislike of the United States would grow over the next few years and that it mirrored the image of Americans being presented by Hollywood, not the real attributes of real Americans. In other words, Hollywood is our ambassador to the world.

The study assumed that: "The collective condemnation expressed by a people when a negative incident occurs does not come out of nowhere. As a general principle, a negative incident can become a *cause celebre,* rallying widespread anger, only if a necessary condition is met. That condition is this: *There must already be in place a foundation of shared negative beliefs and attitudes toward the United States upon which the feelings generated by the specific incident can be based.*"

According to the authors, "The results show that members of the next generation studied in nearly all of the countries appear to hold consistently negative attitudes toward Americans as people."

The study also found that negative depictions of Americans in movies and TV programs have influenced the beliefs of many of the subjects, along with other factors.

The results suggest that problems for Americans are likely to continue into the foreseeable future in terms of terrorism threats, public health issues related to stress, and possible economic problems related to the negative assessments of the next generation.

The study found that good deeds done in the past do not count for much. Although it can be shown that the United States by any overall measure has been a good world citizen and has provided many kinds of assistance to other nations, the study showed that there seems to be no historical balance sheet of international behavior by which people in other countries weigh past contributions of the United States against their current grievances.

The study focused on teenagers because *"they are the ones who are trained and equipped to conduct terrorist acts.* When examining the nature of such threats, and who it is that carries out actual terrorist activities, either in the U.S. or in other countries, one fact becomes very obvious. They are the young. Many Americans have seen televised scenes of youngsters as young as twelve being trained in terrorists' camps to engage in aggression against the infidel [read *Americans*]."

The study noted, "Those who actually flew the airliners on September 11 were young adults, to be sure, but it is clear that their beliefs were shaped earlier, during their teenage years. In the final analysis, then, it is the young who are recruited to do older men's bidding—to deliver their bombs and weapons to the point of impact, even if it means their own death."

Among other beliefs, the study found that teenagers in these countries believe that: Americans are generally quite violent; many American women are sexually immoral; Americans are very materialistic; Americans like to dominate other people; and many Americans engage in criminal activities.

Few of those surveyed had any direct contact with Americans; only 12 percent had visited the U.S. But they did have access to American television programs, movies, and pop music; and, based on that exposure, most of these teens considered Americans to be violent, prone to criminal activity, and sexually immoral.

"These results suggest that pop culture, rather than foreign policy, is the true culprit of anti-Americanism," Melvin DeFleur says. "Hollywood should at least be asked by our public leaders to accept responsibility for the damage it is doing."

Overall Attitudes Toward Americans

Country											
	Very Negative		Generally Negative			Neutral		Generally Positive		Very Positive	
	-5	-4	-3	-2	-1	0	+1	+2	3+	+4	+5
				Negative				Positive			
• Saudi Arabia				-2.13							
• Bahrain				-1.86							
• South Korea				-1.76							
• Mexico				-1.50							
• China				-1.06							
• Spain				-0.89							
• Taiwan				-0.79							
• Dominican Republic				-0.50							
• Pakistan				-0.46							
• Nigeria				-0.05							
• Italy				+0.03							
• Argentina				+0.(							
OVERALL :				-2.13							

Source: Boston University, 2003

Profile of Specific Beliefs About Americans

Saudi Arabia											
	Very Negative		Generally Negative			Neutral		Generally Positive		Very Positive	
	-5	-4	-3	-2	-1	0	+1	+2	3+	+4	+5
				Negative				Positive			
• Americans are generally quite <u>violent</u>				-2.18							
• Americans are a generous people				-1.28							
• Many American women are <u>sexually immoral</u>		-3.23									
• Americans respect people unlike themselves				-0.63							
• Americans are very <u>materialistic</u>				-2.60							
• Americans have strong religious values				-1.80							
• Americans like to <u>dominate</u> other people		-3.60									
• Americans are a peaceful people				-2.25							
• Many Americans engage in <u>criminal</u> activities				-2.45							
• Americans are very concerned about their poor				-0.83							
• Americans have strong family values				-2.10							
• *There is little for which I admire Americans*				-2.68							
OVERALL :				-2.13							

Source: Boston University, 2003

Movies Are a Tool

It is important to understand that each medium has its advantages and disadvantages over the other media. To communicate how something looks, an oft-quoted, ancient Chinese proverb tells us that "a picture is worth a thousand words." If, however, we want to communicate the true nature of some person, event, or thing, then a few words, such as "the Word was made flesh, and dwelt among us" (John 1:14 KJV), says more than a thousand pictures.

Each medium can be seen primarily as a communications tool,[6] capable of accomplishing one or more communications functions. A tool is neither good nor bad. That is determined by how we use it. When we use a tool to perform a function for which the tool is intended, it performs well.

For instance, a screwdriver is useful for driving screws; it is of some value in scraping paint off the side of a house; it is of little value when used to hammer a nail; and it is of no value in gripping a nut.

The screwdriver is neither good when used to repair a church artifact nor bad when used to stab someone. Rather, it is the person using the screwdriver who is responsible, and the same is true of the various media of communications.

Thus, movies and television programs like *The Passion of the Christ* can be used to build up the body of Christ or like *The Last Temptation of Christ* to tear down the church. The filmmaker can use the movie medium for good or ill, so it is up to the filmmaker to develop responsible sense and sensibility.

Just Because You Can Watch Brain Surgery on the Discovery Channel

Since people watch movies and television programs that seem exciting and only last a brief period of time (one hour or two), they assume that making a movie or television program is not that hard. In fact, they are shocked that it costs Hollywood more than $100 million to produce and release a movie. Therefore, it is instructive to a basic understanding of the entertainment industry to turn to an expert who will help us clarify our thinking and start asking the right questions.

Dan Nichols does just that in the following article. Dan has produced and been involved in many movies, including *Raiders of the Lost Ark* and *Always.* Recently he was executive producer of the MOVIEGUIDE® award-winning movie *Luther.* He has taken movies with story problems and made them great. Here he gives us a wonderful insight into getting involved in the entertainment industry.

So, What's Your Story?
J. Daniel Nichols

IT WAS 5:20 AM on a typically beautiful day in Hawaii. On location with a short-lived TV series I was producing for Universal Studios, I stood by the "bottomless" black-stone swimming pool of a hilltop estate, watching my cast and crew rehearse a scene at the far edge of the yard. The camera angle included a spectacular panoramic view of Honolulu, framed by the inevitable morning procession of rainbows floating through Manoa Valley toward the glistening beach of Waikiki.

I was abruptly pulled from the beauty of the view when I heard the AD shouting insistently for silence from the rest of the company, gathered in the distance around the many trailers and trucks in the estate's expansive parking cove. He closed his colorful exhortation with the statement, "*This* is what it's about, ladies and gentlemen," using his entire arm to point toward the two lone actors standing in front of the lens, struggling to make the moment work for the sake of the story they had been hired to tell. His words made clear to everyone that the story was the sole reason for our presence at that place, on that day, at that time, with all of that gear and our 102 people.

To my relief the people who were being exhorted did not respond with resentment or indifference. Instead, they responded with evident agreement that they had been wrong and deserved the correction. Veteran drivers, greenspersons, makeup artists, day players, grips, electricians, and others redirected their focus and attention to the common good. They may have been connected to their work through their expertise in their chosen crafts, but they were connected to the industry and its unwritten rules of purpose in an even deeper, more reverent way.

As for me, I'll never forget the meaning in those words. That simple moment helped define for me what business I was in. I could apply the same skills used to produce a weekly series for primetime TV and make a decent living in many industries, as could any of the other craftspeople on the set that day, but that one incident made clear what our business was. It was not about the beautiful view, or the camaraderie among the talented cast and crew, or the smell of fresh coffee in the early morning, or the laughter, or money, or all of the other feelings of personal enjoyment and belonging experienced on a set or location shoot. The measure in this business that most typically assures another day of employment is, was, and always will be, the story. The question at the end of every day is, "Did we get our day's worth of story?"

Since that incident, I have met with hundreds of young people who have wanted to get into the business of film and television production. I have not met with many who came looking for information about how to get into media marketing or distribution or sales. That fact has always intrigued me. The crafting of film or television product distribution, the marketing of those products, and the development of ancillary markets for film and television program products comprise the components of the industry most directly related to earnings. Yet the industry's appeal to many energetic, purpose-driven people seems to be the process we see and hear so much about on "behind the scenes" programs and DVD extras: the creation, development, and production process and the celebrity relation-ships that result from that business of creativity.

So the first question I ask the rookies is, "Do you know what business you're wanting to be in?" They look puzzled for a moment and then pro-vide an answer as if wondering why I am asking. They usually just say, "The film business," or "Television," or "Interactive media," or "Theater." It's as if they expect me to know which of the many, many occupations within any of those businesses they are talking about. If they respond by answering, "The entertainment business," the number of potential profes-sions they must ultimately choose from has increased exponentially. If they do respond with one of those generic answers, then I know that they have not yet answered the important questions about their involvement in the industry that will bring focus to their life's journey.

To live without focus and purpose by working in any area of the industry that provides employment for the moment provides nothing more than an extended internship in producing and builds no future. Not everyone should be a producer. Not everyone *could* be a producer. Yet producing is the primary skill set within the industry that is best served by knowing at least a little bit about every aspect of the industry from development to exhibition. I'm not saying that it is unbeneficial for anyone interested in the industry to work as a production assistant on a few large productions to decide which aspect of the industry one finds most appealing, but I suggest that a few are sufficient. Thereafter, people need to determine what they truly want to do in the industry and then focus on working in that area of expertise so the appropriate preparation and relationships can be defined and initiated. Choose carefully, then waste no time.

Typically, anyone who has recently entered, or is thinking of entering, the production industry will fall into one of two categories. The first category is the person, or group, who comes as an owner of products. The second category is the person who comes as a craftsperson, looking to use his or her trade to make a living in the production business.

Although the people in either of these groups could probably make a more secure and better work/family-balanced living in the outside world, I will not try to explain the internal drives that make a person want to be associated with the screen arts industry. For each person it is a different set of reasons. However, all should at least ask themselves why they are wanting in. Is it for fulfillment? Freedom? Adventure? Self-validation? Money? Control? Power to make future creative choices? What? Perhaps it cannot be explained anymore than why man creates anything, but the more a person understands one's personal reasons for wanting to be a part of the business, the easier it is to formulate the next questions that must be answered to intensify one's focus even further. With each new set of questions a person can answer related to motive and intention of oneself, the more constructively controlling one is of the industry's impact on one's life.

The first of the two groups I mentioned is producers who believe they have one or more wonderful projects that will succeed in the marketplace if those projects can make it to a screen. These people may also be the writers of their projects, but writers fall into the second category. The producers group almost always comes in search of money or an established person in the industry who can move their project forward. To this producer group I say, be serious about your work. Examine your motives carefully so you understand what the point of reference will be for all of the decisions you will need to make with little time to think about them. What is your true motive? Not the cause-centered one but your personal one, the one in your heart. It is your heart that will be put to the test as you move forward as a producer. The first two questions you will have to answer are, Who am I willing to hurt? and Who am I willing to lose as relationships? Is your motive truly your desire to tell a story? Perhaps you are as altruistic as you believe you are. Will you be willing to give it to someone else to produce just to see it done? Or do you need to control how the story is told? Then your motive may be self-expression. Could nobody do the story as well as you? Perhaps you seek self-validation or just a break. Perhaps you lack humility. Could you have the same impact writing articles? Teaching? What are you using as your benchmark for success? Exceeding Bible sales for the year or exceeding box office receipts for *The Passion of the Christ*? Or just getting your project distributed?

Those in this first group need to understand well that the role of producer is one of the most emotionally demanding positions anyone can fill because the development process can be destructive to relationships. It is common for friends to enter this world together because they have rallied around a particular project they feel is worthy of their collective efforts only to find that the decision-making process required in creative collaboration results in good friends and allies becoming opponents, at least for the duration of development and possibly throughout production. Often relationships are never restored. If you desire to lead the production, will you be willing to hurt your friends for the sake of the production and the quality you deem greater than the quality they define? You may hurt them simply by rejecting their ideas or thinking. But what if you're wrong? Creativity, even in its most collaborative form, is ultimately about control. Who gets to decide what *good* means? Who gets to make the final choices in each of the processes and facets of production? You may find yourself in a position in which everything is at stake because the project has to find distribution if it is going to impact the culture the way you promised your investors it would or if money is to be earned. So whose viewpoint will be used as the point of reference for decisions of taste and quality and, inevitably, conflict resolution? All of this is done every day by many people, but if one has not yet addressed the questions while it is still possible to do so in a mind-rehearsal state, one may not be ready to move forward into an arena in which these questions must be answered through actions that have irreversible consequences.

The second group of entrants is the people who depend on finding an employer who trusts their abilities and believes in their talent. These people range from writers to actors to drivers to wardrobe designers to every other craft that contributes to the success of the industry.

The entertainment industry is comprised of an array of occupations that have little or nothing to do with entertainment as it is talked about in the media but have everything to do with storytelling. Each of these master craftspersons contributes subtly and sometimes not so subtly to what the audience perceives as story. However, it is only because the products created by the craftspeople of these occupations is captured on an audiovisual medium and sold as a product itself that an audience ever sees their work. I recommend that those interested in becoming craftspersons in the industry clearly define the occupation they are interested in and master that skill for use within the industry or in the outside world. The major difference between the production industry and the outside world is that most often production requires faster work, more of it, with greater dependencies, and therefore a greater chance for failure, in a more condensed period of time. It can be a rush for those who thrive on self-satisfaction in their accomplishments.

Writers and actors of film and television are specialized craftspersons, so those specific skills are not as easy to apply in the outside world. However, the basics of the skills can find markets other than film and television. Sadly, one of the misconceptions of our society is that anything other than the public arena of screen arts is a lower measure of success than "making it" in the production business. My response is that I have met many multimillionaires and happy people who have nothing to do with the entertainment business. It's all about focus and purpose and right fit for an individual. No one should perceive the industry as a measure of success, only a measure of personal fulfillment if the industry is one's goal.

I well understand that the *perception* of the industry is appealing to any creative person, whether that person has trade skills in writing, acting, carpentry, interior design, transportation, botany, laboratory sciences, computer sciences, or any other industry that is used in the production industry. It is appealing to people to be part of something that the media exposure can make larger than life. That gives an added value to the work and contribution of an individual, but that credibility by association should never be the measure by which a craftsperson determines a professional value or a retirement plan.

Whichever path a person chooses, it's important to have a clear understanding of one's motives, expectations, and reasons for working in the industry to survive it. When people who love the industry are getting to work in it, there is no better feeling. When we are in pursuit of work that often seems so close yet so far away, it is agonizing. We become like children eating our favorite candy: We relish the flavor and emotional gratification, but when it is gone and the supply is out of reach, we flop ourselves on the floor in wailing misery. When we grow up, most of us know how to balance our desires with the reality of life. If you cannot do that regarding this industry, then it will devour you. Only give it the value it is worthy of, as it relates to the whole of your life. Admire the power and influence of the industry as such, and desire to be an influence in it, but guard your heart from the pain and frustration your personal participation or lack of participation can cause.

As a side note, I often encounter people who love watching television and films so much that they believe they want to be a part of the industry. Many start writing screenplays or looking for opportunities to get into the industry in any way possible, doing whatever they can do, just to get in the door. I try to explain that there is a big difference between being a person who appreciates the industry and the emotions the finished products bring into one's life and making a living, or just working, in the industry. Many people who are attempting to break into the industry are much better off continuing simply to enjoy the industry as viewers. Sometimes, the biggest contribution a person can make to the industry is to appreciate it as a consumer. Ask yourself the question and face the answer even if it is hard to accept.

So how does all of the above relate to the incident in Hawaii and the value of story?

Let me ask you what *your* story is. Are you getting into a business to see how it treats you? Are you getting into an industry because you like how other people's work in that industry makes you feel? I suggest you approach it more seriously than that. Know what the business of entertainment really is. More importantly, know who you are outside the industry and what your relationship to the industry of entertainment should be. If you desire to make a living as a craftsperson within the industry, focus on that craft and master it. Do not relate to it solely as part of the entertainment industry. If you want to be a producer, understand whom you want to tell stories to and be serious about telling those stories in whatever form best affords you that opportunity. Don't always think *big time* if there is no need for a particular story to be big time. Some stories should only be told to small audiences. Never get caught up in the fascination of the production processes to the point you lose sight of why all of the equipment, people, techniques, technology, and money are being used. Make a development plan and work hard to stay on track. Understand what you want out of the industry to a greater degree than you understand what you'll be willing to allow the industry to take out of you.

Don't become engaged in all of the meaningless and endless pursuits that the fringe of this industry disguises as relevant. You will stay busy, but you will not be productive. The cafés of Hollywood and every other media capital in the world are filled with busy people discussing deals and believing their time is being well spent, but the vast majority of those people will never see their projects come to fruition because each step of their process is defined by the previous step and who makes it. They will never see a person's life changed because of their meetings.

To anyone with a biblical worldview interested in pursuing a career within the production industry, I ask you especially to consider what occupation you truly wish to pursue. What is your primary reason for that answer as it relates to the business of telling stories? Is your interest in the viewpoint or the view? In the values or the value? In the result or the process? In the impact to our culture or the personal gain? If your answers are not the first option of each question just asked, then I suggest that you consider a broader market for your talents in which normal hours, good base pay without overtime, and consistency of employment are standard fare.

If you have read all of these words and still have a burning desire to be part of this incredible business, perhaps you should be.

◆　◆　◆

Watch the Credits

Dan points out that there are many people who work on a Hollywood television program or movie; just read the credits at the end of a movie. There are actors, producers, the director, writers, the cinematographer, the director of photography, editors, art directors, soundmen, and others. Just operating the camera requires a director of photography, a cameraman, a person who moves the camera, a person who clears the way for the camera, and so forth. Also, there are coaches, coordinaters, gaffers (electricians), gofers, and costume designers. And these are just a few of the many people who work on a $102 million Hollywood movie (the average cost of a Hollywood movie at the writing of this book).

As Dan noted, you need to decide which area of the entertainment industry is suited for your gifts and talents. This book will help you to do just that.

Asking the Right Questions

Dan has helped us to consider the basic questions of what your story is and to focus on the fact that the movie and television business is all about telling stories. Aside from his cogent direction, he has pointed us in the right direction by asking the right questions. In fact, asking the right questions is the key to making a great movie or television program.

What is your interest in the entertainment industry? Success? Fame? Good relationships? Obedience to God and his Great Commission? Whatever your goal, you must be able to communicate effectively in your chosen medium to achieve it.

In the summer of 1981 I was invited to Knoxville, Tennessee, by nine local churches representing different denominations to consult on the design of an exhibit that would communicate their presence and biblical views to the many people who would visit the 1982 World's Fair. About thirty consultants, media experts, and theologians from throughout the United States came to this consultation to advise the Knoxville churches on their exhibit. The theme of the fair was energy, so the prevailing opinion of those present was that the exhibit should contain posters illustrating energy (e.g., a power plant, an engine, an atomic bomb) with biblical sub-scriptions (e.g., "Blessed are the peacemakers" [Matt. 5:9], "Blessed are you who are poor" [Luke 6:20], and "The land is mine and you are but aliens and my tenants" [Lev. 25:23 NIV]).

This approach sounded dull. As the meeting continued, I recalled the 1964 World's Fair in New York City, where almost all the exhibits had long waiting lines except the Protestant Exhibit, which was decorated with posters with biblical quotations.[7] I reasoned that people came to a World's Fair to be entertained by visionary exhibits that capture their imagination. If the churches wanted to attract people to their exhibit, I suggested that they should use the latest technology and the best creative talent to build the most exciting exhibit at the fair.

The churches asked me to be the executive producer of the exhibit, which we named "The Power." In prayer God gave me a vision of an exciting Disneyland-type exhibit that presented God as the Author of all energy—the Power. A month of meetings with creative talent focused this vision into an exhibit where the audience would step into a time rocket, blast off back to the beginning of time, find themselves plunged into total darkness, watch God create the heavens and the earth, land in paradise, get kicked out for disobedience, enter into man's world, become over-whelmed by the cacophony of voices competing for attention, cry out for help, meet Jesus, follow him though the cross into his body (the church), where they could be filled with his Spirit to do his work, and finish by singing "The Lord's Prayer" together.

After months of hard work by some of the top electronic media and show business talent[8] in the country, The Power became a reality—the most technologically sophisticated exhibit at the fair, visited by more than one million people, and representing the combined statement of fifteen denominations.[9] Newspapers from all over the United States called The Power the most exciting exhibit at the Fair, and children of all ages enjoyed this trip through time and space.

I thank God for all the miracles and the tremendous contributions of all the talented individuals who created, built, and maintained the exhibit. However, the churches, acting together as the communicator, made The Power possible by adhering to the basic principles of good communications.

The churches asked the right questions to determine
- what they wanted to communicate (what story they wanted to tell)
- what the forum and marketplace for their communication was
- who their audience was
- what the appropriate genre (or format) for their communication was
- what the appropriate medium for their communication was
- what the grammar and language of the appropriate genre and medium were

In this process, the churches discovered that for some communications, hands-on do-it-yourself production (such as posters) was not as effective as hands-off production where the communicator discerns what his or her talents and gifts are and brings on board the appropriate professional talent to complement, or supplement, his or her talents and gifts.

The churches wanted to communicate their presence and biblical views to the World's Fair visitors; that was their goal. They succeeded. Moreover, The Power was purchased after the fair closed by the Media Ministry of the Missionary Oblates to be displayed permanently at the National Shrine of Our Lady of the Snows in Belleville, Illinois, just outside of St. Louis, Missouri. Through this permanent display of The Power, the churches will continue to communicate their message to people for years to come.

The story of The Power has a happy ending; however, not all our communications succeed in doing what we want them to do. Sometimes our communications fail because of circumstances beyond our control. As one of Murphy's Laws reminds us, "If you explain something so clearly that no one can misunderstand, someone will." Often our communications fail because we have failed to ask the right questions either because we are lazy, impatient, solipsistic,[10] or fearful.

To communicate through the mass media of entertainment, we must learn the language and the grammar of the medium through which we will be communicating. A broadcaster once told the story of the baby mouse and the mother mouse. The mother told the baby that she was going to look for food and that the baby should not leave his mouse home. While the mother was gone, the baby noticed a delicious piece of cheese on top of a table not far from its home. The baby scurried to get the cheese, and the cat caught it. The mother saw what happened, ran up behind the cat, and screamed, "Bowwow." The cat dropped the baby mouse and ran. The mother said to the baby that the moral of the story is, you must learn to speak two languages.

For Christians, effective communication means much more than achieving one's goals, desires, and needs because communication is at the heart of God's story, and we have been called to communicate that story (Rom. 10:14–15). His story begins with communication: "In the beginning was the Word" (John 1:1). That Word of God is Jesus the Christ, the Son of God, the Author of creation, the great Communicator, who made all things.

Ever since the fall, his story continues. The Word of God has been in the business of rescuing people, created in his image, from death; and he has called us to help him (Matt. 4:19; 28:19; Luke 24:47; Acts 1:8). As Jesus says: "You will receive power when the Holy Spirit has come upon you, and you will be My witnesses" (Acts 1:8).

We want to proclaim his gospel because we love him and because we love our neighbor so much that we want to save our neighbor from death. Our witnessing is a direct, natural, inevitable consequence of our becoming and being Christians, according to Jesus in Acts 1:8. Filled with power, we will witness.

The good news is that "we are God's fellow workers" (1 Cor. 3:9 NIV) called to witness, yet it is he who witnesses through us (John 14:26; John 13). Unlike Islam, where the Muslim must convert the non-Muslim any way possible—whether through argument, persuasion, bribery, or torture—we do not have to worry about converting anyone, for God's Holy Spirit converts (John 3:5–8). We are called merely to communicate Jesus and his salvation.

In preaching Jesus Christ, we must not compromise with the world system, or forsake our zeal for him (Matt. 10:32–33; Rev. 3:1; 3:15–16). Yet, since we love him and our audience, we need to translate our communication into the appropriate language and place it in the appropriate context so that our audience is able to hear and understand what we have to say. We should make ourselves "a slave to all, in order to win more people" (1 Cor. 9:19).

Community

A psychiatrist who was advising me on the production of a PBS (the Public Broadcasting Service) television program on divorce prevention, noted that he had been on a U.S. government commission to discover the reasons for chronic poverty in Appalachia. Before going into the field, the members assumed that the problem had to do with environment or lack of education. In the field the committee found that they could move up a creek beyond so-called civilization and find a house and family that were falling apart, yet they could go further up the creek and find a well-kept home and an industrious family. The difference was not isolation or lack of education; rather, the family that was doing well almost always had a relative nearby, or a neighbor, who cared enough to be demanding and interested in the welfare of that family.

We must be interested in the welfare of the family of believers (1 Cor. 5–6). "I don't care" and "Don't get involved" are negative and destructive adages. Healthy criticism, which is loving and not judgmental, and sincere concern help all of us (2 Tim. 4:2; Titus 2).

Provision

Frequently we do not have the time to love our neighbor. We are too busy worrying about money because we really do not trust God to provide. The good news is that he will provide when we take the time to love him and our neighbor (John 14:12–21; 2 Cor. 9:6ff). Trusting God to provide takes time, and trusting him to the degree that we can be available for and responsive to our neighbor (our families, our friends, and our enemies) takes time and the power of his Spirit.

Sometimes we are just too concerned with our business to pay attention to others, but Jesus, the Communicator, was and is always available and calls us to be available (Matt. 5:42; 10:8). If we focus on him and his grace, we will be freed from fear and available to communicate his gospel. For instance, four days before The Power exhibit was to open at the 1982 World's Fair, we were $150,000 short of funds. We were paid up-to-date (more than $1 million in goods and services, and $600,000 in cash expenditures), but the crew was anticipating that we would not have the final $150,000 to pay them on Friday morning, the day before the grand opening.

The crew was the best talent in the country, chosen because of their skills not because of their religious beliefs. Many members of the crew were more committed to receiving their wages than proclaiming the gospel message. The churches had spent all the money they could and had no idea where they could find the remainder. One of my associates suggested that I should give up, stay in Atlanta, and not bother to go to Knoxville. I countered that this was God's exhibit and he would finance it.

I flew to Knoxville late Tuesday afternoon. My director took me aside to tell me that the crew was going to walk off the job. I prayed. Around 9:00 p.m., a man stopped by the exhibit and asked me how things were going. I quickly told him that we needed $150,000 in the bank in Atlanta by Thursday. He did not have a lot of money, but he felt that the exhibit was the responsibility of the people of Knoxville and invited me to a prayer meeting that the sponsoring churches were holding early the next morning. Thanks to God's grace, we had $175,000 in the bank by Thursday. The extra $25,000 was just enough to pay for maintenance of The Power for the first few months of operation.

We should never worry about finances, time, or any of the other obstacles that seem to stand in the way of our fulfilling his call for us. Instead, we should concern ourselves with doing God's will so we can trust in his provision. "Now this is the confidence we have before Him: whenever we ask anything according to His will, He hears us. And if we know that He hears whatever we ask, we know that we have what we have asked Him for" (1 John 5:14–15).

We learn God's will by studying his Word, the Bible, and by allowing his Spirit to live in us. The good news is that he gives each of us our own unique combination of motivations, talents, and gifts that, when discerned, will help each of us discover how we can best communicate what we want to communicate and what genre and medium of communication is appropriate for each of us and our communications. All too often we become frustrated by trying to communicate in a way and through a medium that does not suit our unique motivational talents. Some of us are chosen to be writers, some executive producers, some directors, some art directors. Chapter 3 will help start you on the road to discovering your unique, God-given, motivational talents.

When you discover your unique, motivational talent and learn the language and the grammar of the medium through which you will be communicating, then you will be able to access any channel of communications (CBS, NBC, television, radio, newspaper, etc.), capture and motivate an audience, and communicate the gospel in all its glory.

Years ago, as president of a mainline church communication ministry, I initiated and produced for the Protestant Radio TV Center (a consortium of four denominations) a television series for PBS television satellite distribution entitled *Perspectives*. After one year on the PBS satellite, *Perspectives* was carried on 120 PBS stations and cable systems. Several programs in the series won important national awards.[11] Furthermore, every program I produced and hosted had a biblical perspective.

One evening, at a benefit dinner, a renowned church organist opened a conversation with me by complaining that Christians could not place programs on PBS television because PBS would not carry programs containing a religious message.[12] A Christian who produced television programs had complained to my new friend that he could not convince PBS to carry his latest program. I mentioned *Perspectives* and suggested that the problem was not necessarily PBS; rather it might have been the quality of the program in question, or the program may not have fit the PBS format. In fact, I was aware of the program, and it was not directed or edited very well, although it had a great message.

Of course the problem could have been with one of the PBS member stations or with personnel. However, all too often the problem is not with the gatekeeper[13] or "the other guy," but instead with the design and quality of our communication. This book will help you overcome those problems and examine the medium of television and how to place your program on the channel of your choice.

W. C. Fields proclaimed one of the most practical rules of effective communications: "Tell them what you are going to say; say it; and, tell them what you said." With that principle in mind, let's look at the structure of this book.

To communicate effectively, you must learn the basic principles of good communications, as well as the language and grammar of the genre and the medium through which you will be communicating. Asking the right questions is the key to applying the basic principles of good communications and the principles of the genre and the medium of choice to a specific communication.

This book is your manual to help you communicate effectively through movies and television programs. I pray that this book will be a blessing to you.

CHAPTER 2

In the Beginning

T he key to winning a war, physical or spiritual, is intelligence. Not the native intelligence that gets a student into the college of choice, but rather the information about the enemy that can help you understand when, where, and how to press the battle. The Bible emphasizes what is required to tackle any task, including movie and television production, successfully in another way: "We are asking that you may be filled with the knowledge of His will in all wisdom and spiritual understanding" (Col. 1:9).

Most people who want to make movies or television programs have no idea what is involved in either. As an analogy, they are like people who watch brain surgery on the Discovery Channel and then attempt to do brain surgery on a friend. Red flags at this thought tell us immediately that one needs to study medicine before attempting such a thing.

Movies and television programs are mainly entertainment that communicates and contains artistic elements. Since the beginning, movie production was called the movie business, not the movie art, not only because the writers and other guilds wanted the legal benefits of the designation as a business but also because they understood that they were supplying a product to the audience for the express purpose of making money. In the 1950s the United States courts started classifying movies as speech because some independent filmmakers wanted First Amendment protection of movies that contained salacious and immoral material. Much later, the word *art* came into vogue to add another layer of obfuscation and protection against the moralists in society and to continue the move from liberty to license. However, even these sobriquets did not change the fact that movies, television, and other entertainment were products of the entertainment industry intended to make money. In this book, however, we will focus on the communication aspects of the mass media of entertainment because Christians are called to preach the Word (2 Tim. 4:2), and most Christians who seek advice about getting into the entertainment industry do so because they want to communicate the good news or they want to clean up the entertainment industry.

Dan Nichols's reflections in the previous chapter opened the door of understanding regarding the complexity of movie and television production. His article "So, What's Your Story?" also suggested many of the questions you should ask before getting into the entertainment industry. Let's consider three of these ascertainment questions.

1. What do you want to communicate through movies and television?
2. Why do you want to communicate through movies and television?
3. To whom do you want to communicate?

"No Man Is an Island"[1]

Communication is basic to our being human. Communication joins us together as a community by giving us the ability to exchange and hold thoughts, ideas, needs, and desires in common. Furthermore, communication gives us the opportunity to be in communion with God. Our God is the God who communicates, who speaks forth creation and who is himself the Word, as John so eloquently proclaims: "In the beginning was the Word, and the Word was with God, and the Word was God" (John 1:1).

Babies come into the world trying to communicate their desires, needs, and feelings. They become frustrated when they are not understood. They are happy about learning to talk, but in the interest of preserving their identity, they want their audience to understand their approach to language, or else. All too often "the child is father of the man" with regard to our approach to communication as adults, although not in the sense that Wordsworth intended.[2]

The alternative to poor communications is for us to stop before we communicate and take the time to ascertain the nature of our audience, our own talents, the nature of the medium we have chosen, and all the pertinent aspects of each communication so that our communication will achieve the result(s) we intend. Effective communication enables us to share our thoughts, achieve our goals, fulfill our desires, and survive as adults, or babies, in a fallen world teetering on the brink of destruction.

The task that confronts us is to continue to strive to produce better, more effective communications that proclaim God's gospel through every medium. In the first forty years of television, the mainline churches produced excellent religious television programs, such as *The Lion, the Witch and the Wardrobe, Insight,* and *Davey and Goliath.* Now parachurch organizations such as the Billy Graham Organization, which produced *The Climb,* and concerned individuals like Mel Gibson, who produced *The Passion of the Christ,* are spreading the Word. Whoever it is, it is important that all Christian communicators strive for excellence and avoid time-consuming sibling rivalries.

Christians often assume that great Hollywood movies and television programs with strong Christian content must be produced by Christians. Several renowned Christian speakers have told me about the influence that the movie *Chariots of Fire* had on their lives. In particular, these speakers note that Eric Liddell's statement in the movie that his running gave God pleasure encouraged each of them to start exercising their God-given talents rather than limit themselves to so-called "Christian" endeavors. I always point out that the actor who played Liddell and the scriptwriter had collaborated on the dialogue that proclaimed the gospel so clearly, yet neither of them was a Christian. In fact, Colin Welland, the scriptwriter, says to this day that the plot of *Chariots of Fire* is about a "couple of young fellows who put their fingers up to the world."[3] Clearly, he has a different perspective on what *Chariots of Fire* is saying than most Christians. Most of the money for *Chariots of Fire* was put up by a Moslem, Mohammed El Dodi Fayed, who died in the car crash with Princess Diana; and the producer was Jewish. In fact, the only committed Christian who was prominent in *Chariots of Fire* was the actor who played Abrahams, the Jewish runner. *Chariots of Fire* shows that God can and will raise up stones to witness to him through the entertainment media if Christians fail to do so.

A Religion of Communication

As Johannes Heinrichs has pointed out: "Theologically speaking, Christianity can be wholly and completely interpreted as a religion of communication, both divine-human and inter-human."[4]

Therefore, as Christians, our ability to communicate effectively and successfully through movies, television programs, and other media is extremely important so that we can witness to the great news of new life available in Christ and minister to the needs of our neighbors.

Our most basic communication ascertainment question is: How do I communicate exactly what I need or want to communicate to the person I want or need to reach, using the appropriate genre and medium properly so that my audience will understand and be convinced, motivated, educated, and/or informed? The key to effective and successful communication in the mass media of entertainment is asking the right ascertainment questions to ascertain exactly what I want to communicate, why I want to communicate it, to whom I want to communicate it, how I want to communicate it, what medium is appropriate with respect to who I am, what my motivational talents are, and what impact or consequence I want my communication to have.

Effective communication always takes work. Communication is a conscious process involving two or more unique individuals. Communication is a bridge for thoughts, ideas, and information between those individuals. Before any bridge is built, it has to be designed properly, or it will collapse. Every detail is important.

As we have heard all our lives, the process of writing (for most of us) is 10 percent inspiration and 90 percent perspiration. The same is true for communication through movies and television: learn and apply the right questions, the right language, and the right grammar, and the communications bridge will be 90 percent built.

Of course, no matter what the medium of communication, like a baby learning to talk, there comes a time when the right questions, the words, and the syntax are second nature to us. Furthermore, once we become adept at talking or communicating, we should not regress into baby talk unless we have just suffered physical or psychological damage or the baby talk is a necessary, conscious, and effective part of a specific communication.

In a wonderful article in *MOVIEGUIDE*® and on www.movieguide.org, producer Bruce Johnson helps us understand the slow, sometimes painful steps of learning a craft and developing one's talent. Bruce is recognized as one of Hollywood's most prolific creative talents, having amassed more than five hundred producing credits, including feature films, television movies, TV series, specials, educational films, and documentaries. A three-time Emmy Award winner, Johnson cofounded PorchLight Entertainment in 1995 with the entire family as its target audience. Since the company was formed, Johnson has executive produced several television series and movies, establishing PorchLight as a leading independent supplier of family and children's content, both as a producer and as a distributor. Please check out his article at www.movieguide.org.

The Right Ascertainment Questions

With these reflections in mind, let's look briefly at some of the right ascertainment questions for us to ask to improve our communications. These questions are grouped in categories chosen to clarify their purpose. In reality, these categories and questions are closely interrelated; however, to help focus our communications, they have been separated and distinguished from one another. Some of these questions will be treated in depth in the chapters that follow. Additional questions, which relate to a specific medium or topic, will also be treated throughout the book. You should adapt, add to, and subtract from these questions to suit your own particular needs. Ask these questions before you begin to communicate.

Power

Yours, LORD, is the greatness and the power and the glory and the splendor and the majesty, for everything in the heavens and on earth belongs to You. (1 Chronicles 29:11)

Are my communications powerful?

What empowers my communications?

Power is by definition the ability, the capacity, the strength, the authority, the energy, the force, and the right to do or accomplish something. As believers, we know that God is omnipotent; God the Father is the source of all power (1 Chron. 29:12); Jesus has all authority in heaven and on earth (Matt. 28:18); and the Holy Spirit gives us power to communicate his gospel (Acts 1:8; 10:44). Therefore, in the final analysis every power question begins and ends with God.

However, there are many levels of power in a communication. To understand what empowers a specific communication, the first question that each of us should ask ourselves before communicating is, "Why do I want to communicate?"

"For this reason I raised you up: so that I may display My power in you, and that My name may be proclaimed in all the earth" (Rom. 9:17).

The essence of powerful and effective communication is passion, and passion comes from self-knowledge, vulnerability, openness, and a clear understanding of "why I want to communicate." Whether you want to reach, teach, serve, proclaim, respond, sell, or ask, knowing the ultimate reason you are motivated to communicate (self? others? God?) will help you evaluate the driving power of your communication.

The question, Why do I want to communicate? refers to the motivational level of power that prompts the communication in the first place and drives the communication to its destination. The motivational level of a communication is comparable to the motivations of the driver of a car who causes the car to drive somewhere. If the driver is out for himself or herself, in a hurry, and thoughtless of others, the power at his or her fingertips may be dangerous or at least annoying to others on the road. If the driver is concerned not only about reaching his or her destination but also about others, he or she can be a rare blessing to those around them.

Furthermore, the motivation of the driver will empower him or her to reach the destination rather than give up when the thrill of the journey starts to wear thin. Most quality communications require perseverance, just as most long hauls require stamina.

The other critical power question we should ask before we communicate is, "What is the premise of my communication?"

"Life and death are in the power of the tongue" (Prov. 18:21).

Although this question is the next power question and is included for discussion at this point, you should ask, "What is the premise of my communication?" after asking the understanding question, "What am I communicating?"

The premise of a communication is the engine or motor that powers the communication, by proposing antecedently the postulate or hypothesis that leads necessarily to the logical conclusion of the communication through the process of proving the argument put forth in the premise. The premise dramatically and logically powers the communication. The premise is the essence of the story, which we will consider later in this book.

Your premise, your motivation, your genre or format, your medium of choice, your gifts, your talents, and your audience will determine what you are communicating, regardless of what you want to communicate. Therefore, it is critical that you state your premise correctly and precisely, and that you distinguish between what you want to communicate, or your idea, and what you are communicating, which depends to a large degree on your premise.

Wisdom

The fear of the LORD is the beginning of wisdom. (Psalm 111:10)

Just as there are many levels of power in a communication, wisdom should be exercised throughout the process of communicating. Wisdom is the ability to make sound judgments and to deal sagaciously with the facts and with every aspect of a communication so that you can make the right choice. With respect to our automotive metaphor, wisdom enables us to stay on the road by helping us make the many decisions involved in steering our car to our destination.

"Now if any of you lacks wisdom, he should ask God, who gives to all generously and without criticizing, and it will be given to him" (James 1:5).

Our wisdom question is, "Who am I?"

"The one who trusts in himself is a fool, but one who walks in wisdom will be safe" (Prov. 28:26).

As Christians, we know that each of us is created by God, in his image, for a special purpose. Each of us has been given the gifts, talents, and desires to fulfill his purpose for us.

Too many of us do not know what God's purpose is for our lives or what our unique gifts and talents are. Therefore, we are often ineffective in our communications because the genre, or the medium, we have chosen is not suited to our talents, or the role we have chosen is not appropriate for us (i.e., we are trying to communicate as an evangelist when we have been called to be a prophet).

This does not mean that some of us are exempt from testifying to the gospel of Jesus Christ. We are all commanded to proclaim the gospel (Matt. 28:19; Rom. 10:14–15). However, how we present the gospel will depend on who we are and what gifts and talents God has given us. Referring back to our automotive metaphor, knowing who I am and what my gifts and talents are helps me to make sound judgments regarding how fast I can take a curve or, for that matter, what kind of a car is best for me to drive in the first place.

The question, Who am I? should be asked in conjunction with our other questions and should not be treated as ontological speculation.

Call

Then I heard the voice of the Lord saying: "Who should I send? Who will go for Us?" I said: "Here I am. Send me." And He replied: "Go! Say to these people." (Isaiah 6:8–9)

We have been called by God out of darkness (1 Pet. 2:9), into the eternal glory of his kingdom (1 Pet. 5:10) to take our place in his body (1 Cor. 12:27–30) to be his witnesses "in Jerusalem, in all Judea and Sumaria, and to the ends of the earth" (Acts 1:8). Responding to God's call involves power, wisdom, and understanding. We have asked the power and wisdom questions; shortly, we will consider understanding. Here we shall look at that aspect of our call that relates to those to whom and with whom we are called to communicate, those who will receive our communication—our audience.

Who is my audience? "After he had seen the vision, we immediately made efforts to set out for Macedonia, concluding that God had called us to evangelize them" (Acts 16:10).

The question, Who is my audience? is in fact a set of questions, including: What are the physical, psychological, emotional, spiritual, racial, political, sexual, and other characteristics of the audience whom I am trying to reach? What do they want to hear? Will they respond to the genre I have chosen? Where do they live? Will the medium I have chosen reach them? Whom will, and whom does, the medium I have chosen reach? Is there a more appropriate, or a more effective, or a less expensive medium that I can use to reach my intended audience?

Our audience must be clearly defined and understood if we want to reach the audience we intended with our communication and if we want our communication to have maximum impact.

If our intended audience is small, then it would be foolish to buy prime time on broadcast television to reach them; however, satellite-casting might be advisable if that small audience is spread out over a large, sparsely populated area, such as Alaska or Minnesota.

Once we have chosen the appropriate medium to reach our intended audience, then we have to determine how we can best adapt, translate, and contextualize our communication without compromising our message so that our audience will not only understand but also relate to what we are communicating. Just as Paul talked to the Epicurean and Stoic philosophers about the "unknown God" whom he proceeded to make known, so we should tailor our communications to our audience, being extremely careful not to lose our message in the process. Part of this process is choosing and conforming our communication to the appropriate genre or format, whether that genre is a story, parable, interview, instruction, sermon, or another appropriate format.

It is not uncommon for Christians to fall into the make-believe mission trap, either by choosing the wrong medium to reach their intended audience, or by failing to speak to their audience in a language the audience can understand, or by failing to adapt their communication to address the audience's cultural perspective, or by all of the above. To say that we are reaching Afghanistan for Christ because we are sending an English-language television program over a satellite whose footprint covers that area of Asia is make-believe mission if almost no one in Afghanistan has a satellite dish and few speak English or cannot relate to the cultural context of our communication.

Whomever we are called to reach, we have to know who they are and where they are to reach them with our communications. In terms of our automobile metaphor, knowing who our audience is and where they live gives us our destination, where we are going, and where we have been called.

Understanding

Look! The fear of the Lord—that is wisdom, and to turn from evil is understanding. (Job 28:28)

Frequently in Scripture, power, wisdom, knowledge, and understanding are mentioned together in discussing the attributes of God (Isa. 11:2) and of those individuals who seek, follow, and love God (Prov. 2). By definition, *understanding* means "to comprehend, or apprehend, the meaning of something." Understanding is the power to comprehend, judge, and render experience intelligible.

God considers understanding so important that he tells us to get it "though it cost all you have" (Prov. 4:7 NIV). To communicate effectively, we must understand our motivation, our premise, our medium of choice, our gifts, our talents, our resources, the truth, and our audience. This may sound difficult; however, by asking the right questions and trusting in his grace, we can communicate powerfully, effectively, and in love.

Although understanding applies to all aspects of our communications, the question that directly involves understanding is, What am I communicating? "Understanding is a fountain of life to those who have it" (Prov. 16:22 NIV).

The first step toward understanding what you are communicating is to set forth exactly what you want to communicate. It would be nice to say that you know exactly what you want to communicate, so do so. However, many people have the desire to communicate, the means to do so, and the ability, but no clear idea of what they want to communicate. Every year movies, television programs, and other big-budget communications fail because the author did not know what he or she wanted to communicate. Anyone who has stared at a blank piece of paper or at an empty computer monitor in the throes of writer's block knows that we do not always know what we want to communicate.

However, for your communication to be intelligible to your audience, you must know precisely what you want to communicate. Asking the questions set forth in this book will help you formulate what you want to communicate. Also, setting forth your thoughts and ideas as briefly and succinctly as possible is an excellent way to get started.

Once you are clear about what you want to communicate, you must determine what format or genre you will use to communicate it, and you need to understand the genre you have chosen and how that genre affects your communication. Also, you must understand the medium through which you will be communicating and how that particular medium affects your communication. You must adapt what you want to communicate to your genre and medium of choice.

Furthermore, you must know your audience and how they will receive your communication. You must adapt your communication to your audience. You must also understand what God wants you to communicate and how that affects what you want to communicate. Finally, after you have communicated, you should seek feedback from your audience so that you can improve and perfect your communication.

In terms of our automotive metaphor, understanding what we are communicating is comparable to being able to deliver our message in an intelligible fashion when we arrive at our destination, the audience.

Truth

Speak truth to one another. (Zechariah 8:16)

We all know what truth is; truth is veracity, sincerity, genuineness, conformity to rule, exactness, and correctness. Truth is the opposite of falsehood. Truth is often defined as that which conforms to reality. As Christians, we know that truth conforms ultimately to the Word of God.

Truth is also necessary in the most imaginative fiction, for such fiction must be true to the rules established by its author; otherwise such fiction will seem shallow, empty, and false to its audience. Christians can and should create great, imaginative communications in all the media in the tradition of C. S. Lewis and Bach, realizing that truth does not demand strict neorealism; rather, it demands an attention to detail so that our communication is true to its own rules. Truth, like all the other categories we have considered, affects the various levels, internal and external, of our communication.

The key truth question is, What does God want me to communicate? "Do not be hasty to speak, and do not be impulsive to make a speech before God" (Eccl. 5:2).

God wants us to "make disciples . . . teaching them to observe everything I have commanded you" (Matt. 28:19–20). God wants us to witness in word and deed to his Word, his salvation, and his good news (Col. 3:17). This is both a simple and a complex task because, although the gospel can be stated briefly (John 3:16), the whole gospel contains eternal, infinite truth, which bursts forth from Scripture to fill every aspect of life and death, even touching the threshold of eternity.

In his Word we are told that "Samson went to Gaza, where he saw a prostitute and went to bed with her" (Judg. 16:1). The Word of God is true

IN THE BEGINNING 55

to life, the good and the bad, because God is interested in saving us from death. Often we create false visions of life because we deny the reality of evil and death. On the other hand, pagans often deny the reality of good and seldom touch on the possibility of real life, eternal life. However, there are instances of nonbelievers clearly communicating his truth, as in paintings of the crucifixion or movies such as *Chariots of Fire, Jesus of Nazareth,* and Pier Paolo Pasolini's *Gospel According to St. Matthew,*[5] produced and written by nonbelievers (God can raise up stones). Saccharine communications are not truthful.

Truth is the gasoline, the fuel on which our automobile runs. Water it down, and our car will run poorly, eventually breaking down completely.

Stewardship

Each one should use whatever gift he has received
to serve others. (1 Peter 4:10 NIV)

We have been appointed by God as stewards over everything he created on earth, in the sea, and in the air (Gen. 1:27ff). As stewards, we are to manage, supervise, harvest, protect, nourish, and care for that magnificent creation that has been entrusted to us. Fulfilling our role as stewards requires effective communication, and to communicate effectively we must be aware of the resources available to us.

Everything said about asking the right questions could be seen as a function of stewardship since the key to good stewardship is accurate ascertainment. In terms of our automobile metaphor, stewardship not only involves determining whether we have enough money, gas, oil, food, water, and other supplies; but also, whether we have the motivation, the ability, the skill, the right car, and a predetermined destination, all of which are necessary for our communications trip. However, to help focus and clarify our ascertainment questions, our stewardship question does not include questions that we cover elsewhere.

Our stewardship question is, What are my resources? "For which of you, wanting to build a tower, doesn't first sit down and calculate the cost to see if he has enough to complete it? Otherwise, after he has laid the foundation and cannot finish it, all the onlookers will begin to make fun of him, saying, 'This man started to build and wasn't able to finish'" (Luke 14:28–30).

At some point in our lives, most of us have fallen into the predicament of not being able to finish a project either because we did not have enough resources (money, time, supplies, energy, and/or assistance), we mismanaged our resources, we failed to recognize our resources, or all of the above. As Jesus notes, this is an embarrassing and usually unnecessary situation, although there are those occasions where unpredictable circumstances sabotage a project. Before we start to communicate, we should count the cost, ascertain what our resources are, choose our medium of communication, and target our audience based on the resources available to us.

Counting the cost and ascertaining our resources does not mean that we forsake our call to communicate to a specific audience. Rather, it means that we take the time to prepare our communications properly by ascertaining what resources are available to us and what resources we will have to secure through fund-raising and prayer, or what steps we will have to take to adapt our communication to our limited resources.

It is important to remind ourselves when we ask this question that, sometimes, trying to do everything ourselves (hands-on production) is the most expensive approach in the long run. The excess cost of hands-on production can show up either in the time that it takes for us to learn how to communicate through the medium of choice or in the lack of quality of our final communication, which prevents it from reaching our audience and communicating what we intended.

Once while I was teaching a Communicate Workshop, a student told me that his church had been talked into purchasing a large amount of video equipment to communicate their presence to their community. The church proceeded to use the equipment to produce a desired communication. To their great surprise, the finished product looked like a home movie. In their disappointment they put their new video equipment in a closet and forgot it. This is a classic case of video burnout.

They would not have burned out on the equipment if they had taken the time to learn about the equipment before they bought it and determined whether they had the resources, including talent, to use the equipment for the production they had in mind. After ascertaining what the equipment could do and what their resources were, then they should have decided whether to buy the equipment. Whether or not they bought the equipment, they should have considered hiring the right talent to produce their communication for them (hands-off production). Note the mistakes inherent in their approach: they put their faith in the new technology to solve their communications problems (this state of mind could be called videolatry); they did not ask the right questions to determine how to communicate what they wanted to communicate; and they did not ascertain their resources.

Hands-off production should not become a shibboleth. There are many instances where hands-on production is appropriate, especially where the talent is available to communicate effectively in the medium of choice or learning the medium of choice is an important part of the communication. At a church in New York City, we involved a group of teenagers in producing their own television program that aired on the local access cable television channel. Producing their own television program helped them to think about the nature of the medium, the nature of the gospel, and how they could communicate the gospel through that medium. Many of the teenagers discovered their motivational talents. Several of them came to know Jesus as Lord and Savior while producing that program.

In counting the cost of equipment, remember that the more sophisticated the equipment, the more it usually costs to maintain. When I was the director of the Television Center at the Brooklyn College Campus of the City University of New York, the chief engineer estimated that the maintenance cost of new equipment per year was equivalent to one-third the purchase price of the equipment.

Advances in technology have reduced these maintenance costs. Less sophisticated equipment and consumer equipment cost much less to maintain. Nevertheless, it is important to count the cost of maintaining your equipment and prepare to meet those maintenance costs before you purchase equipment, or you will find yourself with broken-down, expensive equipment taking up precious space and reminding you of your folly.

You may have more resources available to you than you realize. In many cases, ascertaining what your resources are means becoming aware of what talent and assets are. Often the local television station, cable television system, or radio station will help you with your communication if the medium is appropriate.

In determining your access to the local cable system, television station, or radio station, you should find out who runs it, why they run it, and why they might be interested in your communication. Most often they run their station or system to make a profit, and they will be interested in what you want to communicate if it will help them to make a profit by giving them more viewers or listeners. Your communication may give them more viewers directly, or it may improve their image with the community and thereby help them to attract more viewers.

A few years ago representatives of the Chinese community in New York City approached their local cable system about access to program time on the premier channel on the system. At first the cable system said that no time was available. The Chinese pointed out that many Chinese subscribers would be added to the customer rolls of the cable system and that the appropriate New York City licensing board would be more likely to renew the cable system's license if the system gave them the time they wanted. The cable system changed its corporate mind and gave the Chinese three hours per week on the premier cable channel.

Locating talent may be the most important aspect of ascertaining your resources. Gifted individuals, working together in love, motivated by God, can do wonders with second-rate equipment. There have been many Emmy Award-winning television programs produced on nonprofessional equipment by dedicated individuals. The talent questions in a later chapter will help you find the right talent for your communication.

Try to be a good steward of the talent available. Good talent must be given the freedom to be professional while they are guided toward the communication goal. If you do not have the ability to shepherd the talent necessary for your communication, find a producer who can. Respect is the key to working with talent.

As stated in the introduction, God provides the resources for us to do what he has called us to do. If you count the cost and find yourself short of resources, pray. God answers.

Impact

No one should seek his own [good], but [the good]
of the other person. (1 Corinthians 10:24)

Impact is the other side of power. It is the force with which our communication collides with the audience. The impact of our communication depends on our ability to address our audience where they need to be addressed. To ascertain how to communicate in a way that will have the maximum impact on our audience, we should ask this multilayered question: "What needs to be communicated to my audience? My church? My community? My nation? My world?" "The poor and the needy seek water, but there is none; their tongues are parched with thirst. I, the LORD, will answer them; I, the God of Israel, do not forsake them" (Isa. 41:17).

The advertising industry is built on addressing people's needs so those people will buy a product to meet that addressed need. Often the advertised product will not meet the need the advertiser used to motivate the people to buy the product in the first place. For instance, to sell a product a television advertiser may address the audience's social need for love, claiming that the product, such as toothpaste, will give the audience more friends of the opposite sex, even though that product will not meet the audience's need for love, nor will it give the audience more friends of the opposite sex. Listening to the audience through market research tells an advertiser what needs need to be addressed for their communication to have maximum impact.

In determining needs, advertisers often rely on the research of psychologist Abraham Maslow, Ph.D., who attempted to synthesize a large body of research related to human motivation.[6] Maslow proposed a hierarchy of eight human needs:

1. Physiological: hunger, thirst, bodily comforts, etc.

2. Safety/security: out of danger

3. Belongingness and love: affiliate with others, be accepted

4. Esteem: to achieve, be competent, gain approval and recognition

5. Cognitive: to know, to understand, and explore

6. Aesthetic: symmetry, order, and beauty

7. Self-actualization: to find self-fulfillment and realize one's potential

8. Self-transcendence: to connect to something beyond the ego or to help others find self-fulfillment and realize their potential

This self-transcendence is, in fact, our spiritual need, that can manifest itself as the desire for any or all of the above mentioned needs but is a desire for communion with God—Father, Son, and Holy Spirit—for "man must not live on bread alone" (Matt. 4:4).

Needs are expressed by desires, but desires can be fanned by temptation into all-consuming concupiscence. Hunger is an essential desire that expresses the natural, physical need for food, but gluttony is hunger run amuck.

All of us are sinners, but as communicators who are also Christians, we should not fan natural desires into sins just so we can motivate our audience to buy our products or ideas. The natural desires to procreate, to love and to be loved, have often been fanned and forged into lust so that an advertiser can sell a product such as blue jeans. More often than not, the desire that has been blown out of proportion will not be satisfied by the product in question; the product can't deliver on the promises made for it in the advertisement.

Communicators all too often resort to aggravating desires to give impact to their communication because they are too lazy, or rushed, to ask and answer all the other questions that would help make their communication effective. Addressing and aggravating desires becomes a quick fix, an easy way to impact an audience, rather than building a truly powerful, effective communication.

For our communications to have a powerful impact on our audience, we must ascertain and address our audience's needs, wants, and feelings by listening to them. To do so, we should undertake the appropriate market research. Furthermore, our communications will deliver on God's promises if we are communicating his truth. If we discipline ourselves to ask and apply the right questions and learn the language and grammar of the medium of choice, then we will communicate powerfully and effectively.

Prophesy

The men of Nineveh believed in God. They proclaimed a fast and dressed in sackcloth—from the greatest of them to the least. (Jonah 3:5)

Jonah did not want to go to Nineveh to proclaim God's judgment because he knew that God would relent from sending destruction on Nineveh if the Ninevites repented (Jon. 4:1–3). Jonah wanted sinful Nineveh destroyed. He wanted the prophecy God gave him to preach to be fulfilled. He preached destruction, and he wanted the destruction he preached to occur to prove his status as a prophet of the one true God. He was concerned with his image and his righteousness. He was not concerned about the people of Nineveh. He did not want his prophesying to result in active repentance by the Ninevites, but it did.

By definition, *prophesy* means "to foretell or forthtell under divine inspiration." All our communications should be divinely inspired because God's Holy Spirit dwells in us. Our communications should forthtell, and/or foretell, in that they proclaim the truth.

As was the case with our other categories, to prophesy relates to and affects all aspects of communication. To distinguish our ascertainment questions, our prophesy question will focus on the consequences of prophesying.

The key question that relates to our call to prophesy is, Will my communication result in action? "John came baptizing in the wilderness and preaching a baptism of repentance for the forgiveness of sins. The whole Judean countryside and all the people of Jerusalem were flocking to him, and they were baptized by him in the Jordan River as they confessed their sins" (Mark 1:4–5).

Unlike Jonah, most of us want our communications to result in action. In one sense every communication results in action, even if that action is only the internal decision to perceive the communication and reject or ignore it. However, we are not concerned here with an internal decision to ignore a communication, nor are we concerned with communications that are received and then forgotten. Rather, to prophesy is to demand a reaction, a movement of the heart, a conscious decision, a motivation to do or reject the necessary consequences of the communication. If you have clearly stated your premise, which you will learn how to do if you don't already know, and you have answered all the pertinent ascertainment questions prior to this one, then your communication will result in action.

To prophesy is to proclaim our communication with such inherent power that our audience climbs into our car and drives with us into the kingdom of God.

Revelation

For now we see through a glass, darkly; but then face to face: now
I know in part; but then shall I know even as also I am known.
(1 Corinthians 13:12 KJV)

From the first chapter of Paul's letter to the Romans, we know that all of creation reveals God's eternal power and divine nature. God communicates himself and his will to us through revelation, and we reveal his revelation to others. Communication should make the unknown known to those to and with whom we are communicating. Therefore, our revelation question is, Did my communication succeed? "The Spirit searches everything, even the deep things of God" (1 Cor. 2:10).

"Did my communication succeed?" may be restated in several ways to help us evaluate the effectiveness of our communication: Did my communication make the unknown known? Did my communication communicate what I intended? How did my audience react to my communication?

To reveal the effectiveness of your communication, you must have feedback. Feedback simply means taking the time to listen to your audience after your communication, whether or not they have joined us on our drive in the eternal kingdom of God.

There are many methods and devices for obtaining feedback from your audience, but regardless of what listening technique you use, the important point is that you seek feedback from your audience and God, and that you heed that feedback. Feedback continually helps us to reevaluate our communications and improve upon them.

This does not mean that we compromise or dilute our message because we receive negative feedback. Instead, this means that the feedback allows us the opportunity to improve our presentation of the revelation that we have received from God so that we can help to bring more people into the kingdom. Feedback should bring us closer to God and to the joy (and cost) of communicating his good news. As Jesus said, "For I gave them the words you gave me and they accepted them. They knew with certainty that I came from you, and they believed that you sent me" (John 17:8 NIV).

At the beginning of this chapter, we asked the most basic communication question: "How do I communicate exactly what I need or want to communicate to the person I want or need to reach, using the appropriate medium properly so that my audience will understand and be convinced, motivated, educated, and/or informed?" The answer we have seen is threefold:

1. Ask and answer the right ascertainment questions to arrive at exactly what I want to communicate, why I want to communicate it, to whom I want to communicate it, how I want to communicate it, what genre and medium are appropriate with respect to who I am, what my motivational talent is, and what impact or consequence I want my communication to have.

2. Learn the language and grammar of the appropriate genre and medium of choice.

3. Apply the ascertained answers and the language and grammar of the genre and medium of choice to communicate effectively.

To simplify our task in the future, let us review the ascertainment questions posed in this chapter, keeping in mind that there are other questions we may add to this list depending on the nature of a particular communication and that a specific communication may not demand that we ask all these questions. Furthermore, the chapters that follow will treat some of these questions in depth and pose other ascertainment questions.

- Why do I want to communicate?
- Who am I?
- Who is my audience?
- What are the physical, psychological, emotional, spiritual, racial, political, sexual, and other characteristics of the audience I am trying to reach?
- What do they want to hear?
- Will they respond to the genre I have chosen?
- Where do they live?
- Will the medium I have chosen reach them?
- Who will and who does the medium I have chosen reach?
- Is there a more appropriate, or a more effective, or a less expensive medium I can use to reach my intended audience?
- What am I communicating?
- What is the premise of my communication?
- What does God want me to communicate?
- What are my resources?
- What needs to be communicated to my audience? My church? My community? My nation? My world?
- Will my communication result in action?
- Did my communication succeed?

CHAPTER 3

Places Please

This above all: to thine own self be true, and it must follow, as the night the day, thou canst not then be false to any man.
—William Shakespeare, Hamlet

W ho are you? What is God's plan for your life?

When he was four years old, our oldest son wanted to be a government official (the president) and a baseball player. Today, an adult, he is translating the Bible in Papua, New Guinea, for Wycliffe Bible Translators. Most of the students in my Communicate Workshops, whatever their age, come into the workshop wanting to be the star, the director, or the producer of their own television program. Philip Carey, in Somerset Maugham's *Of Human Bondage,* wanted to be an Anglican priest in his youth, then he decided to become an artist, then an accountant, and finally he finds out that he is called to be a doctor. The question arises, Does it matter which profession Philip chooses? Or what my son becomes (aside from his father's pride)? Or what roles the students take in the Communicate Workshops?

With regard to Philip, the answer is a resounding "Yes, it matters!" because Maugham has so drawn Philip's character that he has no alternative other than eventually to become a doctor. In drama, novels, and other storytelling genres, the dynamics inherent in a character's bone structure determine the character's development and actions as that character reacts to the other characters within the context of the premise. If an author has done his or her job of getting to know a character by determining every aspect of the character's physiology (such as sex, age, posture, appearance, defects, and heredity), sociology (such as class, occupation, education, race, and home life), psychology (such as temperament, attitude, complexes, motivations, and abilities), and spirituality, then that character will develop in the story as the author intended because the character's makeup is such that the character cannot do otherwise. If any other alternative is available to the character, then the author has not done his or her job, and the bone structure of the character has to be rethought.

As Henrik Ibsen emphasized:

> When I am writing I must be alone; if I have eight characters of drama to do with, I have society enough; they keep me busy; I must learn to know them. And this process of making their acquaintance is slow and painful. I make, as a rule, three casts of my dramas, which differ considerably from each other. I mean in characteristics, not in the course of the treatment. When I first settle down to work out my material, I feel as if I have to get to know my characters on a railway journey; the first acquaintance is struck up, and we have chatted about this and that. When I write it down again, I already see everything much more clearly, and I know the people as if I had stayed with them for a month at a watering place. I have grasped the leading points of their characters and their little peculiarities.[1]

Philip has to become a doctor because Maugham has constructed Philip so that he will become a doctor. However, what about our eldest son? Or youngest for that matter? Or the Communicate Workshop students?

Unlike a character in a story, our son or a student can persist in pursuing a job or role that is not suited for him or her. According to some studies, three or four out of five people are in the wrong jobs. However, just because we persist in the wrong job does not mean that we are not designed to excel in a job that suits our motivational talents and gifts. We are.

According to many career counselors, every individual has a unique combination of characteristics that give him or her the ability to excel in a particular career. Of course, different people perform the same job differently. In fact, saying that a person creates a job is probably a more accurate point of view than saying that a person adapts to a job.

As Christians, we realize that these findings by scientists and career counselors are nothing more than an affirmation of the fact that God has designed each of us for a particular purpose. God created and is interested in the real world. Just as he became a carpenter, so he chooses some of us to be rulers, some to be bankers, some to be craftsmen, some to be scientists, and each of us to be what he has created us to be (Rom. 13:1; 1 Cor. 12; Col. 1:16). He tells us: "I create the blacksmith, who builds a fire and forges weapons. I also create the soldier, who uses the weapons to kill" (Isa. 54:16 GNB).

He gives each of us those talents and desires to excel in a particular role. He also gives us the free will to choose to flourish by fulfilling his plan for our lives or to choose to be frustrated by rebelling against him and ourselves.

Even before the fall, work was a part of God's plan for man's life: "The LORD God took the man and placed him in the garden of Eden to work it and watch over it" (Gen. 2:15).

After the fall, work became difficult and exhausting. However, in spite of our fall, God wants to bless and prosper us and wants us to rejoice in all that we do because he created us for his pleasure. He rejoices over us, and he loves us. This is great news: God wants us to be joyous and enjoy our work; however, to do so, we must submit to his glorious plan for our lives, give thanks, and be content in all circumstances.

In the church we sometimes assume that God's plan for us is limited to prayer, praise, worship, social action, evangelism, Bible reading, and the other aspects of spirituality we discern in the New Testament. Living a holy life is a worthy goal (even if it is only fully attainable in heaven); however, since work is part of God's plan for our lives, our sanctification takes place in our living out his plan, not in our escaping the secular work world to adopt a religious role for which he has not created us or called us.

God may call us to be apostles or clergy, but too many Christians upon conversion drop out of the so-called secular world to pursue so-called Christian careers. The institutional churches have recently come to the realization that they are partially responsible for this rush to change from a secular to a sacred career by sometimes adopting a low view of the laity and an exalted view of the clergy. (The opposite perspective is also wrong.) Churches must learn to recognize, bless, and ordain nonclerical jobs, as Jesus did. As Martin Luther said: "Be the monk never so holy, his work is no more holy than the farmer in the field, or the housewife at home."

Another influence causing this leap into the clothe or into so-called Christian professions is the prevailing, unbiblical view that wealth and profits are bad, when, in fact, God protects property ("Thou shall not steal"), wants us to prosper, and praises the man who makes a profit. It is not money that is bad but the love of it.

Several times a year I meet a successful communicator who has come to know Jesus as Lord and Savior and who wants to know how to get into "Christian" communications. Many of these influential individuals leave prominent positions at network television stations, advertising agencies, or editorial boards of major newspapers where they can impact the mass communications industry. They enter the Christian communications industry where they are never heard from again, or their voice is limited to the Christian communications enclave.

When we come to know him, God frees us from bondage to sin not so we can escape from the world but so we can witness to him in word and deed in the marketplace where he called us, unless he indicates otherwise. God calls us to "occupy till I come" (Luke 19:13 KJV) by working in and taking charge of the mass media and all areas of life. His plan is for us to be coworkers with him in redeeming the world by doing that which he has designed us to do best in his name.

Every individual has a specific contribution to make to society and civilization. Every job that each person performs within our society is important to our society whether that person is working as a doctor, a corporate executive, a shoemaker, a homemaker, or a janitor, even though, in our fallenness, we tend to glamorize some jobs, belittle others, and discount the remainder. We should, however, respect every job, even though some jobs demand, deserve, and receive more compensation and/or authority than others. In the biblical model of the world, there is a definite hierarchy, but that chain of authority is qualitatively different from any social hierarchy we experience because each person is dedicated to loving, respecting, and serving God, and to one another.

This brings us back to the question: What is God's plan for your life? In other words, what has God designed you to do? And how do you find out what God has designed you to do?

Since each of us has many talents and motivations that come together to determine who we are and in what job we will flourish, we can be defined by that point where our motivations, talents, physiology, sociology, psychology, and spirituality meet, almost like a character in a story—God's story. Just as Philip Carey's future occupation was clear from his bone structure as revealed in the beginning *Of Human Bondage,* God's plan for us is revealed in those talents and motivations we exhibit throughout our personal history. Even our weaknesses are instruments of God's grace. By discerning and analyzing our characteristics as they reveal themselves in our own history, we can discover what those jobs or roles are.

At age seventeen, Joseph, although he was the youngest brother, clearly exhibited talents and motivations that would make him the leader of his family, his people, and the Egyptians. Joseph was respectful of authority, responsible, obedient, intelligent, wise, and a man of vision; furthermore, Joseph was motivated by his dream of leadership.

As a youth confronted by a messenger of God, Gideon exhibited the fearlessness, cunning, and drive to save Israel. Later in his life these same characteristics would propel him to become a mighty warrior judge of his people, even when God put him in impossible positions so that God's glory was revealed through Gideon's triumph.

Daniel, as a youth, exhibited those characteristics that were to make him a leader and a prophet:

> The king ordered Ashpenaz, the chief of his court officials, to bring some of the Israelites from the royal family and from the nobility—young men without any physical defect, good-looking, suitable for instruction in all wisdom, knowledgeable, perceptive, and capable of serving in the king's palace. . . . Daniel determined that he would not defile himself with the king's food or with the wine he drank. So he asked permission from the chief official not to defile himself. . . . God gave these four young men knowledge and understanding in every kind of literature and wisdom. Daniel also understood visions and dreams of every kind. (Dan. 1:3–4, 8, 17)

From Noah through Abraham, David, and Solomon to John the Baptist, Peter, and Paul, those characteristic talents and motivations that determine each one's role in history can be discerned at the beginning of their lives, including the weaknesses that caused any victories to be attributed to God rather than to a man. God has his plan for each of us. All we need to do is discern it.

Two articles from our contributors, Donzaleigh Albernathy, a wonderful actress, and Randall Wallace, writer of many epic movies, including *Braveheart, The Man in the Iron Mask, Pearl Harbor,* and *We Were Soldiers,* director of *The Man in the Iron Mask* and *We Were Soldiers,* producer of many movies, musician, and father, will help out here. Go to www.movieguide.org to read these articles.

As indicated by Donzaleigh's and Randall's experiences, if you read their articles on our Web site, there are as many ways to discern God's plan for our lives as there are people, careers, and career counselors. Most systems boil down to designating several distinct periods in your life, recalling four or five of your achievements during each period, and then analyzing what motivations and talents went into those achievements. From this analysis, your motivational talents, thrust, characteristics, and pattern may be discerned and related to those jobs for which that combination of motivations and talents is a prerequisite.

Research indicates that companies structured according to motivational talents are much more productive and successful than companies that hire and organize people on the basis of a job description. The classic example is hiring a secretary because she can type one hundred words a minute without a mistake, only to find that she doesn't fit into the position because she is motivated to lead and organize the office, not type. If her history had been reviewed with an eye toward discovering her motivational talents, it would have been clear, for example, that she was a leader throughout her childhood, and she was best suited to be an office administrator.

Of course, this is a simplistic example. All of us have many talents, motivations, and gifts. Someone, for instance, may be motivated to race cars, read books, compile statistics, and design houses; however, they may be talented at learning languages, playing chess, and persuading audiences of logical imperatives; furthermore, they may have the gifts of helping and teaching. Our hypothetical person should clearly not run off and race cars without considering the total picture defined by motivational talents and gifts. Furthermore, as noted in the last chapter, motivation is often more important than talent, although both talents and motivations should be considered in choosing a profession.

If you want to communicate effectively, you need to know your motivations, talents, and personal characteristics as they relate to communications. Communication impacts all aspects of life, and there are many different methods of communicating effectively involving many different motivational talents. As a medium, television involves a constellation of motivational talents—from financial wizardry through electronic genius to a highly developed sense of time, space, and rhythm, to the motivated ability to project an image through time and space to a faceless audience.

To know which method and which medium of communication you should use, you should know what your motivational design is. Not knowing your motivational design, you can find yourself frustrated, communicating ineffectively through a medium that is alien to you in a style that works for others but not for you.

Pick out a few of the better preachers in your community and analyze their preaching. You will no doubt find that some of them are good story-tellers, some are good exegetes, some are good teachers, and some are powerful prophets. For you to choose to be a storytelling preacher when nei-ther the method of storytelling nor the medium of preaching is appropriate for your motivational talents would be extremely frustrating and perhaps self-destructive.

In the Communicate Workshops, the students work through a few exer-cises where each of them tries their hand at being the star or director in accordance with their fantasies. They quickly discover whether they have the aptitude for that role and whether they really like being in their fantasy role. More often than not, many find that they really do not want to be the star or the director, but they do enjoy doing what they do best, whether it is lighting, set design, engineering, or another important television task. In fact, they find that they excel at those jobs for which they have the propen-sity and the right motivational abilities.

This is not a career counseling book, but each of us needs to be aware of our motivational talents if we want to communicate effectively. Not only does the specific motivation for a particular communication, as discussed in the last chapter, flow from who you are; but also, the intensity of the moti-vation for a specific communication is determined to a large degree by your God-given motivational thrust. Therefore, on www.movieguide.org, we have posted an article under "So You Want to Be in Pictures?" to help acquaint you with the process of discovering your motivational talents by giving you several practical exercises that demonstrate the methods used by several career counselors. Included later in this chapter is a brief exercise for determining your role in movie and television production.

Knowing your motivational picture will enable you to communicate more effectively by helping you to determine what you want to communi-cate, why you want to communicate, to whom you want to communicate, and through what genre and medium you want to communicate. Your motivational direction and motivational talents will tell you what matters most to you and why you want to communicate. Your motivated characteristics and talents will indicate to whom and in what circumstance you are most comfortable and effective communicating. Your motivational picture will guide you into using the appropriate medium for your gifts and talents once you are aware of the nature of the available media.

Of course God and unique circumstances can make you an effective communicator of subjects and in media that are not predictable by your motivational pattern. Also, God frequently uses our weaknesses to accomplish his purpose. Moses with his speech problems is a good case in point. In most instances, however, by being sensitive to your motivational picture, you will communicate much more effectively than you would if you ignored your own motivated talents and characteristics.

For example, an acquaintance of mine is an excellent lecturer/teacher of memory techniques. Reviewing his personal history, it is clear that he has been driven by the desire to memorize (his motivational thrust is to memorize); his secondary motivational talents are to promote, solve problems, teach, and overcome, in that order; his motivated faculty is charisma; his motivated object is images; his motivated relationship is leadership; and his motivated circumstance is in a lecture hall in front of an audience. He knows what he wants to communicate—memory techniques; why he wants to communicate—to help others by teaching them; who his audience is—a live audience whom he can lead; and what his appropriate medium is— lecturing. He is an effective communicator because he is true to his motivational pattern.

In the fall of 1984, the Continental Basketball Association (CBA), the minor league of professional basketball, held an amateur contest to find the official CBA television "color" commentator. About three hundred lawyers, accountants, doctors, salesmen, and even an FBI agent showed up to try out for CBA sportscaster. Having to keep up with a four-minute segment of fast action on a television monitor, one Connecticut man blurted out in frustration, "The players are running around everywhere." A New York equipment operator sat through the four-minute segment in embarrassed silence. Hal Lancaster, reporting on this modern-day *Ted Mack's Amateur Hour* in the *Wall Street Journal,* captured these comments: "'It's a lot tougher than you think,' says Rick Hansen, a computer researcher for International Business Machines Corp. 'It looks so easy sitting at home.' Adds Robb Larson, the CBA's vice president of entertainment services: 'One guy said it was worse than his first date.'"[4]

Most of the contestants did not take into consideration their motivational talents before they tried out to be a sportscaster.

As you learn more about the various media, you will be able to discern how you can communicate most effectively through each particular medium. The following exercise illustrates through talent questions the different major roles involved in a simplified movie production. Ask these questions of yourself with reference to your motivational pattern to see where you would fit in a television production.

Simplified Televison and Movie Talent Exercise

For each role or job, a series of questions follows that briefly sketches the major motivational talent required for that role. These questions are also useful for recruiting talent to produce a television program or a film.

Executive producer
- Can you raise money and secure resources and talent?
- Are you good at getting?
- Can you wheel and deal?

Producer
- Can you get a group of creative individuals to work together and finish a project?

Line producer
- Can you take orders and execute them?
- Can you keep track of resources?
- Are you careful with your bank balance?

Director
- Can you bring the best out of people?

Author
- Can you articulate your ideas dramatically?

Scriptwriter
- Can you take ideas and develop them into a story?
- Can you write dialogue?

Production manager in television
- Can you keep people working on time?
- Can you organize people?

Director of photography
- Can you visualize stories?
- Do you recognize authenticity?

Cameraperson
- Can you frame a picture?
- Can you focus a camera?
- Can you compose a picture?

Audio engineer in television and post-production sound mixer in movies
- Do you like music?
- Do you dislike a bad recording?

Soundperson
- Do you like sounds?
- Can you tell the difference in the quality of a recording?

Art director in television and production designer in film
- Can you capture a period? A look? A moment in time?

Video engineer in television
- Can you make sure that the video equipment is doing what it is supposed to be doing?
- Can you think and act immediately?
- Are you an electronic whiz?

Technical director in television
- Are you good at running a model railroad?

Location manager
- Do you know your way around?

- Do you have a good sense of direction?
- Can you get the cooperation of the people affected by the production?

Prop manager

- Do you enjoy rummaging through thrift shops?
- Are you good at treasure hunting?
- Can you find just the right thing?

Grip

- Do you like to help?
- Are you strong?

Gaffer/chief lighting technician in movies and lighting director/engineer in television

- Do you see things in dark (black) and light?
- Are you good with electrical wiring?
- Can you fix an electrical appliance?

Secretary/continuity

- Can you keep track of details?
- Do you follow through?

Editor

- Can you make sense out of chaos and throw away surplusage?

Makeup

- Can you see the best in people?
- Can you see the character in people?
- Can you paint?

Wardrobe

- Do you like designing clothes?
- Can you capture a look?

Special effects

- Did you have a chemistry set as a child?
- Can you make the impossible possible?

Sound effects

- Can you mimic sounds?
- Are you aware of noises?

It should be noted that each one of these production roles is important in producing a movie. Without a continuity person, scenes shot on different days will not match, and the movie will fall apart. Every production person is important and worthy of respect.

Having discerned your motivational talents and related them to production roles, you can do the same with any other medium by simply analyzing the talents required by each role involved in that medium and comparing those talent questions with your motivational picture. Furthermore, since every career, job, or activity requires communication, you can analyze the communication talents required in that career, job, or activity and compare those required talents with your motivational picture, keeping in mind that almost all careers, jobs, or activities can be modified to some degree to fit with your motivational talents.

One area of God-given talents that we have not considered in depth is the spiritual gift or gifts God gives us when we become a member of his body. These gifts are set forth in 1 Corinthians 12, Romans 12, and Ephesians 4. They are an integral part of who *I* am if the *I* is a Christian. Many of these God-given spiritual gifts relate directly to communications, and you should take the time to review them as set forth in the above mentioned chapters of the Bible.

Using the same method that you used to discern your motivational talents, you can discern your spiritual gift or gifts by focusing in on those achievements that relate to your Christian walk.

It has been said that only a fool would distrust his Creator. God has created us, giving each of us a unique combination of motivations and talents so that we can glorify him and enjoy his creation. Furthermore, as Christians, we are his children and heirs to his kingdom, anointed with spiritual gifts. We should know who we are so that we can fulfill his plan for our lives and communicate effectively in the position or role for which he has designed us.

He calls us into his body so we can occupy every area of life for him. We should praise him not only with our lips but also by loving ourselves, whom he has created us to be. As Paul said, "But each person should examine his own work, and then he will have a reason for boasting in himself alone, and not in respect to someone else" (Gal. 6:4).

However, knowing who I am and acting accordingly is only part of the process. To communicate effectively we must ask, answer, and apply each of the ascertainment questions. Furthermore, each of us must persevere in being the person God has called us to be in spite of the opposition inherent in our fallen world. Trust God and follow him. "For it was You who created my inward parts; You knit me together in my mother's womb. I will praise You, because I have been remarkably and wonderfully made. Your works are wonderful, and I know [this] very well. My bones were not hidden from You when I was made in secret, when I was formed in the depths of the earth. Your eyes saw me when I was formless; all [my] days were written in Your book and planned before a single one of them began" (Ps. 139:13–16).

CHAPTER 4

If It's Not on the Page

The first sign that a baby is going to be human comes when he begins
naming the world, demanding stories that connect its parts.
—Kathryn Morton[1]

Actually, babies are human because God created us in his image, not because they demand, or tell, stories. Communication, however, is an important part of the uniqueness of humankind, and the human drive to communicate through a variety of forms, formats, and media is remarkable. Furthermore, the primary job that God gave to Adam in the garden was to give names to the animals.

Christians and Jews have been known as people of the Book, the Bible. Since the Bible is full of stories and Christians are called by Jesus to communicate the good news, which he did through parables, Christians are a storytelling people. In faithful obedience to this call, they tell the good news through every conceivable medium and genre. Thus, the church invented modern drama with the medieval mystery plays. And since the beginning of the motion picture industry, Christians have used movies to communicate the gospel because movies and television programs are the most powerful audiovisual storytelling media.

Powerful Emotional Images

Around the world, viewers seek out, see, and hear the stories told on television and in movie theaters every day. Not only are movies and television pervasive in our society, but they also are the most powerful tools of communication. They plant powerful emotional images in our minds, direct our purchases, influence our lifestyles, and redirect our hopes and dreams.

Gary Smalley, president of Today's Family, has pointed out that altering people's actions or attitudes has always been difficult, but in 1942 Walt Disney demonstrated the power of movies to blast through the defensive barriers people erect to change their lives and the world around them. Disney's animated movie *Bambi* painted a picture that went straight to the heart. Almost overnight this Walt Disney film nearly bankrupted the deer hunting industry. As Gary notes: "The year before the film was released, deer hunting in the United States was a $9.5 million business. But when one particularly touching scene was shown—that of a yearling who sees his mother gunned down by a hunter—there was a dramatic change in men's attitudes. The following season, hunters spent only $4.1 million on tags, permits, and hunting trips!"[2]

We may applaud this use of the emotive power of film to save wildlife, but we cannot overlook the power of film to negatively affect people and our civilization. The heinous power of the emotive, emotional pictures was dramatically brought to the world's attention by Dr. James Dobson's television interview with Ted Bundy just hours before Bundy was executed in Florida's electric chair. To the dismay of newscasters across the nation and to the shock of many Americans, Bundy acknowledged that pornography had played a critical role in leading him to murder as many as twenty-eight young women and children.

In a poignant excerpt, a tearful Bundy noted that in the many years he had spent in prison with violent criminals: "Without exception, every one of them was deeply involved with pornography—without question, without exception—deeply influenced and consumed by an addiction to pornography. The FBI's own study on serial homicide shows that the most common interest among serial killers is pornography."[3]

Exclusion

Because every communication excludes what it does not include, its omissions create powerful secondary messages in the mind of the audience. An Annenberg School of Communications study on "Television and Viewer Attitudes about Work"[4] found that in the television environment blacks and other minorities were generally excluded from prestige professions. These omissions had a profound effect on specific demographic groups; some groups were demoralized by the exclusion, and others affirmed.

In a similar study a little black girl is recorded saying that she wants to be a doctor so she can travel a lot and have a big house, a pool, a plane, and a yacht. Her perception of the medical profession had been totally distorted by television's portrayal of the medical environment. Instead of being attracted to medicine as an opportunity to heal, serve, and help, she was drawn to medicine as a way to acquire things.

Selling Murder

For another poignant illustration of the power of movies, consider the work of Dr. Joseph Goebbels, the National Socialist (Nazi) propaganda minister from 1933 to 1945. He exploited radio, press, cinema, and theater in Germany to destroy the Jews, evangelical Christians, handicapped Germans, and other groups of people. In 1994, the Discovery Channel aired *Selling Murder,* an important documentary investigating how Goebbels used mass media to influence the German people to accept the mass murder of human beings. The documentary shows that a majority of German people rejected mercy killings (a euphemism for murder), even though the ministry of propaganda had released several clinical documentaries trying to convince the German people to accept the inhuman practice. Finally, Goebbels produced a dramatic movie called *I Accuse,* an emotive feature film about a beautiful, intelligent woman who is dying of an incurable disease and begs to be allowed to commit suicide. After the movie was released, a majority of German people said they had changed their minds and now supported mercy killings. After a few more of Goebbels's films about invalids and handicapped people, the German people voted for mass mercy killings.

As an insight into the power of the mass media, historian Paul Johnson writes in his book *Modern Times,* "Hitler appears always to have approached politics in terms of visual images. Like Lenin and still more like Stalin, he was an outstanding practitioner of the Century's most radical vice: social engineering—the notion that human beings can be shoveled around like concrete. But, in Hitler's case, there was always an artistic dimension to these Satanic schemes. Hitler's artistic approach was absolutely central to his success. [Historians all agree] the Germans were the best-educated nation in the world. To conquer their minds was very difficult. Their hearts, their sensibilities, were easy targets."[5]

Indoctrination, with specific use of newsreel and films, was vital to Hitler's control of the new generation. Gerhard Rempel, in his book *Hitler's Children: The Hitler Youth and the SS,* wrote: "Each day began with a newsreel, followed by the various types of training. On Sunday mornings, an ideological program was substituted for church services, and Sunday nights were set aside for motion pictures."[6]

On the Other Hand

On the positive side of the influence of the mass media of entertainment equation, the Mel Gibson movie *The Passion of the Christ* convinced millions, including criminals, to repent; the epic television program *Jesus of Nazareth* introduced millions of people throughout the world to Jesus Christ; *A Man Called Peter,* about the preacher Peter Marshall, brought a flood of young men into the pulpit; and *Chariots of Fire* brought many to Jesus and gave many more a sense of God's purpose in their life.

Story, Image, and Effect

Three elements of a movie or television program help capture the attention of the audience: story, image, and effect.

When I was director of the TV Center at City University of New York (CUNY), Brooklyn College, one of the professors, Jim Day, had been a founder of Children's Television Workshop (CTW), which produced *Sesame Street.* CTW would test every program. In one segment they wanted to show the difference between an internal skeleton and an external skeleton. The animation showed an ant while a voice-over said that the ant had an external skeleton so it could not grow as big as an elephant, which had an internal skeleton. As the narrator spoke, the animated illustration showed the ant growing as big as an elephant and then exploding. When CTW tested the segment and asked the audience whether an ant could grow as big as an elephant, 90 percent of the audience said, "Yes, an ant can grow as big as an elephant," because they had just seen it in the animated sequence, and the visual was much more powerful than the audio.

CTW also tested the extent to which each *Sesame Street* program would capture and hold the attention of the audience. CTW would show a program segment and have a distracter machine next to the TV set. (The distracter machine was merely some blinking lights.) Observers would watch the eyes of the audience to see when they looked away from the TV program and at the distracter machine. At that point CTW would put in another effect, such as a cut, dissolves, pan, wipe, or animated move, that would hold the audience's attention.

For Better or Worse

Communicating effectively requires learning and applying basic principles that are the language, grammar, rhetoric, techniques, and rules that govern each genre and medium. There are three levels of principles that govern a communication:

1. General principles that apply to most communications

2. The principles that apply to the genre through which you are communicating

3. The principles that apply to your medium of choice

Furthermore, several steps are involved in producing powerful communications, including movies and television programs. Here is a brief outline of the most important foundational steps in preparing your communication. Each genre and medium will modify this outline by adding or subtracting steps or substeps. However, this outline is your basic guide to the steps required to communicate effectively.

Twelve Basic Foundational Steps to Communicating Effectively

1. In light of who you are, why you want to communicate, and well-thought-out research and ascertainment, make a brief note of what you want to say—your idea, conviction, or key thought. This idea, thought, or statement must be something you believe and want to communicate through a movie or television program.

2. Ask and answer the appropriate ascertainment questions to target your audience, determine your genre and medium, and plan the execution of your communication.

3. Rephrase your idea or key thought into an active premise that you can prove in your communication, taking into consideration your answers to the pertinent ascertainment questions.

4. Identify the elements needed to prove your premise, most of which are inherent within your premise. In drama these elements are your characters, conflict, climax, and resolution.

5. Structure these elements, taking into consideration your audience, genre, medium of choice, and your answers to the ascertainment questions that are appropriate for your communication.

6. Write out, plan, or script your communication, punctuating it with technical, dramatic, or literary effects to capture and retain audience interest.

7. Prepare, storyboard, and/or rehearse your communication.

8. Produce, polish, or otherwise finish your communication.

9. Edit, review, and revise your communication.

10. Deliver, distribute, or broadcast your communication.

11. Survey your audience to find out how effective your communication was and how it can be improved.

12. Review and revise your communication to improve it if possible.

Half of this process is preparation. Many people fail to prepare, or they dash off a script and believe that they will perfect it when the right person buys it. However, you never have a second chance to make a first impression, so you need to get the script right, right from the beginning, even if you need to change it later.

Remember that the average movie takes nine years from start to finish. *The Passion of the Christ* took ten years. *Evita* took twenty-three years. *Batman* took seventeen years.

There are several reasons it takes so long. First, only one out of every one thousand scripts submitted every year to the Writers Guild of America makes it to movie theaters. Thus, most scripts never make it into production. Second, Hollywood movies cost more than $102 million to produce and distribute in 2003, and it takes a long time to get all the elements together so that some distributor or investor will want to put up this kind of money. Third, most people take years to get the script right. The *Los Angeles Times* interviewed a woman who had been trying for twenty years to sell her script. She said that in all those years she had not had the time to take a scriptwriting course or read a book on scriptwriting. The *Los Angeles Times* and all of us should be perplexed: What was she doing all that time that she could not take a moment to learn her chosen craft?

Before examining how to write a good script, read the words of the novelist who wrote the powerful book *Once upon a Time When We Were Colored*, Clifton L. Taulbert. See his article in *MOVIEGUIDE*® or in the "So You Want to Be in Pictures?" section on www.movieguide.org.

Screenwriting is a difficult task, full of rejection. As Clifton points out, you need to be rooted in God's loving grace. Some valuable insights into the process of scriptwriting will help, however.

In this regard most screenwriting books specialize in some aspect of screenwriting. For instance, if we looked at the whole process as a car, then the following must-read books focus on components of the vehicle: Lajos Egri's *The Art of Dramatic Writing* would be the engine of the car; Robert McGee's *Story* would be the transmission, taking the power from the engine to the wheels; Linda Seger's *How to Make a Good Script Great* would be the body of the car; Syd Field's *Screenplay* would be the paint job; and Linda Seger's *Creating Unforgettable Characters* would be the driver and the passengers.

Once upon a Time

A story is a connected narration of real or imagined events. There are many types of story, including science fiction, romance, myth, fairy tale, tragedy, and adventure. The full range of storytelling is limited only by the human imagination, yet key principles apply to all stories, and all stories can be classified in different categories or subgenre.

Stories have an internal logic driven by a premise acting through characters and conflict to move the plot from a beginning point of attack through one or more crises to a climax that moves toward a resolution. There are a wide range of variations on this approach, but the key principles apply to almost all of them, and the rare exception proves the rules.

The classic story formula goes something like this:

1. The hero wants something enough to do anything to get it.
2. The hero faces a difficult adventure or problem in trying to get what he wants.
3. The hero faces serious obstacles.
4. The hero overcomes the obstacles.
5. The hero reaches his goal and gets what he wants (the princess, the money, revenge, etc.).

Here are the steps and key principles involved in constructing your story:

Constructing Your Story

1. Start Your Engines—Formulate Your Premise

The engine of your communication is the premise that your communication must prove in a logical, impressive way, given your genre and medium of choice, in order for your audience to be affected by your communication in exactly the way you desire. In most cases an impressive proof of your premise will require lots of interesting illustrations, verbal or pictorial, and plenty of technical, dramatic, or literary effects.

For another perspective: the premise is where you are going (let's say Hollywood); the plot is how you get there (let's say you miss your plane and decide to take a car, but the car breaks down, etc.); the people who travel with you are the characters (let's say that each one is a friend of yours who does not get along with anyone else); and the themes are the continuing interactions between different sets of characters (let's say your friend Joe wants to lead your friend June to Jesus Christ).

The audience will want to know where you are going up front. In *The Lord of the Rings* trilogy, the audience knows right from the first act that Frodo has to take the ring to the mountain where it was originally forged and destroy it. From the beginning of *Finding Nemo,* the audience wants the father, Marlin, to find Nemo. How the hero achieves his goal in spite of all the obstacles the writer throws at him produces the excitement in the story.

Thus, the key element is your premise. The premise is the motivating power that drives your communication. Your premise is an active, dynamic statement of the argument that you will prove in your communication. Your premise is the essence of your communication. Within your premise are the key elements of your communication. Quite simply, your premise is a simple sentence with an active verb, a subject, and an object, that summarizes your communication and tells you where you are going—your goal.

In discussing the role of a premise and those elements that emerge from the premise in a dramatic play, Lajos Egri has noted: "A play can be judged before it reaches actual production. First, the premise must be discernible from the beginning. We have a right to know in what direction the author is leading us. The characters, growing out of the premise, necessarily identify themselves with the aim of the play. They will prove the premise through conflict. The play must start with conflict, which rises steadily until it reaches the climax. The characters must be so well drawn that, whether or not the author has declared their individual backgrounds, we can make out accurate case histories for each of them."[7]

A writer has many ways to arrive at the premise. You may have an idea or a conviction that you will convert into a premise. You may be intrigued by an obligatory scene, event, or situation and want to develop that scene, event, or situation into a premise that will drive your communication. To convert your scene or idea into a premise, look for the drama, the meaning, the conflict, and the purpose inherent in that idea or scene and then state that purpose, meaning, and conflict in a simple, active sentence, which is your premise.

Suppose your idea is to communicate that God is love. Ask yourself what your purpose is in communicating that idea. Your answer may be that your purpose is to show your audience that God loves them, us, mankind, and/or the world. Be as specific as possible by refining your purpose in light of the answers you have found to your ascertainment questions in combination with the question, How does God love them, you, or us? Your answer may be that he loves us by comforting us in sorrow, by delivering us from fear, by forgiving us our transgressions, or by rescuing us from drug addiction—depending on your answers to your ascertainment questions.

For example, let's say your purpose is to demonstrate the forgiveness inherent in God's love. In light of your answers to the ascertainment questions, state your premise in a simple but specific sentence, such as "God's love forgives the transgressor."

What does that mean? What is the conflict inherent in that statement? Forgiveness must mean that a wrong was committed that has alienated the wrongdoer, perhaps because of his or her feeling of guilt or knowledge that a just judgment is awaiting him or her. God's love conflicts with and triumphs over that alienation by forgiving the individual from judgment and healing him or her of his or her guilt.

Your premise gives you the direction, the basic elements, and the conclusion of your communication. In our example the direction and the conclusion of your communication is inherent in the active verb *forgives*. Since you are going to demonstrate how God's love forgives the wrongdoer, you will conclude your communication at that point where the forgiveness is a reality for the transgressor. The initiating force in your communication is God, and the object of your communication is the forgiven transgressor. The conflict is the negation of the verb-object combination, which, in terms of your premise, is the transgressor's alienation that resists forgiveness. By resisting the direction and conclusion of your premise, the conflict forces your proof and propels your communication along.

Let's assume that you decide, because of the audience and medium that you have chosen, to demonstrate your premise through a story. You could choose to make the wrongdoer a young woman who decides to run away from home to live the good life. After several adventures, she ends up destitute. She feels guilty for running away and for ending up destitute. You might decide, because of your audience, to represent the subject of your premise as the girl's father who manifests God's love. His love for his daughter causes him to go search for her. She sees him but avoids him because of her guilt and fear of judgment. In the process of avoiding him, she is thrown in jail. The father finds his daughter, spends all he has to pay her fine, and takes her home. When the father finds the daughter and forgives her, and she accepts his love and forgiveness, your premise is proved and the story is resolved, although you may want to top and tail your story to highlight the message of your premise.

Because of the nature of your audience, you may want to prove your premise in another genre. Whatever method you choose to prove your premise, by rephrasing your idea into a premise, you have given yourself a clear direction to follow in your communication. Any idea, scene, thought, or conviction may be converted into a premise that will drive your communication to a powerful conclusion.

In every story the premise can be found by analyzing the story. In the *Star Wars* trilogy, the evil empire is taking over the universe. A young man who is full of goodness, perseverance, and integrity is forced to fight the empire. He wins. "Good triumphs over evil" is clearly the premise. Every film or television program with that clear-cut premise, "Good triumphs over evil," tells a different story by proving that premise in a different way. However, it is the process of proving the premise that satisfies the expectations of the audience.

Every one of Jesus' parables has a premise. As an exercise, you may want to try to discover the premises in some of Jesus' parables.

Also, every one of Shakespeare's plays, every good story, and even every commercial has a clear-cut premise. The next movie or television commercial you see, try to find and state the premise.

Many well-produced films, television programs, or other media communications fail not because of the quality of the production but because of an unclear premise, double premise, or another defect in the premise. The movie *2010* was beautifully produced but failed because three-fourths of the way through the movie the premise changed, and the second premise was never proved through the medium of the story to the audience's satisfaction. The first part of *2010* told the story of how cooperation triumphs over adversity; then, after proving that premise—a second premise, supernatural being(s) bring peace—was introduced, taking the movie in another direction.

As Lajos Egri has noted, without a clear-cut premise no idea, thought, or conviction is strong enough to carry you through to a logical conclusion.[8] Furthermore:

- A badly worded or false premise will force you to fill space with pointless and irrelevant material.
- A communication with more than one premise is confused because it is trying to go in more than one direction at once. Note, however, that an anthology, variety, or series of separate and distinct communications will have separate premises for each communication, but no one distinct communication should have more than one premise.
- A premise that says too much is ambiguous and says nothing.
- A premise that does not take a position is ambivalent and says nothing.
- Don't write what you don't believe.
- In most communications you should not mention your premise in the body of your communication; however, your audience should know what it is, and whatever it is, you must prove it.
- In the storytelling genre, if there is no clear-cut premise, your characters will not live because without a clearly defined premise, it is impossible to know your characters.
- No one premise expresses the totality of universal truth. Every premise is limiting. For example, poverty does not always lead to

crime, but if you have chosen the premise that poverty leads to crime, then it does in your case, and you must prove it.

The elements of a premise are a subject; an active, transitive verb; and an object. The verb must be active, present tense (not future or past tense) to give direction to your communication. If the verb is past tense, the goal of your communication has been achieved historically, and there is nothing to prove. If your verb is future tense, then your premise is purely speculative.

Furthermore, the verb must be transitive to motivate your communication. An intransitive verb states a fact and portrays a static picture, giving you no basis for proving your premise and reaching a conclusion. To say "Jesus is love" is a static portrait of a fact; however, to say "Jesus loves you" sets up a dynamic situation where, starting with Jesus, there has to be a demonstration of his love for whoever *you* is, and the questions how? why? where? when? and what? become relevant and necessary to answer.

Here are some sample premises:

- Hope triumphs over despair.
- Greed consumes itself.
- Great love conquers death.
- Ruthless ambition destroys itself.
- Jealousy destroys love.
- Love conquers jealousy.
- Poverty encourages faith.
- Faith conquers fear.
- Honesty defeats duplicity.
- Pride leads to a fall.
- Good triumphs over evil.

You can find premises all around you. Look at an interesting situation and ask what motivates that situation. The best premises and characters come out of genuine experience.

Look at a strong, even militant, character and ask why he or she is motivated to do what he or she is doing. Look at an idea and ask what that idea means translated into action. Your premise expresses the motivation, the action, and the reaction through a subject, active verb, and object, which drive your story to its conclusion.

If you are starting with a novel, before you write the script, write your premise. In this regard, the great director Alfred Hitchcock said that the worst books make the best movies. The corollary that good books often make bad movies can be seen with movies such as *Midnight in the Garden of Good and Evil.* Often a good book is too complex with too many goals and too many characters. You must first choose the story line you want to follow in the book and express that story line as a premise.

For Every Action, There Is a Reaction

In every premise, conflict drives the communication forward. To prove your premise you must disprove the negation of your premise. This process propels your communication. If there is no negation and no conflict possible in your premise, your communication will be stillborn, with no direction and no goal.

Most Christian movies fail from lack of conflict. Writers should keep in mind that the world is caught in a spiritual battle. Furthermore, no two people are the same, so they fight. Finally, *drama* means "to do" or "to perform," and for every action, there is a reaction.

To illustrate this, try asking two friends to stand five feet apart, face each other, and tell each other "I love you" in as many ways as they desire for no less than two minutes. After a short period of time, this dialogue without conflict will become boring. However, if you ask one to convince the other of his or her love for the other, and you ask the other to resist this advance, the dialogue will be entertaining. One or the other will have to relent, thereby establishing the premise for that brief scene as either "love triumphs over rejection" or "resistance destroys love."

Some Christian radio and television interview programs are boring to all but a few loyal supporters because the host avoids conflict or loses sight of the value of loving conflict. In these boring programs the host and the guest spend all their time affirming each other so that the program remains static and uninteresting. If the host defines what he wants to discover in the interview (which is his premise) in such a way as to probe who his guest is and why the guest is there by asking the tough questions the audience needs and wants to know, then there will be real dialogue. The interview will be interesting because conflict is built into the program, even if only on the level of a premise such as "curiosity discovers important information."

This conflict does not have to be mean, petty, or angry, as so much conflict is on nonreligious television. The conflict can and will be loving if the tough questions that prove the host's premise are asked in love. A thoughtful, loving host can ask tough questions in a loving way to reveal the interesting story that every guest has to tell. The conflict in the interview is merely the vehicle by which the guest proves his or her story to the host and the audience. Without a clear-cut premise, there will be no conflict, and neither the host nor the audience will have any idea what the host is trying to communicate.

Outlining four basic plots, Aristotle highlighted the conflict inherent in drama in his categorization of dramatic stories:

1. Man against man
2. Man against nature
3. Man against himself
4. Man against the supernatural or subnatural, including aliens

Aristotle's categories help us to evaluate the premise or main proposition in a story, but they may not help us determine whether the story fits the Christian worldview.

Another traditional literary approach proposed by Northrop Frye[9] may be more helpful. It divides stories into five different kinds:

1. Mythic, in a traditional sense: The hero or protagonist(s) triumphs by an act of God or gods.
2. Heroic: The triumph of the hero or protagonist(s) by his or her own means.
3. High Ironic: The triumph of the hero or protagonist(s) by a quirk of fate.

4. Low Ironic: The failure of the hero or protagonist(s) by a quirk of fate.

5. Demonic: The defeat of the hero or protagonist(s) by evil, demons, etc.

A story that fits the Christian version of the traditional mythic story, where the God of the Bible or Jesus Christ helps the hero or protagonist overcome his or her antagonist, is a story that fits the Christian world-view. A story, however, where the hero or protagonist, especially a Christian, is defeated by demons is probably not a story Christians should want to see because it contradicts their worldview and the worldview of the Bible.

Beyond the basic story types, there are various themes. The eight basic themes are:

1. Survival
2. Redemption
3. Revenge
4. Betrayal
5. Coming of age
6. Love/romance
7. Mistaken identity
8. Fish out of water

The Notion of Genre

The notion of genre is a simple way of talking about the different kinds, types, or formats of communications. George Gerbner has reduced human communication to three genres: stories that tell about how things work, stories that tell about what things are, and stories of action.[10] Aristotle was most likely aware of the three ultimate categories of drama, epic, and lyric, which have evolved into drama, fiction, and poetry according to some contemporary literary critics.[11]

Other philosophers and pundits have proposed other generic classifications, such as comedy, epigram, satire, epic, and tragedy. Often, movie reviewers classify movies in genres such as the following (this list is suggestive, not exhaustive):

Romance	Comedy	Detective/Police
Action Adventure	Children's	Thriller
Drama	Religious	Horror
Tragedy	Fantasy	Sports

Remember: Schopenhauer said, "Write the way an architect builds, who first drafts his plan and designs every detail."[12]

2. In a Galaxy Far, Far Away—Define Your Environment, Subgenre, Style, and Point of View

Your environment must be real, even if it is far, far away in time and space.

Before you start constructing your story, you must define in detail the environment in which your story takes place. The environment and the laws that govern that environment create the illusion of reality in your story. The more detail you know about when and where your story takes place, the more real your story will be to your audience.

The novel *Time and Again* by Jack Finney works in spite of an implausible plot—the hero wills himself back in history—because Mr. Finney has defined the setting of the novel with such meticulous care.

Many movies, especially science fiction, fail because the setting of the movie is only partially realized. *Battleship Earth* has many scenes where the sets look like sets—unreal, with no sign of having been inhabited. *The Lord of the Rings,* on the other hand, has outlandish sets that look real because time was taken to make them real through detailed definition.

You must learn, define, and obey the rules of the subgenre you choose.

Whether you choose to construct your story as romance, science fiction, comedy, contemporary stream of consciousness, history, or detective story, you must obey the rules that the subgenre imposes on your story.

Note that the principles of the genre to which the subgenre belongs apply to the subgenre as well as the particular principles or variations on major principles that define the subgenre.

Select your style to fit your premise, your environment, your characters, and your subgenre.

The style, rhythm, and tone you establish are as important as your plot. A satiric or low ironic style may be appropriate for a detective story but not for a historic portrayal of Jesus' ministry, unless you are attacking the gospel or you have chosen Judas Iscariot's point of view.

Within a style—

- to shock, you must make the incredible credible.
- to create irony, the audience's assumptions must be contrary to the outcome.
- to create a paradox, logic must be contradicted by fact.
- to create satire, the normal is exaggerated.
- to create suspense, withheld information must confront the desire to know.

Your point of view affects your characters.

The first-person point of view involves the audience in the thoughts of one of the characters. The first person *I* is not necessarily the protagonist or the antagonist. The *I* can be any character in the story.

The first-person point of view may be pure stream of consciousness, but the rules of storytelling still apply. The first person may be established in a neutral style, which overcomes the limitations imposed by the *I* speaking in dialect. If you choose a first-person point of view, you must define that person in the same detail as you would define any other character.

The third person is the most common and flexible point of view. The third person allows for different perspectives, involving the audience with different characters or establishing an omniscient perspective.

3. Who Is the Hero and Why Isn't He Always the Protagonist?—Define Your Protagonist

In a dramatic communication, the subject of your premise is your protagonist who initiates the action of the verb and carries that action through to the conclusion. The protagonist takes the lead in the movement of the story, creates the conflict, and makes the story move forward. The protagonist knows what he or she wants and is determined to get it. The protagonist can be the hero, the villain, or any other character in the story. The protagonist may not be the central character in the story, but without the protagonist the story flounders.

Your protagonist is the driven, driving subject inherent in your premise who forces the conflict that moves your story to its conclusion. Your protagonist takes the lead in your story. He or she knows what he or she wants and will act to get it. Not only does your protagonist want something badly enough to act, but he or she will go after it until he or she has obtained it or been completely defeated in the process.

Your protagonist must have something important at stake. The character acts out of necessity and is forced by who he or she is and by circumstances to do what he or she does and become what he or she becomes.

Your protagonist has one highly developed motivation such as love, hate, revenge, greed, envy, caring, faith, and hope, that drives him or her to act until he or she succeeds or is defeated.

Even if the motivating characteristic of your protagonist seems passive, it must be active in terms of your premise and his or her situation. For instance, if your protagonist is motivated to patiently endure, then he or she must be willing to act on that motivation even if it brings him or her to martyrdom, as is the case with many Christian martyrs.

Your determined protagonist will not grow as much as your other characters. The other characters will grow a great deal, even from one emotion to its opposite, because of the strength of will of your protagonist.

For instance, if your premise is "love conquers death," your protagonist must love his or her beloved enough to do everything possible, including die, to save the beloved from death. Your protagonist could be a loving father who risks his life to save his son who has fallen through the ice, a loving mother who will give up everything to save her family from destruction, or Jesus, who gave his life so that death would be defeated.

As a guide to the impact a hero who may or may not be the protagonist has on a story, the following restating of the archetypal story styles are helpful:

- In the mythic story, such as *The Lord of the Rings,* God triumphs, or Frodo the hero triumphs because of an act of God and the help of supernatural forces.
- In the heroic story, such as *Harry Potter,* the hero triumphs because he or she is superior.
- In the high ironic story, such as *Forrest Gump,* the hero triumphs because of a quirk of fate or circumstances.
- In the low ironic story, such as *Death of a Salesman,* the hero fails because of a quirk of fate or circumstances.
- In the demonic story, which includes not only many horror films but also psychological movies and political films such as *The Diary of Anne Frank,* the hero is hopelessly overwhelmed by evil or wields evil to fight evil.

4. Make Beautiful Music Together—Define and Orchestrate Your Characters

All these elements are embodied in your premise and are important to understand and define clearly so that your audience will know exactly what you are trying to communicate. If you have decided to communicate dramatically through a story, then you must define your characters carefully and get to know them inside out. Get inside your characters, live with them, find out and define what makes each character unique.

Well-orchestrated characters are one of the primary reasons for rising conflict in any story. Their differences distinguish each of your characters and move your story from start to finish through conflict. You may have two apostles, two tax collectors, or two thieves in your story, but they must be different. They must contrast each other so that they move the story along. The contrast between them must be inherent in their character as you define them.

Orchestration is simply creating well-defined, strong characters who are in conflict and therefore move your story along. Through this conflict your characters will grow, and your story will develop, proving your premise.

If you really want to define your characters, use the process for motivational talent set forth in chapter 3. At a minimum, define each of the following elements of each character's bone structure. These elements will help you to define and orchestrate your characters.

Name of character

Physical characteristics

Sex	Eyes	Posture
Age	Skin	Deformities
Height	Race	Abnormalities
Weight	Ethnic group	
Hair	Appearance	

Background

Class	Nationality	Hobbies
Education	Politics	Parents
Home	Relationships	Relatives
Occupation	Marital status	Children

Psychological characteristics

Ambition	Fears	Qualities
Preferences	Wants	Intelligence
Motivations	Likes	Emotional state
Temperament	Relationship patterns	
Attitude	Talents	

Religious characteristics

Beliefs	Worldview	Religious environment
Hopes	Cares	
Faith	Religious background	

Use this information, or modify it, to define each of your characters. Your story is built by your characters, so be as thorough as you can. The difference between a simple and a sophisticated story is primarily determined by the complexity of the characters. Visualize your characters as if they were people you have known all your life.

5. Good Versus Evil—Define Your Antagonist in Opposition to Your Protagonist

The antagonist is the conflicting force inherent in the premise who opposes the protagonist. The antagonist can be the hero, the villain, or any other character in the story. The antagonist has to be as strong as the protagonist so that the conflict between the two will carry the story forward to its natural conclusion. If the antagonist gives up at any time, then the story will die. There must be a unity of opposites between the protagonist and the antagonist.

Your antagonist opposes your protagonist. He or she wants to prevent your protagonist from acting, from doing what your protagonist is driven to do. The will of your protagonist must clash with the will of your antagonist, and your antagonist must be as strong and as driven as your protagonist.

Your antagonist and your protagonist must be locked in opposition. There must be a unity of opposites that can only be broken by the death of the motivating characteristic in either one or the other of these two characters. Either your antagonist or your protagonist must be completely defeated for your story to reach its natural conclusion. Because of the strength of will of these two characters, the initial conflict between them must lead to a crisis that must lead to a climax that must lead to a resolution.

If one or the other of these two characters gives up early, your story will stop. If one or the other of these two characters is a pushover, if they are unequally matched, then you have no story because there will be no conflict to drive the plot. Compromise is out of the question unless it is the result of a completely realized conflict that has proved your premise. If one character is determined to win and the other doesn't care, there is no challenge, no battle, and no story. A strong person pitted against a weak one is a farce unless the weaker has the courage, will, and hidden ability to put up a real fight and perhaps win.

Every character will fight back under the right circumstances. It is up to you to catch your character at that point where he or she will carry the premise through conflict.

Your antagonist is inherent in your premise. He or she is what your subject/protagonist must oppose to fulfill his or her goals. He or she reacts against the action of the subject. Depending on the outcome determined by your premise, he or she must change for your protagonist to reach his or her goal, or your protagonist must change in the face of opposition.

6. En Garde—Define Your Starting Point, a Crisis, Which Must Lead Your Story to a Climax That Must Result in a Conclusion or Resolution

Your movie or television program should not start at the beginning of someone's life (he was born in a log cabin) but at a critical point of attack where something worth living or dying for is at stake (as he was being born, the villain attacked), thereby creating jeopardy (or something at stake) that propels the plot to its destination, thus fulfilling the premise. Every Hollywood movie should start with a bang, as opposed to European movies, that take some time to develop the situations involved in the story.

If you want your story to move and capture your audience, you must choose the right point of attack. The right point of attack is that moment in time and space when your protagonist is at a critical turning point where he or she must act to achieve his or her goal, thereby initiating the action of the premise. This turning point is a crisis point where a decisive change one way or another must occur. Because of your premise, this opening crisis can only lead to the climax inherent in your premise that must be resolved in such a way that your premise is proved.

No story starts at the beginning. There is always something that occurred prior to the beginning of the story. Genesis starts with God acting to create our universe, but it does not tell us what was going on in eternity before God decided to create. In the beginning of Genesis, God as the protagonist is at a turning point where he acts to create the heavens and the earth.

Rather than ramble, looking for a place to begin, start your story at the moment when the conflict starts, when the protagonist acts to achieve his or her goal. This moment occurs when circumstances and motivation force your protagonist to act. He or she acts out of necessity because something extremely important is at stake, such as love, survival, health, or honor. This point could be where your protagonist has made a decision, has reached a turning point, or where something important is threatened.

Whatever precipitated this moment has already occurred when your story begins. Your story grows out of whatever happened to cause your protagonist to act, and that action forces the climax, which proves your premise in its resolution.

7. Avalanche—Develop Rising Conflict

Your story builds through a rising series of conflicts, each one building in intensity on the previous conflict until the climax is reached and the premise is proved. Each conflict moves your story forward through action and reaction, attack and counterattack, which cause change, growth, and new conflict until you have reached the proof of your premise. The first conflict in your story comes from your protagonist consciously trying to achieve the goal that you determined by your premise.

Conflict will grow out of the characters who are in opposition. The more evenly matched your characters are, the more real rising conflict will move your story to its resolution.

Conflict Exposes Your Story and Your Characters

Through conflict your characters and your story are revealed and exposed. Each dialogue, every interaction between characters, reveals who they are, what their background is, what the environment is, what the plot is, and where the plot is headed.

Conflict Causes Change and Growth

Every conflict causes change. At no two points in your story are any of the characters, or situation, the same. As a result of conflict, each character will change emotionally, psychologically, and spiritually. Growth occurs continually until the story proves your premise.

In your story, if your premise is love conquers hate, the conquered character must grow from hate to love. To do so he or she must go through every step, every change, that leads from hate to love: hate, dislike, annoyance, understanding, interest, attraction, caring, love. Each conflict will move this character along the road from hate to love, where his or her growth will be complete.

Avoid Static Conflict

Static conflict occurs because:

- One or more of your characters can't make a decision. Each of your characters has to grow from one emotional, psychological, or spiritual point to another in your story. If he or she stops at one of the intermediate steps along the way because he or she can't make a decision, then you will have static conflict, and your story will stop.
- Your story lacks the motivating force of a premise.
- Your characters share exactly the same point of view because you have not orchestrated them by carefully defining them as unique individuals.

Static conflict will bring your story to a halt. No dialogue, effects, descriptions, or rhetoric will move your story if the conflict is static.

The exercise suggested earlier where you ask two friends to try to tell each other that they love each other for two minutes is an example of static conflict. Since they are both starting at the same point of view, there is no conflict to generate a story.

Here is an example of a character who is indecisive:

Jane: Do you want to go out, my darling?

Jack: Maybe.

Jane: When will you decide?

Jack: Sometime.

Jane: Do you care?

Jack: I don't know.

Jane: When will you know?

Jack: Soon.

Jane: Will you tell me?

Jack: Sure.

These characters and this story are going nowhere because Jack is indecisive.

Avoid Jumping Conflict

Jumping conflict occurs because:

- One or more of your characters has skipped one or more of the important stages of growth through which he or she must go to reach the conclusion inherent in your premise.
- You are forcing one or more of your characters to do something that is not within his, her, or their uniquely defined characters.
- You have not given one or more of your characters a chance to grow steadily and realistically through rising conflict.
- You have not thought through the process of proving your premise.
- You have not defined your premise clearly.

Here is an example of jumping conflict:

Jane: Do you want to go out, my darling?

Jack: Maybe.

Jane: Well, if you don't know for sure, I'm walking out
  on our marriage.

Jack: But I'll make up my mind.

Jane: It's too late, you inconsiderate slob. [She
  leaves, slamming the door.]

To avoid jumping conflict, determine the stages of growth through which each character will progress from where they are emotionally, psychologically, and spiritually when your audience first meets them to where they must end up as dictated by your premise. As your characters grow through conflict, they are only allowed to choose those solutions to each conflict that will help prove the point of your premise.

For instance, if your character has to go from rebellion to submission in your story, make sure you have predetermined each one of the stages he or she must pass through in the process: rebellion, alienation, loneliness, insecurity, fear, need, longing, desire for help and protection, submission.

Conflict Foreshadows Itself

Each minor conflict in your story leads to the next conflict because none of the intermediate solutions will resolve your story until your premise is proved. Each conflict foreshadows the next conflict because it contains the seeds of the next conflict by the very nature of how you have defined and orchestrated your characters in light of your premise.

Conflict is the product of the tension that is inherent in your characters. Every conflict contains all the elements of a story in brief.

8. Talking Pictures—Dialogue Quotes a Character's Words or Thoughts

You have defined each of your characters; each character defines the dialogue he or she utters. Dialogue that does not flow clearly and validly from the character who uses it is unnatural and defeats your story unless it is a science fiction effect. If dialogue is an effect, it still must be true to the character of its real source.

Dialogue reveals who a character is and hints at who he or she will become. Each character should speak in his or her own language and dialect, but too much dialect will usually sound phony and should be avoided. Informal, natural dialogue is most effective.

Rising conflict produces healthy dialogue that foreshadows the direction in which the premise is leading.

Dialogue should be concise and succinct. In most cases surplusage vitiates. Sacrifice brilliance for character. Do not preach through dialogue unless that preaching reflects who a character is and occurs naturally in context. Never overemphasize dialogue. Don't be didactic.

9. Reel Versus Real—Observe, Experience, Be Unique, and Create the Illusion of Reality in Your Story, Even If That Reality Is Set in a Cosmos Far, Far Away

But Even So

Television series do not follow the typical movie script in that television series are character driven. The audience tunes in to follow their favorite or most hated characters.

Our friend Gary Johnson presents some interesting insights into becoming a television writer in *MOVIEGUIDE®* and in our "So You Want to Be in Pictures?" section on www.movieguide.org. Given our nation's often trashy, MTV, R-rated mentality of the past decade or two, who would have believed that PAX TV's wholesome, charming, family-values programs, *Doc* and *Sue Thomas: F. B. Eye,* would be top-rated television fare in the 2000s? And who writes such popularly unconventional shows? The answer is people like Gary R. Johnson, along with his wife, Joan, and his brother, Dave.

You Have the Answers

Once you have determined who you are, why you are communicating, and what the idea, scene, or conviction is that you want to communicate, every other element, including your premise, should be fashioned, structured, and constructed in light of all your answers to the ascertainment questions that apply to your communication. Use the information you have discovered by answering the ascertainment questions to shape your communication. If your audience likes to ski, frame the elements of your story or your proof in terms of skiing. If your audience is preoccupied with the human condition, design your premise and your proof thereof with the human condition in mind.

Designing your premise and its proof in light of the answers to the pertinent ascertainment questions does not mean that you need to dilute the gospel; rather, it simply means that you need to consider what is the most effective way in which you can communicate the gospel.

Throughout the process of constructing your communication, use your imagination and allow your communication to be emotional. Powerful emotions and images will give life to any communication whose premise is well defined and proved. Whether you are communicating through movies or television, concrete, emotional images created in words, pictures, and/or sounds will cause your communication to impact powerfully on your audience. Allow yourself the privilege of imagining your audience and their reaction to your communication because that process will help you to make your communication more interesting.

◆ ◆ ◆

The Mechanics of Transforming Your Story into a Script and Beyond

We have considered the script process from the foundational dynamics necessary to create a screenplay that will capture the audience. Now let's consider some of the mechanics you need to turn your story into a script, unless you hire a scriptwriter to do so, assuming that you did not start out with a script.

In many cases a producer will start with a script that he or she will boil down to a one- or two-page treatment to sell the story idea to the networks. If you start with a story or a book, usually you will want to turn it into a script and a treatment before you can make the sale to a network or interest prominent talent in your production.

The author of a book is not always the best person to transform their own work into a script. The author often has trouble sacrificing scenes, devices, or characters to meet the time and space limitations of movies or television. In a book, for instance, you can carry on several complex subplots with many minor characters who come and go. Also, the author of a book can describe characters, feelings, situations, and motivations in great detail, whereas a scriptwriter can't. Movies and television force you to simplify and condense most books, discarding characters, scenes, and situations if necessary.

A play is easier to adapt in terms of condensation, but the problem can arise that the original author can't shift his or her thinking from the stage to the big or the little screen environment. With regard to TV, a television audience is not captive, as is an audience in a theater, so you have to capture your television audience.

Bringing in a scriptwriter to reformulate a book, play, or short story can save time and money and often improve the final teleplay or film. If you bring in a scriptwriter, you must work to keep the author's intent because that is the reason you bought the story in the first place.

Finally, you should involve a script doctor like Linda Seger, who invented the profession. The script doctor will help you take your script from good to great and help you sell your script by giving the major movie studio the confidence that the script doctor has given their imprimatur to the script. Please note that the script doctor will not pitch or sell your script for you, but their coverage of your script will help the studio decide to take your script seriously. More than 300,000 scripts are written every year, and fewer than 300 movies reach the theaters. Thus, the studios are trying to defend against a flood of scripts. Your job is to get your script moved beyond their defenses. A script doctor can help you do just that.

The script, rights, financing, access, and talent steps of a movie or television production often occur simultaneously, with each affecting the others. If you have a script, in most cases, the major movie studio/distributor or television network who picks up your story will want to review and revise it, as will the big-name talent that you bring on board. On the other hand, the talent and the network will often defer making a final decision on your story until they know how good your script is, because many great stories defy scripting.

The Treatment

Whether you have a script or a story, the first step in selling either is often a short treatment. Entertainment industry executives do not have the time to read every story or script that is submitted, so they will give the property to a reader who will boil it down to one or two pages and give an opinion of how good the story idea is. Rather than leave your story to a reader to turn into a treatment, which may not do justice to your story, it is better to prepare your own treatment and present that treatment with your story or script.

A treatment should set forth the log line that is the basis of your pitch, the premise of your story, your main characters, and a brief synopsis of the story itself. The more concise your treatment is, the better. Many movies and television programs have been sold to the networks solely on the basis of a one-sentence, *TV Guide* log line/synopsis/premise. One producer, after failing to sell a complex story idea, said, "How about a Grand Hotel on the water? A Love Boat?" That brief statement of the story sold the television network on the program *Love Boat.*

Sometimes you will be required to expand your story into a full-length synopsis of thirty to fifty pages. Do so, keeping in mind the principles you have learned.

Formatting

If you have not hired a scriptwriter and you are adapting your story into a script, you will find that there are many formats for scripts. Most books on scriptwriting will give you these formats, or a quick search of the Internet will find the many computer programs that will help you format your script for the appropriate medium. The computer program Final Draft is one of the best, but newer and better programs are released all the time, so a little research on the Internet will be invaluable. These programs, by the way, will not help you with the foundational dynamics of story that have been covered above in brief. For a commercial and public service announcement (PSA), the script[12] may look like this:

30 SECOND PSA[14]

LOVE IN ACTION

VIDEO	AUDIO
1. SOUP BEING SERVED TO A	V.O.[15]: For I was hungry,

STREET PERSON IN A SHELTER.	and you fed me . . .
2. A YOUNG BOY HANDING A HOUSE PAINTER A DRINK	V.O.: Thirsty, and you gave me to drink . . .
3. A COUPLE WHOSE CAR BROKE DOWN IN A STORM ARE BEING WELCOMED INTO A HOME.	V.O.: I was a stranger and you invited me in . . .

◆ ◆ ◆

News programs, variety programs, game shows, documentaries, teleplays, live-taped teleplays, and Hollywood movies have different script formats and layouts. Before you start writing, research these different formats because you want your script to be professional so you can sell it to a movie studio or network.[16]

The degree of detail in a script will vary depending on the scriptwriter, the director, and the producer, as well as on the use of the script within a production. A master script will not have the detail of a shooting script prepared with the director, nor will it include the camera shots and angles that are found in the camera script. The master script is the beginning of a long process. The scriptwriter who prepares the master script may have nothing to do with the final shooting script.

You write a traditional script in scenes. The reason for this is that film is shot by location, so that once you set up your equipment in a location, you film all the scenes associated with that location to save money, time, and energy.

Master Script

What follows is an example of a master, or master scene, Hollywood-style script for an excellent television movie. Note that there are few directions, such as "wipe to," "dissolve to," "close shot," or "high angle shot." The keys to a good script are in-depth character analysis, the action spelled out, and the dialogue completely realized. Often the visual and the action move the story along as much as the dialogue.

As noted, once you have written your script, you should hire a script doctor to analyze your screenplay. The amount of money you spend on a script doctor will be more than made up in the money, time, and energy you save trying to sell a script that is good but not great. As lyricists Alan and Marilyn Bergman note, "Whether it be a lyric, a novel or a screenplay, what separates the professional from the amateur is not so much the ability to write, as the ability to rewrite."[17]

Stage directions, shots, video and audio directions, and other details will be added by the producer, the director, the director of photography, the editor, the actors, and even the scriptwriter as the production planning process refines the script. A movie or television program is rarely the product of one man or woman; and if it is, it is rarely any good.

"MY PALIKARI"[18]

BY GEORGE KIRGO & LEON CAPETANOS

FADE IN

1. INT. OLYMPIA RESTAURANT—NIGHT—CLOSE ON PHOTO

A large framed panoramic view of Athens, featuring the Acropolis. HEAR recorded Greek music. PULL BACK slowly to REVEAL PETE PANAKOS, wine glass held high. Pete is handsome, powerful, vigorous, full of himself. The toast:

PETE

To the greatest country in the world—after the U.S.A., natch
—my Greece! Yiassou!

2. FULL SHOT

His celebrants respond: "Yiassou, To Greece, L'Chayim, Salud, Bon Voyage Pete!" . . .

◆ ◆ ◆

CUT TO:

9. EXT. SEA—DAY. (Stock or 2nd Unit or 1st Unit)

As the ship comes toward Piraeus. The Ionian. In the distance: a large ocean liner. Sound of ship whistle.

10. EXT. SHIP—DAY.

That's Pete on the forward deck, scanning the sea ahead. Passengers pass. Impatient, Pete lights a cigar, a chore in the wind. He paces a few steps. Stops. Peers out again.

11. POV and ZOOM IN TO ACROPOLIS.

Big rush of emotion.

◆ ◆ ◆

PETE

Chris, Chris, come here!

CHRIS

What?

PETE
(exasperated)

What? I'll show you what. Come on!

The passengers sit up to stare at this crazy man. Pete glares as Chris slowly saunters over. Pete grabs him and LEADS him to the forward deck.

PETE

Look, look!

CHRIS

Where?

PETE

There, there—

14. POV.

Land. Acropolis, Port, Hills, etc.

15. PETE AND CHRIS

Pete grins at Chris as his son coolly studies the sight.

PETE

Huh? Huh?

> CHRIS

It's nice.

16. ANOTHER ANGLE.

On Pete and Chris with land in b.g.[19]

> PETE
> (incredulous)

Nice?

> CHRIS

Yeah. Kind of like . . . Brooklyn.

> PETE

Brooklyn—! This is Greece! Alas!

He crosses himself and whispers, as the tears almost fall from his eyes—

◆ ◆ ◆

This script is intended for film production, but it could be shot with video using electronic field production (EFP). You could also adapt this script to shoot it in a studio with inserted stock shots, as is the case with many programs, such as *JAG*.

Helpful Hints

Here are some hints for writing your script, teleplay, or screenplay.

In building your script:

Organize flow—Make sure it flows smoothly and continuously, resulting in a unified, coherent, and entertaining program. If you prove your premise with rising conflict, then your story will flow.

Organize pacing—Make sure the length of your shots, scenes, and sequences develops the tempo that is required by the story while also enhancing it. Rapid sequences provide excitement and stimulation. Slower cutting slows the pace and induces a feeling of serenity and ease.

Organize rhythm—There should be a definite rhythm to a series of cuts, dissolves, and devices that will match the rhythm, mood, and action of your story.

Organize interrelationships so that motion is established by a continuous sequence of images.

A sense of action is suggested at all times. Even when there is no physical motion during a particular scene, action can be suggested through contrast or repetition.

Organize visually for progression, opposition, and repetition of image size. Generate variety through camera position, lighting, and shading.

Organize effects—Dissolves are usually one to five seconds in length and will establish a smooth transition between scenes.

Fades in and out usually open or close an independent segment and can be considered a curtain that opens on new material and closes at the end of an act.

Lap dissolves, where one image is faded over another, and matched dissolves, where two items of similar or identical shape are matched in the dissolve, are used to create effects, mood, and to promote action.

Superimpositions, frame buffing, and more contemporary technical effects should be studied before incorporating them into your script so that you are aware of the effect they have on the audience. New effects and new devices for creating effects are continually being developed. Use any one effect sparingly; overuse will intrude on your story.

Remember: your story is the heart of your production. Effects can enhance a good story, but they cannot make a bad story better.

Organize sound so that it is established before or during the picture. Avoid sound on cue. If sound comes on at the same time as the picture, it will be unnatural and mechanical. If you are about to have a train come into view, introduce the distant sound of the train first. Or, if you have someone walking across the desert, show them and then bring up the sound of walking on sand. Also, avoid music that calls attention to itself unless that is your purpose.

Dialogue should be natural. It should consist of short speeches. Long speeches impede action and bore the audience. Clichés and colloquialisms should be used carefully and sparingly.

Actions should be described thoroughly, precisely, and yet briefly. Rather than having someone simply walk over to someone, have them walk fearfully or forcefully over.

Use present tense directions.

Be unique. Do not fall into the trite.

Chart the rising tension and rhythm of your script:

OVERALL TENSION

Tense

| Open | Crisis | Exposition | Conflict | Climax | Resolution | Close |

Relaxed

Chart each factor that contributes to the rising tension, such as image, effects, sound, music, and scene lengths. Together these charts will add up to your master chart of the rising tension and rhythm of your script. For example, for dialogue your chart might look like:

DIALOGUE TENSION

For action, your chart might be:

ACTION TENSION

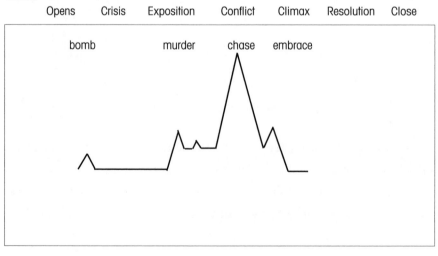

As the production of your program progresses, you should add charts for factors that contribute to dramatic tension and revise the original charts you prepared to keep them current. Eventually these charts will graphically show the rhythm, flow, and tension embodied in your program. These charts will be useful for analyzing how well your program is going to emotionally grab and entertain your audience.

Effects

Technical, literary, and dramatic effects help to capture and hold an audience. Every communication should be punctuated by effects, even if it is only a turn of phrase, a change in perspective, or whatever is appropriate to retain the audience's attention.

In television and film, both real-time media that reach out to their audience, technical effects are particularly important. Watch several minutes of different movies and television programs and count the technical effects, such as cuts, camera moves, action, and scene changes per minute. You will find that most television programs have ten to fifty technical effects per minute to capture and hold your attention, and those with less effects will not keep your attention unless the premise, its execution, and the emotive images that constitute the fabric of the program are unusually powerful.

Your Voice

Aside from the effects you use, where appropriate, keep your communication simple, as the anagram KISS notes: "Keep It Simple Somehow." This does not mean that you should force yourself to communicate in a manner that is alien to you. If your communication is unnatural, it will fail. Be true to yourself, your own voice, your premise, your medium, your audience, and your characters. Where appropriate, be brief. Where your communication demands, capture the tone, language, and grammar that will be most effective.

Be truthful in your communication, true to its demands on you and your demands on it, taking the time to edit, cut back, and/or elaborate as needed to be perfectly clear and coherent. Articles abound in literary magazines urging communicators to be ruthlessly plain and natural. Just as many articles appear urging writers to recapture the beauty of the romantic flights of fancy of the great nineteenth-century novelists. There is room for both if they communicate effectively, clearly, and coherently what the author wants to communicate. In an article in *The New York Times Book Review* entitled "Is Fiction the Art of Lying?" Mario Vargas Llosa notes: "In fact, novels do lie—they can't help doing so—but that's only part of the story. The other is that, through lying, they express a curious truth, which can only be expressed in a veiled and concealed fashion, masquerading as what it is not. . . . Every good novel tells the truth and every bad novel lies. For a novel 'to tell the truth' means to make the reader experience an illusion, and 'to lie' means to be unable to accomplish that trickery."[20]

For a communication to be true is for it to be true to the rules you have set up as the communicator, given that you have good reasons for setting up those rules.

If at one point in planning your movie or television script you feel that you want an objective reaction to it, do not have your friends review your communication, they will be prejudiced and will not give you an objective evaluation. Have your most critical enemy look at it. However, if you must have your friends review your script, then ask them to stop when they feel bored. That point is where your communication has failed.

If you state your premise clearly, define all of the elements contained therein with great precision, and carefully prove your premise, then your premise will powerfully drive your communication no matter what genre and medium you choose. If you follow the twelve basic foundational steps, or your own variation in light of your answers to the ascertainment questions then you will communicate what you want to communicate to your audience. Finally, your communication will be effective and successful if you "commit your activities to the LORD and your plans will be achieved" (Prov. 16:3).

CHAPTER 5

Lord of the Box Office— Making Sure Your Script Pays Off

E very once in a while, a movie like *The Passion of the Christ* or *My Big Fat Greek Wedding* will come along and make the elite decision-makers in Hollywood scratch their heads. Then someone in the press will remark that it's impossible to know what movies will be successful and what movies will flop.

Balderdash!

The unique success of movies like *The Passion* and *Greek Wedding* is not a strange occurrence striking out of the blue. The tremendous success of these two movies, and many others like them, can be attributable to major factors that have always driven the movie industry, ever since D. W. Griffith, Charlie Chaplin, and Cecil B. DeMille started making movies.

Our annual analysis of movie content and the cinematic box office at MOVIEGUIDE® proves beyond a shadow of a doubt that writers, film-makers, and studio executives have a much better chance of being financially successful if their scripts and movies contain positive Christian content, bib-lical principles, godly virtues, and traditional moral values. Contrary to pop-ular thinking in today's "anything goes" culture, graphic violence, sexual immorality, nudity, foul language, and substance abuse usually don't sell all that well.

This is especially true if you look at the top box office champs of all time, whether you adjust for inflation or not. For example, if you adjust for inflation, the top two box office champs of all time, *Gone with the Wind* and *Star Wars*, beat their closest rivals by nearly $300 million or more. Also, there are no R-rated movies among the Top Ten Movies at the Box Office of All Time, whether you adjust for inflation or not.

All the information you need to make informed decisions is noted in the charts and analyses in our Annual Report to the Entertainment Industry. Therefore, you need to get copies of our annual reports if you wanna be in pictures.

Return of the King

The phenomenal success of Mel Gibson's *The Passion of the Christ* in 2004 sent a lot of tongues in Tinsel Town wagging, but the success of this strongly pro-Christian movie came as no surprise to me. There have been plenty of successful pro-Christian movies in the last five to seven years. For example, *Spider-Man* and *X2* were the two most popular comic book movies in the last two years, and they both contained positive, strong references to New Testament passages and the Christian worldview. Other extremely popular movies have contained positive Christian content, including such movies as *My Big Fat Greek Wedding, The Patriot, Signs, Minority Report, Bruce Almighty,* the *Spy Kids* movies, *Pearl Harbor,* and *The Lord of the Rings* trilogy.

Not only did the king return in *The Lord of the Rings* in 2003, but also, the King of kings returned in *The Gospel of John* and *The Passion of the Christ.* What is more incredible is that Jesus Christ will return in six or seven more faithful movies and television programs about his good news, including *The God/Man, The Lamb, The Gospel of Mark, The Alpha/The Omega,* and *The Greatest King.*

Bringing Down the House!

The good news is that in our comprehensive analysis of the box office in our Report to the Entertainment Industry, we found that movies with strong moral, biblical, and/or Christian content do much better at the box office than movies with excessive or graphic foul language, sex, nudity, violence, alcohol use, and substance abuse. Although some movies with graphic or excessive violence, sex, and sexual nudity, such as the *American Pie* movies, are doing better, they still cannot match the financial success of movies with strong positive content, according to MOVIEGUIDE®'s Christian, biblical standards.

Also, movies with occult and anti-Christian content are not doing as well as they have been doing in recent years. In fact, when you combine all the negative worldview elements together, it is clear that movies with anti-Christian worldviews and strongly immoral, unbiblical content don't do well on average, especially when compared to movies that fit more in line with MOVIEGUIDE®'s high biblical standards.

Furthermore, movies with strong moral, redemptive, and Christian content are much more likely than movies with strong immoral, non-Christian or anti-Christian content to make it into the Top Grossing Movies at the Box Office. As noted in the Report to the Entertainment Industry in recent years, 70 to 100 percent of the Top 5 and Top 10 movies have a Christian or moral worldview, and 90 percent of the Top 10 had at least some moral or Christian content in them. In fact, one of the top two movies of the year in 2003, *Finding Nemo*—written by a Christian, directed by a Christian, and produced by a Christian—was one of the most Christian-friendly movies, thematically speaking, of the year. The other top movie in 2003 was *The Return of the King,* based on one of the most popular Christian novels ever written, J. R. R. Tolkien's *The Lord of the Rings.*

Year in and year out, I and my staff find that movies with very strong Christian content and very strong moral/biblical content earn four to six times as much money per movie as movies with strong negative content!

Master and Commander of the Box Office

One thing that separates MOVIEGUIDE® from its competitors is its analysis of the dominant philosophical, theological, and political worldviews of movies and television programs.

A worldview is a way of interpreting reality. Although political ideologies are not technically worldviews, they often display attributes or qualities similar to worldviews. For example, the communist writer Karl Marx said that his communism was the ultimate humanism and advocated that a humanist society should abolish religion, family, nation, and private property. That is one reason MOVIEGUIDE® has a separate worldview content category for communism. MOVIEGUIDE® also shows readers when a movie merely has a moral or biblical worldview as opposed to an explicit or implied Christian worldview.

Since 1999, movies with a strong Christian worldview have steadily done better at the box office. In 1999, movies with a strong Christian worldview earned an average of $30.1 million per movie, while in 2003, they earned $77.3 million per movie, a significant increase of 157 percent in five years! In general, the more Christian a movie's worldview is, the better it tends to do at the box office.

MOVIEGUIDE® Picks the Pix

MOVIEGUIDE®'s aesthetic standards match the aesthetic standards of the general moviegoing public. Entertainment industry executives and readers can depend on MOVIEGUIDE®'s quality ratings when they're deciding which movies to pay their hard-earned money to see!

In fact, since we've been tracking our quality ratings, the movies that rate excellent quality (four stars) from *MOVIEGUIDE®* earned nearly 100 percent more than movies that earn three stars, two stars, and especially one star from us.

Lord of the Box Office

Looking at MOVIEGUIDE®'s Moral and Spiritual Acceptability Ratings clearly shows that movies that reflect MOVIEGUIDE®'s Christian, biblical standards do better at the box office on average than movies that don't. Thus, movies with positive acceptability ratings from MOVIEGUIDE® (+1 to +4) earn significantly more money than movies with negative ratings (-1 to -4), and especially better than movies with the two lowest ratings

(-3 and -4). The same results hold true for movies rated G and PG as opposed to PG-13 and R. When adjusting the All-Time Box Office Champs for inflation, the most successful movies, hands down, are movies with only G or PG ratings, like *Gone with the Wind, The Sound of Music, Star Wars,* and *The Ten Commandments.* All of these movies appear on my Best Movies of All Time list.

Mr. Smith Goes to Washington

Our Annual Report also shows that moviegoers not only favor family-friendly, Christian-friendly movies with traditional moral values, but they also favor family-friendly, Christian-friendly movies with patriotic, pro-American, procapitalist values that reject radical left-wing viewpoints. Every year these movies make far more money at the box office than movies with anticapitalist, anti-American, socialist, feminist, radical homosexual, Communist, atheist, anti-Christian, and politically correct content.

Terminator

Obscenity, sexual immorality, and graphic violence rarely make the most money. That's the continual lesson that MOVIEGUIDE® discovers every year in its Annual Report.

In fact, our statistics generally show that the more foul language, sex, and sexual nudity in a movie, the worse it did at the box office. Conversely, movies with strong moral, biblical, and/or Christian content do far better than movies with strong and excessive foul language, violence, sex, and nudity!

Thus, sex, violence, vulgarity, and immorality do not sell as well as many people think and as the news media often report. That's because God is still sovereign. His abiding love does not delight in evil but rejoices with the truth.

If you want your movie to make a significant amount of money, you must drastically reduce, and preferably eliminate, all scenes of explicit sex, violence, nudity, and vulgarity from the script. People really want to see wholesome, quality movies, like *Finding Nemo, Toy Story 2, My Big Fat Greek Wedding, Spider-Man, The Princess Diaries, Elf, Shrek, Spy Kids,* and *Ice Age.*

They don't want to see, much less buy, movies with false, immoral, radical, or non-Christian worldviews that violate the intelligence and beliefs of the 172 million people who go to church once a month or more in the United States.

By the way, contrary to the current conventional wisdom in Hollywood, our analysis and box office statistics show that movies with pro-homosexual content in them do poorly on average. In fact, we have found repeatedly that the stronger the homosexual content in a movie, the less it does at the box office, in significant numbers.

A Mighty Wind

Fueled by DVD mania, home video sales and rentals have been sky-rocketing the past three to four years. MOVIEGUIDE® has found that the Top 5 and 10 Home Video Sales and Rentals during these years tend to be family movies like *Finding Nemo, Ice Age, Shrek,* and other movies with strong moral, biblical, or Christian elements in them. Also, most of the Top 5 and Top 10 Home Video Sales (70 to 100 percent) contain no depicted sex scenes, little foul language, no sexual nudity, and no graphic or excessive violence.

American Splendor

Some in the entertainment business think that moral, Christian movies might be successful in the United States but not overseas. This however, is definitely not true.

Year in and year out, most of the Top Five Movies Overseas win top MOVIEGUIDE® Awards, including such movies as *Finding Nemo, Spider-Man, The Lord of the Rings* trilogy, *Pearl Harbor, Pirates of the Caribbean, Monsters, Inc., X2,* and *Shrek.* Most of these also contain either no foul language or only a few light obscenities or profanities, little or no sexual content, no explicit nudity, and no graphic violence.

Furthermore, most of the Top Movies Overseas making $100 million or more have moral, biblical, and/or Christian content, usually earning 80 percent or more of the money among the Top Movies Overseas every year.

The Curse of the Bad Movie

Finally, if you look at the All-Time Box Office Champs and Top Movies at the Box Office in our Annual Reports, you will find that the most popular movies are science fiction adventure (*Star Wars, Jurassic Park, ET,* and *The Matrix* movies), comic-book movies (*Spider-Man* and *X2*), fantasy adventure (*Lord of the Rings* and *Harry Potter*), big budget comedies (*Greek Wedding* and *Bruce Almighty*), supernatural horror movies (the *Mummy* movies, *The Blair Witch Project,* and *The Ring*), computer-animated comedies and comedy adventures (*Finding Nemo, Toy Story 2, Monsters, Inc.,* and *Shrek*), and hand-drawn animated movies with spiritual Christian themes (*Beauty and the Beast, The Lion King,* and *The Prince of Egypt,* which is the most successful hand-drawn animated movie other than *Lilo & Stitch* since *The Lion King*). Thus, if you combine positive moral, biblical, Christian, and conservative values with these kinds of movies, and if your script is well-written, entertaining, and even exciting, you are well on your way to making a blockbuster hit.

Another safe conclusion looking at these numbers is that most people love uplifting fairy tales and heroic adventure stories that take them to worlds they don't see in their normal daily lives. These and popular biblical epics such as *The Ten Commandments, The Passion of the Christ,* and *Ben-Hur* are the kinds of movies that delight and inspire viewers. Believable, honorable characters overcoming huge, difficult obstacles or finding a bit of God's grace will always be the kind of stories that touch our lives and help us to endure. That's the kind of stories you should be writing if you want to be in pictures.

CHAPTER 6

Understanding Your Audience

But if anyone causes one of these little ones who believe in me to sin, it
would be better for him to have a large millstone hung around his neck
and to be drowned in the depths of the sea.
—*Matthew 18:6* NIV

A few years back the evening news broadcast a story about a babysitter in Dallas, Texas, who had molested the baby she was supposed to protect. The parents, who had become suspicious of the sitter, installed a hidden camera in their living room. The evening news showed what the parents saw—the babysitter starting to undress in front of the baby—then the newscast cut away. The news anchors were horrified and wondered how the parents had failed to check this sitter's credentials. The news team closed by remarking that this type of abuse probably occurred more often than anyone knew.

They were right. There is one babysitter who is constantly abusing millions of our children. That babysitter is a television set. No one fires this babysitter or brings criminal charges against it, nor do many people try to rehabilitate it.

No matter how much we condemn the mass media for influencing the behavior of our children, we must admit that there are several accomplices in this tragedy. They include churches that don't teach parents how to teach their children discernment; parents who allow their children to watch television, go to movies, or surf the Internet without adequate supervision or training in the necessary discernment skills; and the creative people in the entertainment industry who do not care about protecting the children.

Child Abuse via the Silver Screen

Even the secular press understands the problem of exposing children to violent and improper television and movies. In an article in the *Los Angeles Times,* James Scott Bell,[1] a writer and novelist in Los Angeles, noted:

> The country was rightly repulsed at the videotape of Madelyne Toogood beating her 4-year-old child in an Indiana parking lot. We know such mistreatment can have a terrible effect on a child's mental health. But, how many Americans indulge in a worse form of abuse without a second thought? I'm talking about taking kids to the movies. The wrong movies.

> The other night I saw *Red Dragon,* the third installment in the Hannibal Lecter series starring Anthony Hopkins. When the bad guy (Ralph Fiennes) bites off the tongue of a screaming reporter, then stands up, mouth bloody, and spits out the offending organ, I squirmed in my seat. What I couldn't stop thinking about, however, was the little girl in the seat in front of me.

> She looked about 6-years-old. . . . Two hours of mayhem ensued. People stabbed, set on fire, tortured. Your average day at the office for serial killers. Every now and then I'd lean over and see the little girl with her eyes fixed to the screen.

Seek Understanding

Understanding why and how the mass media affect children is an extremely important step in producing worthwhile movies and television programs.

Many scientists have argued that there is such a significant body of evidence on the connection between the content of the mass media and behavior, especially aggressive behavior, that researchers should move beyond accumulating further evidence and focus on the processes that are responsible for this relationship.

According to Dr. Victor Strasburger, chief of the American Academy of Pediatrics' section on adolescents, "We are basically saying the controversy is over. There is clearly a relationship between media violence and violence in society."[2]

A report on four decades of entertainment TV from the media research team of Robert Lichter, Linda Lichter, Stanley Rothman, and Daniel Amundson found about fifty crimes, including a dozen murders, in every hour of prime-time television. This indicates that our children may see from 800,000 to 1.5 million acts of violence and witness 192,000 to 360,000 murders on television by the time they are seventeen years old.[3]

This contrasts radically with the generations of men and women who grew up *without* this flood of violent images from the entertainment media. Lichter and his fellow authors wrote: "Since 1955 TV characters have been murdered at a rate 1,000 times higher than real-world victims."[4] If the same murder rate were applied to the general population, everyone in the United States would be killed in just fifty days.[5]

If you are more than forty years old, you probably watch only six movies a year in theaters, most of which are family films. In contrast, teenagers watch an average of fifty movies, 80 percent of which are rated R or PG-13. They watch another fifty movies a year on video.[6]

Five Seasons

To understand why children are affected by the mass media, we need first to understand cognitive development itself. In this regard, it is important to note that psychology, including the field known as cognitive development, is descriptive in that it helps us to classify and understand human beings (after all, God gave man the job of naming what he saw). For many Christians, psychology falls short of being prescriptive in the sense of curing a problem that it identifies, whereas the Bible has the cure for what ails us.

In the late 1970s, building on the research of renowned child psychologist Jean Piaget,[7] television researcher Robert Morse[8] adapted Piaget's stages of cognitive growth so that they can be more effectively applied to research into the mass media.

Every child goes through the stages listed below. Please note that the use of masculine pronouns throughout the following sections is simply for ease of grammatical transition and is not intended as exclusionary language. These stages and principles apply to girls as well as boys.

• The *sensation stage*[9] (approximately ages 0 to 2 years old) where the child's sole means of processing reality is his senses. These young children think that they are the center of the universe, that something exists only if they can see it, and that everything around them serves them.

• The *imagination stage*[10] (approximately ages 2 to 7 years old) where the child's cognition is dedicated to the acquisition of representational skills such as language, mental imagery, drawing, and symbolic play and is limited by being serial and one dimensional. During this stage the child has an active imagination, often confusing fact and fiction, making him uniquely susceptible to what he sees on television and in movies. It is not surprising that a four-year-old girl was critically injured after she apparently tried to fly after watching *Harry Potter and the Sorcerer's Stone*. Authorities in Shelby, North Carolina, said that the girl watched the movie and then crawled onto a kitchen counter, straddled a broom, and jumped off.

• The *concrete operational stage* (approximately ages 7 to 11 years old) where the child acquires the ability of simultaneous perception of two points of view, enabling him to master quantities, relations, and classes of objects. At this stage there is such a strong correspondence between the child's thoughts and reality, he assumes his thoughts about reality are accurate and distorts the facts to fit what he thinks. Younger children react to direct violence but not to suspense. Children in the concrete stage of cognitive development are more upset by suspense than direct violence. Thus, little children will get bored by *Jaws*, which is mostly suspense, while older children may be traumatized by it.

• The *reflection* or *formal operations stage* (approximately ages 12 to 15 years old) where abstract thought gains strength. In this stage differentiation is still incomplete as a result of the adolescent's inability to conceptualize the thoughts of others, as exemplified by the assumption that other people are as obsessed with his behavior and appearance as he is. For example, if he has a pimple and walks into a room filled with friends, he will usually think that everyone is looking at his pimple. In this stage, the adolescent will take risks because he still has difficulty conceptualizing the consequences of his actions. For instance, when the movie *The Program* was released, several teenagers mimicked the main characters by lying down in the middle of the road to prove their courage. Some of these teenagers were seriously injured, and some were killed.

One national radio personality said that these teenagers were really stupid. However, one of the teenagers who died was at the top of his class. What the radio personality did not understand was that these teenagers were in a stage of development where they were the most impulsive and the least able to consider the consequences of their actions. Like most adults, the radio personality didn't remember what it was like to be in a previous stage of cognitive development.

• The *relationship stage,* wherein the adolescent grows into a mature adult, shows complete differentiation. As a result, the adult understands that others are different and accepts those differences by learning to relate to others. Furthermore, the adult is able to conceptualize the consequences of his actions and take the necessary steps to reduce his risks.

Babes in Toyland

Children experience fear reactions to horror entertainment. Exposure to large amounts of violence can produce either desensitization or imitation as a way for the child to cope with the emotions raised by the violence.

Researchers Barbara J. Wilson, Daniel Lynn, and Barbara Randall have examined the harmful effects of graphic horror on children and have discovered some important distinctions:[11]

Visual versus nonvisual threat—The principle of perceptual depend-
ence suggests that younger children are likely to be frightened by movies
and television programs with visually frightening creatures like witches
and monsters. Older children will focus more on conceptual qualities, such
as the motives of a character[12] and are likely to be more upset by an evil,
normal-looking character or by an unseen threat than by a benign but
grotesque character. Therefore, *The Wizard of Oz* is more frightening for
younger children than for older children, while older children are more
frightened by movies such as *Poltergeist* and *Jaws,* which rely more on nonvisual threats.

Reality versus fantasy—Younger children are unable to distinguish fully
between reality and fantasy.[13] Although the terms *real* and *make-believe* may
be used in conversation, younger children do not understand the implications of these terms. The notion that a character or an event is not real has
little impact on a younger child's emotions. Therefore, fantasy offerings
involving events that could not possibly happen, such as *Harry Potter,* are
more frightening to younger children, whereas fictional programs involving
events that could happen, such as *Jaws,* are more frightening to older
children and adults.[14]

Abstract versus concrete events—A concrete threat is explicit and tangi-
ble. For example, an evil character might attack a victim. In contrast,
abstract threats must be inferred from information in the plot. Examples
might include movies about evil conspiracies or disasters such as poisonous
gases. Younger children have difficulty drawing inferences from entertainment and are more likely to focus on explicit rather than implicit cues in the
plot,[15] and so they will be more frightened by a movie depicting a concrete
threat than one involving an intangible or obscure hazard.

Threat versus victim focus—Also, cognitive stages are distinguished by
the degree to which the scenes concentrate on the actual threat versus the
victim's emotional reactions to the threat. Movies that require viewer
involvement and focus primarily on the victims' emotional reactions are less
upsetting for younger than for older children. *Jaws* is a good example

because the viewer often sees only the upper bodies of the victims as they are attacked by the unseen shark.

More important than the sheer amount of mass media horror and violence children watch is the way in which even small amounts of violence are portrayed.[16] Therefore, "a number of contextual features of violence are critical determinants of whether such depictions will facilitate aggressive behavior."[17] According to Wilson, Lynn, and Randall, these contextual features are:

Reward versus punishment associated with violence—Violent depictions for which the aggressor is rewarded are most likely to produce imitation effects or foster attitudes supportive of aggression.[18] In fact, characters need not be explicitly rewarded for such effects to occur. As long as no punishment is associated with a violent act, young viewers will often imitate such depictions.[19] The lack of punishment is a reward for such behavior. Much media violence is portrayed without negative consequences; neither perpetrators nor victims suffer much, and the perpetrator is often rewarded for antisocial actions, as in *Harry Potter.*[20]

The timing of the reward or punishment has important developmental implications.[21] In many movies the perpetrator receives material rewards immediately after performing an aggressive act. Punishment, however, is typically delivered toward the end of the movie. Since younger children are less able than older children to coherently link scenes together and to draw inferences from them,[22] younger children are more likely than older children to see the violence as acceptable and to imitate such behavior when rewards are immediate and punishment is delayed in a movie.

Degree of reality of violence—Violence perceived to be realistic is more likely to be imitated and used as a guide for behavior.[23] Older children are better able to distinguish reality from fantasy and are more emotionally responsive to programs that depict realistic events. Thus, older children are affected more by violent movies that feature events that are humanly possible, such as *Scream*. Younger children are responsive to both realistic and unrealistic violence as long as the acts are concrete and visual.

The nature of the perpetrator—Children are more likely to imitate models who are perceived as attractive or interesting.[24] Children who strongly identify with violent media characters are more likely to be aggressive themselves than are those who do not identify with such characters.[25]

Younger children are more likely to focus on the consequences of a character's behavior in determining whether the character is good or bad, whereas older children focus more on the character's motives.[26] Such age differences are presumably due to the fact that motives are typically presented early in a plot so that the viewer must be able to draw inferences in order to link them to subsequent behaviors. Therefore, younger children will be more likely to emulate bad characters as long as they are rewarded, whereas older children presumably will be cognizant of the characters' motives in selecting role models.

Justified violence—Violence that is portrayed as justified is more likely to be imitated.[27] A common theme in many movies is the portrayal of a hero who is forced to be violent because his job demands it (e.g., *Dirty Harry*) or because he must retaliate against an enemy (e.g., *Harry Potter*). Although the message may be ultimately prosocial (e.g., "don't be a criminal"), the moral is conveyed in a violent context.

In one experiment examining mixed messages,[28] children viewed either a purely prosocial cartoon or a cartoon that contained a prosocial message delivered through justified violence. Kindergartners were more likely to hurt than to help a peer after watching the prosocial-aggressive cartoon. Moreover, both younger and older children showed less understanding of the moral lesson when it was conveyed in the context of violence versus no violence. Therefore, a hero who commits violence for some "good" cause is likely to be a confusing and negative role model for younger and older children.

Similarity of movie situations and characters to viewer—Viewers are more likely to imitate media violence if cues in the program are similar to those in real life.[29] Also, children are likely to imitate models who are similar to themselves.[30] Thus, movies depicting children as violent are more problematic than those involving violent adults. Preschool and early elementary schoolchildren focus on younger characters who are violent, whereas pre-teens and teenagers attend more to aggressive teenage characters.

Amount of violence—Although the way in which violence is portrayed is more critical than the amount of violence in facilitating aggressive behavior, the sheer amount and explicitness of the violent content is important with regard to the viewer's emotions. Excessive exposure to violence may produce a "psychological blunting" of normal emotional responses to violent events. Children who are heavy viewers of television violence show less physiological arousal to a clip of filmed violence than light viewers.

In one experiment, children who watched a violent film or television program were subsequently less likely to seek help when the other children became disruptive and violent. Thus, exposure to media violence leads to a lack of responsiveness to real-life aggression.[31]

Dangerous Minds

Part of the problem with television programs as well as movies is that they are so effective at propelling powerful, emotional images into the viewers' mind in real time with no time for the viewer to reflect, react, or review the information he or she is receiving—processes that are absolutely necessary for cognitive development.

Therefore, the act of watching is harmful to the cognitive development of children and, as a consequence, adversely influences their moral, social, emotional, and religious development. Videos/television also "debilitates an important cognitive function in adults, the one that permits abstract reasoning—and hence related capacities for moral decision making, learning, religious growth, and psychological individualization."[32]

Rush

Watching fighting or other violence can make the mind believe that it is about to engage in life-threatening activity, so the body will often respond by releasing adrenal epinephrine into the bloodstream, giving the viewer an adrenal rush without the threat of actual violence. Watching sexual activity and nudity makes the mind think that the person is about to mate, so the body releases raging hormones that can often cause an addictive adrenal rush without the psychological burdens attendant to most human relationships. These physiological phenomena will engage and attract the viewer, often causing him or her to want more and more exposure to the stimuli that cause their artificial physical elation.

Scientists have discovered that mass-media violence leads to aggressive behavior by overstimulating children. The more intense and realistic the violent scene, the more likely it is to be encoded, stored in the memory, and later retrieved as model behavior.

Another study showed that boys who watch a great deal of violent programming may exhibit less physiological arousal when shown new violent programs than do boys who regularly watch less-violent fare.[33] This study seems to explain why consumers of mass-media sex and violence need more and more prurient fare or more and more violent fare. Of course, all of this can add up to addiction (best summed up by the phrase the "plug-in drug" as applied to television) because most of the offerings of the mass media are emotive, not intellectual pursuits.

The impact of excessive movie and television sex and violence on teenagers is aggravated by the fact that their raging hormones give them a predisposition to seek arousal. They are subject to tremendous peer and media pressure at an age where fitting in with their peers is extremely important even if that fitting in means rebelling against their parents. They have a predisposition to seek out movies and programs that arouse them. Some are so aroused that they seek to replicate the emotive sexual or violent situations portrayed in the movie or television program in their own lives.

Truth or Consequences

Since 1966 (the year the church abandoned Hollywood), violent crime has increased in the United States by 560 percent, illegitimate births have increased 419 percent, divorce rates have quadrupled, the percentage of children living in single-parent homes has tripled, the teenage suicide rate has increased more than 300 percent, and SAT scores have dropped almost eighty points. Rapes, murders, and gang violence have become common occurrences. While many factors have contributed to our cultural decline, it is clear that the mass media have had a significant influence on behavior.[34]

Researchers affiliated with the National Bureau of Economic Research and Stanford University wrote in the journal *Science*[35] that America's children are fatter, more suicidal, more murderous, and scored lower on standardized tests in recent years than in the 1960s. After years of denial, even 87 percent of the top media executives now admit that the violence in the mass media contribute to the violence in society.[36] And children, too, are aware of the ability of the entertainment media to influence their behavior.[37]

Yet, in spite of the clear correlation between violence in the mass media and violence on the street, few people are yelling, "Stop!" The growing American tolerance for brutal sex and violence in the mass media suggests the proverbial frog who calmly dies as he is slowly brought to a boil.

The following verses from Paul's letter to the Romans describe the conditions in which we find ourselves today:

> And even as they did not like to retain God in their knowledge, God gave them over to a debased mind, to do those things which are not fitting; being filled with all unrighteousness, sexual immorality, wickedness, covetousness, maliciousness; full of envy, murder, strife, deceit, evil-mindedness; they are whisperers, backbiters, haters of God, violent, proud, boasters, inventors of evil things, disobedient to parents, undiscerning, untrustworthy, unloving, unforgiving, unmerciful; who knowing the righteous judgment of God, that those who practice such things are deserving of death, not only do the same but also approve of those who practice them. (Rom. 1:28–32 NKJV)

A Sample of the Violence

The suggestion that the mass media of entertainment spawn violence is not anecdotal; it is real. Over the years there have been innumerable reports of grisly crimes that were inspired by and mimicked the fictional product of the entertainment media. It is important to take note of these stories to realize the scope of the problem and the powerful influence of movies, television programs, music, and the other mass media. A small sampling of specific films and their violent outcomes is outlined below.

Child's Play?

It is clear to any parent that children learn to a large degree by mimicking the behavior of the adults around them, including those on television and in movies.[38]

One of the most famous examples was the connection that a judge in Liverpool, England, made between the horror movie *Child's Play 3* and the murder of two-year-old James Bulger by two eleven-year-old boys, Robert Thompson and Jon Venables.[39] According to the judge, the horror movie *Child's Play 3* presents some horrifying parallels to the actual murder of little James Bulger, and the movie was viewed repeatedly by one of the killers just before the murder took place. The judge noted:

- The horror movie depicts a baby doll who comes to life and gets blue paint splashed in its face. There was blue paint on the dead child's face.
- The movie depicts a kidnapping. James was abducted by the two older boys before they killed him.
- The climax of the movie comes as two young boys murder the doll on a train, mutilating the doll's face. James was first mutilated and bludgeoned by the two older boys and then left on a railroad track to be run over.

This story was widely publicized around the world, but the link to *Child's Play 3* seldom made the news. Why were these facts overlooked or withheld by the mainstream media?

Slasher Movies and Stephen King Novels

In Houston, Texas, Scott Edward May, a seventeen-year-old obsessed with slasher movies, the occult, and heavy-metal music, attacked a girl during their first date, stabbing her when she closed her eyes for a good-night kiss.[40] They had just seen the movie *The Cutting Edge.* May told police he had had urges to kill since childhood. "I love knives," May's statement reads. "I like to go to the movies a lot. A lot of people get stabbed in the movies. I really liked the *Texas Chainsaw Massacre.* A lot of people got stabbed in that."

Natural Born Killers?

The Oliver Stone movie *Natural Born Killers* has produced a slew of copycat murders.

Nathan K. Martinez, an unhappy seventeen-year-old obsessed with the movie *Natural Born Killers,* murdered his stepmother and his half sister in their suburban home fifteen miles southwest of Salt Lake City.

In Georgia, Jason Lewis, a fifteen-year-old, murdered his parents, firing multiple shotgun blasts into their heads. Letters found in his room indicated he worshipped Satan and, along with three friends, had formulated a plan to kill all their parents and to copy the cross-country swing of violence portrayed in *Natural Born Killers.*

Christopher Smith, an eighteen-year-old, shouted at television cameras, "I'm a natural born killer!" echoing the words of actor Woody Harrelson in the movie *Natural Born Killers,* following his arrest for shooting to death an eighty-two-year-old man.

One gruesome incident prompted novelist John Grisham to suggest that the survivors of these killing sprees should sue Stone.[41] The incident that incensed Grisham occurred in March 1995 when two teenagers saw *Natural Born Killers* in Oklahoma, then drove to Mississippi and killed Bill Savage in the same randomly violent way as the movie's protagonists do. They then went to Louisiana and nearly killed a woman in a convenience store (she is now a quadriplegic). One of the two said the movie led directly to their actions.

What Else?

Increased violence in our society would be more than enough, but it is not the only effect of the mass media of entertainment on children. Five other consequences are discussed below: decrease in creative imagination, concentration, and delayed gratification; false memory syndrome; movies/TV as religion; spiritual warfare; and the transference of spirits.

The Twilight Zone

Children who are heavy users of the mass media of entertainment demonstrate decreases in the capacity for creative imagination, concentration, and delayed gratification. With regard to imagination, they are less able to form mental pictures, and they engage in less imaginative play. With regard to concentration, children become lazy readers of "nonbooks," with greatly decreased attention spans (you have to exercise concentration or it atrophies). With regard to delayed gratification, the children have less tolerance for getting into a book or other activities.

Symbolic function, perception, and abstract reasoning are damaged in a manner that resembles dyslexia. The rapid increase in reading disabilities, or dyslexia, in the United States may be, in part, attributed to heavy television and movie viewing. Television in particular inhibits eye movement and, thereby, the acquisition of reading skills.

False Memory Syndrome

Another area of research on the influence of the mass media on children and adults is false memory syndrome, unchained memories, memory therapy, and associated psychological insights that have captured the national imagination.

One area of life that most likely contributes to the false memory syndrome is the tremendous amount of movie and television sex, violence, and occultism that has filled the minds of youth over the years. Nefarious films and other mass media have planted images in the minds of our youth that they have processed in the same manner as the daily activities in which they engage. However, unlike the many daily activities, which are repetitive and dull, most of these entertaining movies and television programs are a potent and often cognitively dissonant, if not traumatic, brew of emotive visual and audile messages that lodge in the nooks and grannies of the child's memory, waiting to pop into their dreams or consciousness.

Research indicates that the minds of our youth are overflowing with movies and television programs that they confuse with reality and history. Everyday examples abound, from the woman who saw the movie *Independence Day* and afterward told a reporter that she believes the government is hiding a flying saucer, to those who saw the movie *The Wind and the Lion* (including a media literacy teacher) and assume that this historical incident involved a beautiful woman and a dashing desert chieftain, rather than the real characters, an old Greek immigrant and a Moroccan thief.

Memory therapists have been able to induce adults to fabricate a childhood history from disjointed memories. Regrettably, some of these adults have acted on these false memories.

God Rewritten Hollywood-Style

The mass media influence not only our behavior but also our beliefs. Therefore, it is important to realize that religion is alive and well in the mass media, though it is not the predominantly Christian faith of our founding fathers. It is, instead, a cacophony of ill-conceived religions such as materialism, consumerism, eroticism, hedonism, naturalism, humanism, cynicism, stoicism, the cult of violence, and a multitude of other modern variations on pagan practices that now vie for renewed homage in the mass media.

Kathleen Waller, Ph.D., and Michael E. O'Keeffe, Ph.D., team-teach the popular Religion and Film course at Saint Xavier University in Chicago, Illinois. They note that movies deeply influence how their students see God and theology. They wrote in *MOVIEGUIDE®*:

> We have come to two conclusions about our students that give us pause. The first is the relative insecurity many of our students feel when explaining their faith; and, the second is the undeniable influence that the mass media has on the religious ideas they do hold. . . .
>
> These students certainly consider themselves good Christians, but they lack the ability to discuss their faith with anything more than a surface understanding of who Jesus is and what Christianity is about. In short, they are unable to "explain" their

views, particularly to classmates who come from religious traditions that do not use the same terms or speak from the starting point as they do. Thus even discussing something as seemingly straightforward as "the Bible is the Word of God" is difficult for them, particularly if they are called upon to explain the theological presuppositions that stand behind such a claim.

Perhaps because of this naivete, many of our students also struggle with the second fact; namely, their almost wholesale acceptance of the culture's understanding of religion. In other words, they are relatively uninformed about the faith given to them by their parents and their churches, and they are uninformed about the distinction between that faith and the "faith" packaged for them by the mass media, especially films and television. Hence our task is doubled: we not only have to help students sort out and explain the inherited faith of our fathers and mothers, but we have to distinguish true faith from the faith of Hollywood. In many cases, the faith of our students is more indebted to *The Simpsons* and movies such as *Stigmata* and *Dogma* than to traditional Christianity. . . .

Our experience confirms it is more difficult to dislodge Hollywood's version of Christianity, for Hollywood's version eventually becomes "real," becomes the way they see God, or heaven and hell, or sin and virtue, or the lives of believers vis-a-vis the lives of others.

The themes portrayed are consistent: malevolent supernatural forces are real, humans are powerless in the face of evil, Christian doctrine and religious training provide no recourse or significant spiritual guidance in the struggle with evil, and the Christian Church and its leaders are powerless before Satan and his minions. In addition, God is too distant, or uncaring, unable, or unwilling, to check Satan's power. These films, and others like them, borrow freely from Christian teachings and symbols, but usually subvert them beyond recognition or take such dramatic license that any sound theological insight is lost. They often purport to quote from the Bible or to interpret biblical eschatology, but these interpretations are horribly skewed at best. Several of the movies are visually stunning in their special effects so, even if one is able to recognize the faulty theology, the world they portray is so compelling that it is hard not to accept Hollywood's version as true. Thus it is not surprising that many of our students are unable to distinguish the unorthodox teaching in these films. Instead, they come away convinced they have learned something valuable about Christianity and its inability to deal with evil.[42]

As theologian Paul Tillich explains, "Your god is that reality which elicits from you your deepest feelings and ultimate concerns," and "Religion is the state of being grasped by an ultimate concern, a concern which qualifies all other concerns as preliminary and which itself contains the answer to the question of a meaning of our life."[43] British playwright J. M. Barrie summarizes that "one's religion is whatever he is most interested in."[44]

The Internet, computer games, prime-time entertainment television, movies, and popular music have become a religion for too many, especially some of those employed in the entertainment industry.

Sadly, children have lost all memory of the Ten Commandments with the prohibitions against murder, theft, and adultery, among the other absolute moral values, as illustrated by the following chart:

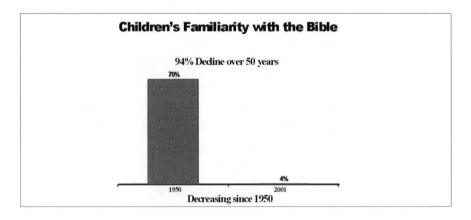

Spiritual Warfare

The cognitive/psychological and physiological influence of the mass media has a spiritual impact. The images of the mass media that tug at our desires, seduce our thoughts, and lodge in our memories are the demons of our age. They claw at our consciousness and entice us to do things we would not otherwise do, whether to buy a product we don't need or worse.

We often forget there is a war raging around us. It is a war being waged inside our minds, a spiritual war for our souls. The adversary is using every possible tactic to control our minds: materialism, secularism, humanism, and all the other *'isms* that conflict with Christianity. He is using the most effective weapon to win: the power of the mass media of entertainment. With the corrupted movies and television programs of our age, the adversary is fueling our sinful propensity to lust and hooking us on our desires. Once hooked, he drags us down to hell.

As the apostle Paul notes in 1 Corinthians 15:33 (AMP): "Do not be so deceived and misled! Evil companionships (communion, associations) corrupt and deprave good manners and morals and character."

The key is for Christians and the church to develop wisdom, knowledge, and understanding by rediscovering a biblical theology of art, entertainment, and communication. Thus equipped, it becomes much easier to comprehend and produce great movies and television programs.

CHAPTER 7

The Producers

M otion picture and television technology is continually changing. By the time you read this, many changes will have occurred, and most of the equipment used as I write may be obsolete. However, if you learn the basic principles and techniques of production, you will be able to use whatever equipment comes along.

These techniques and principles will help you communicate through other audiovisual media. However, you should acquaint yourself with the unique principles and techniques of those other audiovisual media to use them effectively.

To understand the techniques and principles that apply to movie and television movie production, let's examine the steps involved in producing a movie. A movie involves the most talent, the most equipment, the most resources, and the widest range of artistic and technical creativity and decisions. Reviewing the basic steps required to produce a movie will give you an overview of the medium and allow us to touch on most of the pertinent principles and techniques of production. In the process, specific aspects of television movie production will also be addressed.

With regard to television movies, *Hallmark Hall of Fame* has made some of the best. Hallmark is certainly a household word in America because of the company's outstanding greeting cards and other products. Hallmark Cards, Inc., is based in Kansas City, Missouri, and Hallmark Hall of Fame Productions is its television moviemaking subsidiary, with an additional office for production based in Studio City, California. The Hallmark Hall of Fame Series is now fifty-three years old and is considered to be the most honored series in television history. The company has produced more than two hundred movies, or about four two-hour programs a year. They have won a total of seventy-eight Emmys, plus numerous Peabody, Golden Globe, and other awards throughout the years.

Audience favorites include such recent movies as John Grisham's *A Painted House, Sarah, Plain and Tall* starring Glenn Close, and *Fallen Angel,* with Gary Sinise. Other popular titles, still available at Hallmark Card Shops, include such productions as *What the Deaf Man Heard* and the recent *The Blackwater Lightship.* Brad Moore is the president of Hallmark Hall of Fame Productions, which he says is the best job in the movie business. In *MOVIEGUIDE®* and in the "So You Want to Be in Pictures?" section on www.movieguide.org, Brad shares a bit of his life experience and wisdom for people of faith pursuing filmmaking or television production.

Producing Your Movie

The following steps will take us through the production process involved in producing a hypothetical movie from idea through follow-up. The assumptions made throughout this process will guide you through the basic principles and techniques of a typical production.

1. Review your choice of theatrical movie. To reach your decision to produce a movie, you had to work through the appropriate ascertainment questions, discern your talents, target your audience, formulate your communication, determine your genre, and choose your medium—motion picture for theatrical distribution. You decided that you are called to communicate the gospel to a mass audience and that you have the motivation and talents to do so.

At first you may have considered communicating through a television interview program but realized that genre would limit your audience because television is best suited to communicating stories, whatever form they take: commercials, reality-TV, variety, contests, and sports. Lack of audience appeal has caused television executives to relegate most public affairs programs to poorly watched time periods, PBS, or certain cable television channels. Producing your program for a secondary time period or PBS would limit the size of your targeted audience. (PBS offers advantages if you are targeting professionals.)

You may have considered producing a commercial, but you decided that genre did not give you the broad impact you wanted, and ten, thirty, or sixty seconds was not enough time to present your communication. Sports, contests, and variety programs did not give you the logical, emotive power you wanted. Although your communication was good news, it did not lend itself to a current events format. Therefore, you decided to use a story genre, a movie.

2. Transform your story into a script and a treatment. Once you have decided to produce a movie, you have to secure the rights to a good story and transform your story into a great script. Since the story and script are the foundation of your movie, the subject is covered in chapter 4. Either you need to turn your story into a script or hire a scriptwriter to do so, assuming that you did not start out with a script.

3. Secure rights, financing, and access to distribution. Once you decide to produce a movie the question arises, how are you going to get your movie distributed? This question should be answered before you go to the trouble and expense of producing your movie. Your answer may change your mind about producing a movie, or it will affect how you produce your movie.

Preproduction

4. Establish breakdown, budget, schedule, and timetable for your production. As soon as you have a story, you should have it broken down so you can start estimating the cost of producing your movie. The distributor, the networks, and the financiers will ask you how much your movie will cost to produce. Before you go to a movie studio/distributor, you turn your story into a script and prepare a budget based on that script, unless you are seeking development funds to prepare a script, in which case you need to budget the development funds you need.

5. Storyboard and plan your production. So that you can accurately plan your production, turn your script into a rough storyboard that you will want to revise and perfect as you proceed. A storyboard is a visual representation of the script as a series of sketches that can be very rough (using stick figures) or very detailed.

6. Bring your key above-the-line talent on board. Your above-the-line talent will be determined to a degree by whom you need to bring on board to make your production bankable. What big names, or talent with track records, will cause a major movie studio or private capital to finance your production? Sometimes all you need is one star, such as Pierce Brosnan or Julia Roberts. Sometimes a director, such as Stephen Spielberg of *ET*, *Indiana Jones*, and *Schindler's List*, will make your production bankable. Often you will have to join forces with a coproducer, who may end up with the credit, such as George Lucas of *Star Wars* and the *Indiana Jones* series. Of course, getting either of these two megatalents is close to impossible, but look for available talent who appreciate the type of movie you are producing.

7. Finalize your script and organize inserts. (This is primarily for television.) With your key talent, finalize your script. Then working from your final script, obtain or arrange for graphics, photography, film, stock shots, film clips, properties, and everything that needs to be in your production.

8. Enlist cast and staff. Casting is critical and so is below-the-line staffing. Be selective. Be careful.

9. Organize artistic and technical services and facilities.

Production

10. Rehearsals. (This is primarily for television.) At this point you will start rehearsing your cast and crew.

11. Prepare camera and other scripts. Prepare breakdown sheets and other scripts.

12. Prepare studio and locations. All too often studios are rented and the personnel rushed in to produce the program only for the producer and director to find that the studio is not prepared to do the type of production work required. You, your producer, and your director should meet with the studio to confirm the availability of everything that is essential to your production, such as, space, equipment, back-up facilities, crew, storage space, time to set up, technical equipment, dressing rooms, green room, etc.

13. Determine camera blocking and equipment preparation. Before your production starts, you need to know what you want your camera, sound, and other equipment to do, and when and how.

14. Run through and final rehearsal. (This is primarily for television.) Run through your script to remove any kinks and timing problems.

15. Complete location production. If you have planned carefully for shooting on location, things should go well.

16. Complete studio production.

17. Celebrate with a cast party. Establish a good rapport with your cast. Plan to work together again. Be supportive.

Postproduction, Distribution, and Beyond

18. Add music and sound. Music and sound effects will make or break a movie or television production.

19. Edit. You will want to spend a great deal of time off-line[1] reviewing your production.

20. Review. Does your program work? Reedit if necessary.

21. Move to distribution/sales. You are ready to distribute.

22. Follow up. Check the ratings, promotion, advertising, and any payments and billings that are due.

Having set forth most of the steps in a production, let's hear from one of the best what it is all about. In May 2003, everyone from toddlers to grandparents, and all those in between, lined up at the box office to purchase tickets for *Finding Nemo*. From the very first scene, audiences were captivated by the breathtakingly beautiful, realistic animation and the heartwarming story of the love of a worried fish-dad for his son. According to one *MOVIEGUIDE*® reviewer, the movie was the first "perfect" family movie ever to be made. With no offensive elements in it, it is an entertaining, captivating, hilarious story filled with memorable characters from the sea.

One of the most memorable characters is the turtle dad named Crush, with his hilarious surfer-dude accent. Little do some audiences know, however, that the man who voiced Crush is also the man who wrote and directed *Finding Nemo.* Go to our Web site at www.movieguide.org and read the interview with Andrew Stanton, where he shares with us some of his wisdom and experience in his exciting industry of animated filmmaking.

To produce a movie or a television program, you have to be creative, self-disciplined, organized, unstructured, persistent, flexible, imaginative, and practical. As a rule of thumb, 50 percent of your energy will be expended doing the work of producing your program. Another 50 percent will be expended fighting for your production. If this seems overwhelming to you, trust God and you will succeed in producing a powerful program telling the story he has given you to tell.

This overview of the techniques and principles that apply to producing a movie is applicable to your production no matter what size, but smaller productions will require less of everything. If you are embarking on producing a video on your church, review the steps necessary for a movie or television program and select those principles and techniques that are relevant to your production. By familiarizing yourself with the most complex form of production, you will excel in simpler productions, including productions in other audiovisual media.

An excellent exercise is to assemble a group from your church and produce a movie in miniature with amateur equipment. If you take care to follow all the appropriate steps, you will end up with a successful production. If not, you will know it because of the glaring flaws in your final product. Having trained many communicators, I have found that such an exercise is the most effective way to learn about the nature of the media of movies and television.

Try it. Have fun and apply yourself to achieving excellence in his service.

CHAPTER 8

The Art of the Deal

Once you decide to produce a movie, the next question you should ask is, "How are you going to get your movie distributed?" This question should be answered before you go to the trouble and expense of producing your movie. Your answer may change your mind about producing a movie or may affect how you produce your movie. This question involves financing and rights, two of the basic building materials of movies.

Financing and Access to Distribution

Every year around nine hundred movies are rated by the Motion Picture Association of America (MPAA), but fewer than three hundred make it to your local theater. Furthermore, for more than seventy-five years, seven major studios, which own and control the MPAA, have controlled theatrical distribution in spite of mega-anomalies like *The Passion of the Christ, My Big Fat Greek Wedding,* and *The Blair Witch Project.* Although these studios have been releasing about 120 to 140 movies per year for several years, they often control around 98 percent of the box office net or distributor's gross. That means that the 60 percent of the movies that are released by truly independent distributors usually earn less than 2 percent of the box office.

In the entertainment industry, there is a tight concentration of power in the hands of a few executives, producers, and agents who make it difficult for a producer with no track record to break into the movie business. With regard to television, the major networks have to fill twenty thousand hours of programming time every year and need new ideas to capture and hold their audience. On the other hand, there is also a tight concentration of power in the hands of a few producers, agents, and network executives who have little contact with religion and make it difficult for a producer with no track record to break into the network program schedule.

For forty years a religious program producer had reasonable, though difficult, access to the networks because they scheduled a certain amount of religious programming as part of their obligation to operate "in the public interest, convenience and necessity."[1] Since the late 1970s, however, the Federal Communications Commission has been relaxing the public interest obligations of broadcasters. Therefore, to get on the air today, you have to sell the networks on your concept, convince them that they should air material with religious content, and/or buy airtime.

At this point you may decide to reconsider producing a movie for theatrical release or a major television network. You could retarget your audience and use a medium that is easier to access, such as cable television, PBS, independent television, or Christian television.

You should not aim for theatrical distribution unless that is the right medium for you and your communication. However, if your communication demands the most prestigious release in the entertainment industry and you have the patience and stamina to go for it, you can get a distributor or even get your program on the air with God's help. Movies like *The Passion of the Christ, Gods and Generals, Luther, Master and Commander: The Far Side of the World, The Lord of the Rings* trilogy, *Spy Kids,* and *Finding Nemo,* and television programs like *Doc, 7th Heaven, Sue Thomas: F. B. Eye, The District,* and *Jag* are good examples of entertainment with strong Christian content.

The more you understand the entertainment industry, the more likely you will be able to succeed. What follows are brief snapshots of aspects of the entertainment industry that will help you avoid some common mistakes or help you choose among your several options.

Movie studios are financing, production, and distribution companies.

Once upon a time, once a month for several years, I brought together a group of wealthy investors who were united in their desire to make movies in order to help them understand the entertainment industry. Each month they were introduced to a top executive in the entertainment industry or a top talent.

During one of these meetings, one investor asked the president of a major movie studio if the investor brought the studio a great movie that would cost the studio $50 million to make, but only cost the investor and his team $5 million, would the president want to distribute his movie. The president asked, "Why would we want that?" The investor said, "To make more profit." The president asked, "Why would we want that?"

Then the president added, "If you want to make movies, we will set you up with an office on the studio lot, which costs ten times more to rent per foot than it would across the street. And we will sell you supplies from the studio store for ten times more than you could buy them outside the studio store. Then we will assign you movies that we agree to produce and use your money to produce them." The investors were overjoyed at the opportunity.

I told the investors that what they didn't understand is that a movie studio is in part a production company. As such, the studio writes off some of its tremendous overhead in the $50 million movie production budget. If the investor produces the movie outside the studio, the studio cannot write off its sound stages, shops, personnel, utilities, etc. Therefore, the studio is interested in movies being made within the system, even if those movies are filmed in Hollywood, New Zealand, or Canada, so that the costs of the production cover its unfair share of the overhead of the studio.

Producers with movie studios resemble sharecroppers or employees in a company town.

As the president noted to our investors group, come to work with the studio and you pay the studio for everything.

After the Civil War many plantations substituted sharecropping for slavery. Instead of providing the slaves with food and lodging, no matter how meager, the plantation rented the new sharecroppers their shacks and all the equipment the sharecroppers needed to farm the plantation. When the harvest was brought for sale to the plantation silo or warehouse, the price for the harvest was paid after deducting all that was owed for the shack, the farming equipment, and the supplies that were leased to the sharecropper. Often this meant that the sharecropper got practically nothing.

Producers for the studios are often in the same position. The producer rents his office space, pays for the development of his movie or television program, and leases all his equipment from the studio. When the box office returns arrive, all these costs are deducted, often leaving the producer in debt.

Hollywood doesn't need your money.

The major studios not only produce movies, but they also finance them and place the financing for them with banks and institutional investors. As of this writing, the average Hollywood movie costs $102 million to produce and distribute. When an outsider comes into Hollywood thinking that the studios need the outsider's money, he is usually treated as a dude from the east, a greenhorn, or a naïf who will soon be parted from his money by the studio that does not need it.

The history of Hollywood is filled with brilliant, wealthy outsiders who lost a lot of money and left in disgrace. Joe Kennedy became infatuated with a starlet, was fleeced by Hollywood, made some rotten movies, and high-tailed it back to Boston to rebuild his fortune so he could eventually bankroll his son John F. Kennedy's run for U.S. president. The brilliant Howard Hughes lost bundles of money and acquired syphilis for all his efforts. Billionaire Kirk Kerkorian lost MGM twice and told the press that he never knew what went wrong. And the list goes on and on.

On February 29, 2004, a *Los Angeles Times* article by Patrick J. Kiger entitled "Chew. Spit. Repeat. The Movie Industry Consumes Carpetbagging

Investors Like Prime-Cut Steak. What's the Appeal of Being Eaten Alive?"
exposed the treatment of wealthy outsiders:

"We don't go for strangers," spoke one of F. Scott Fitzgerald's
characters in the writer's final, unfinished Hollywood novel. But
he didn't get it completely right. The Industry likes interlopers
just fine—as long as they empty their wallets and don't overstay
their welcome. That scenario has been repeated in Hollywood
almost as often as the two-unlikely-cops-become-wisecracking-
crime-fightin'-buddies action thriller. An outsider, flush with
success in some other industry or bankrolled by a family fortune,
bursts onto the scene with dreams of becoming the next Louis B.
Mayer, only to slink away a year or three later in ignominious
defeat. The most recent, high-profile examples—Messier and
Edgar Bronfman Jr., the Seagram heir whose Hollywood ambi-
tions were intertwined with Vivendi's—are only the latest in a
series that goes back to the early days of Hollywood, when
sharpies such as William Randolph Hearst and Joe Kennedy came
West to get their pockets picked.

Since then, scores of other West Coast carpetbaggers have met
with varying degrees of failure—old-line industrialists, Wall
Street financiers, insurance conglomerates and corporate raiders,
New Economy wunderkinds from this country, plus Dutch,
Japanese, British, Italian and Israeli hopefuls. . . . But with few
exceptions, such as Australian media baron Rupert Murdoch, the
movie industry has chewed up and spit out newcomers like
hunks of Morton's prime-cut steak.

Why do all these powerful, wealthy alpha males venture out of
their comfy enclaves and plunge into an utterly unfamiliar, noto-
riously Byzantine business that they often approach with distain
and condescension? What sort of mass-induced hypnotic state
convinces a German investor, for example, that it's a sensible
idea to sink millions into a film homage to L. Ron Hubbard's
Battlefield Earth? Or an otherwise adroit telecommunications

mogul into putting his name in the credits of an unnecessary remake of *Around the World in Eighty Days*? Is there some sort of semiotic explanation for why otherwise astute people from another culture—whether it's Amsterdam or Peoria—get hopelessly tangled up in movie industry lingo and end up mumbling about "synergy" after that disastrous first-cut screening? . . .

"Outsiders who've been very successful and made a lot of money rightly think they're smarter than the average person and perhaps even somewhat creative," explains Roderick Kramer, a onetime Hollywood script reader who is a professor of organizational behavior at Stanford University's graduate business school, where he also teaches a course on the movie industry for MBA students. . . .

Unfortunately, the world's dream factory, by its very nature, doesn't quite work that way. And it could be that even the business world's richest and smartest minds are helpless to resist a fate that may be determined, in part, by our genes. . . .

Instead of locking horns like real bulls, the in-group may resort to trickery and exploitation. "The in-group members may look at the outsider and think, 'I'm not going to have reciprocal relations with this person in the future, because he's not going to be allowed to stay.' So instead they go after whatever he's got that's of value."

"The most important thing is [your] knowledge base, the contacts that give you 'reputational capital,'" Kramer says. "That's what gets you in. An outsider has a lot of trouble breaking into that kind of network, because outside money and power aren't going to trump those connections. They don't really have time for you. The ones who are willing to let you into a network are the ones who are less reliable, the ones who are out to take advantage. Because the only thing an outsider brings to the network is money—while he still has it. . . ."

"They don't do the same sort of traditional business analysis that they would if they were entering, say, the machine-tool business," says Dartmouth College business school professor Sydney Finkelstein, author of the book *Why Smart Executives Fail*. "Then again, when you're making machine tools, you're not seduced by the idea of sitting in the audience with a bunch of movie stars at the Academy Awards. Instead, you get seduced by the glamour and it screws you up. . . ."

From an empirical point of view, though, an outsider would have to be totally insane to try the movie industry in particular, because the economic model is bizarrely different from just about any other business. The movie industry actually earns only a 3% to 4% return on investment, which is lousy when compared with steel-making or book publishing.

To make it worse, the statistical curve for movie profits isn't much of a curve at all. If the movie industry followed a bell curve, the typical movie would make money, and it would be extremely rare for a movie to take in more than three times the standard deviation—the average amount that the films differ from the middle. Instead, it's shaped more like a playground slide—6 percent of the product earns 90 percent of the money, and 70 percent to 80 percent of the product sinks into oblivion. This results in what economist De Vany calls an industry of "extreme uncertainty." That is, successes are aberrantly rare and outlandishly enormous. The movie *Titanic*, for example, grossed $600 million domestically in 1997, in a year when the average film grossed $23 million. Results like that are impossible to predict. . . .

Another added complication: Most industries don't have Hollywood's peculiar distribution system, in which a would-be blockbuster suddenly covers most of the nation's movie screens like kudzu and competitors get what's left. That's the equivalent of one brand of microwave oven getting all the shelf space at Best

Buy, Target and Wal-Mart for a week, but then disappearing instantly if it doesn't sell. . . .

The carpetbagging mogul usually doesn't realize that until it's too late. Early in his Hollywood misadventure, William Randolph Hearst was so confident that he brushed off Adolph Zukor's offer of management help. "Making pictures is fundamentally like making publications," proclaimed Hearst, who orchestrated such flops as 1933s *Going Hollywood*, in which Marion Davies starred with Bing Crosby—an unfortunate bit of casting because the two shared an interest in alcohol and spent much of their time on the set intoxicated. The movie lost $250,000. Just a few years later, Hearst was ready to quit the movie business, despairing: "I don't think I can make any money at it."

Stripped of his competence and confidence, the outsider is vulnerable. Stuart Fischoff, a sometime screenwriter and professor of media psychology at Cal State L.A., compares the process by which outsiders get sucked in by the Hollywood culture to cult recruiting or North Korean prison camp brainwashing. The would-be mogul is "brutalized and humiliated, then infantilized and reduced to a helpless state, and then introduced to the new set of values," Fischoff says. . . .

Language also can be a problem for outsiders. . . . "The language of Hollywood is so filled with hyperbole that you have to be able to decode it," behavior expert Kramer explains. "Otherwise, you don't pick up that when a guy tells you that your project is fantastic and it'll be exciting to work with you, he really means that he's going to tell his assistant not to put through any more of your calls."

In a follow-up article by Kiger entitled "Bitten by the Movie Bug" the *Los Angeles Times* listed the common delusional defenses of the investor seduced by Hollywood:

1. Denial: Keep telling yourself that you're the exception to the rule, the outsider who can swim with the sharks.

2. Anger: When you're in that inevitable meeting with backers who've lost faith in your leadership, go ahead and curse the unfairness of it all.

3. Bargaining: Find another naïf from the outside world and convince him that he's smarter than you. Remember that even after Coca-Cola paid more than half a billion dollars for Columbia, it still was able to sell it to Sony for many times that amount.

4. Depression: It's OK to feel a little down in the dumps. Indulge yourself. After Howard Hughes lost RKO, he retreated to a rented studio for four months and sat around naked, watching movies for days without sleep, gobbling junk food and befouling the floor like a caged animal.

5. Acceptance: Hire a ghostwriter to do a defensive memoir. Even if nobody is willing to pay $22.95 to read it, you'll feel much better.

On the other hand, if you don't have money, you are not a player.

Once upon a time, several of the investors whom I had assembled to learn about the entertainment industry decided to go to the Cannes Film Festival. I had lunch with some of them when they came back. They were derisive of the others who went to Cannes because they did not have a yacht and stayed in hotels. Thus, the studios pay attention to your financial status although they do not need your money.

Hollywood is a club.

If you have ever belonged to a club, you know that you can bring your friends and treat them to dinner, but they can't come back to eat the next day if they are not members. Whatever race or creed, they must be members of the club to use the club. Good clubs recognize their members. Hollywood is just such a place.

Hollywood is a poker game.

Literally, the top studio executives have weekly poker games where they share information and discuss the entertainment industry. If you are not in the game, well, . . . you are an outsider.

Hollywood is the lawless wild, wild West.

While a millionaire was buying a famous movie studio, his lawyer was selling the studio's assets to a competing studio that the lawyer in question also represented. The lawyer would be disbarred in any other area of the country for doing this, but no one tackles the ethics of Hollywood because the mass media shape the culture and elect the politicians.

Hollywood is a family.

For years Hollywood executives have hired their family and friends to fill the key roles at the studios. The nonfamily members are the exception rather than the rule.

Hollywood is the dream factory.

The entertainment industry gives us our dreams. America, in contrast, was founded on a vision of freedom, justice, and property ownership for each and every person. For the last hundred years, the Hollywood dream has been replacing the American vision. Perhaps we should wake up to Proverbs 29:18 (KJV): "Where there is no vision, the people perish."

Watch out for the glass ceilings.

The entertainment industry has many different invisible barriers or glass ceilings. Minorities and women often complain that they may be hired as window dressing on the set (as actors or on-air anchors), but they have little power in the boardroom. Other barriers are the implicit assumption that television producers, actors, and crew can't do movies, and commercial talent can't do television or movies, and industrial talent can't do commercials, television, or movies. Of course there are exceptions, but built-in biases impose invisible barriers on the "lesser" genre of the mass media of entertainment.

Development hell is "Yes, we will look at your project."

The entertainment industry does not produce widgets or gadgets such as mousetraps. If they did, then producing a better widget, gadget, or mousetrap would bring great success. Instead, the entertainment industry is the dream factory, and dreams are ephemeral. Who can evaluate which dream will sell this year? The major studios have spent billions trying to ascertain what dreams the moviegoer wants to buy, only to be frustrated when the requisite movie is produced and no one wants to see it. Therefore, the entertainment industry executives are always concerned that the next big dream will pass them by or that they will back a dud. To avoid making a tough decision on a project that could go either way, the executive will often say that they will look at the project and then let it languish in development hell. As long as they have the project, you cannot go anywhere else with it, so you are trapped unless you can figure out a way to push it forward.

Don't try to bluff an insider.

One studio head said that they were seriously considering picking up for distribution an independent movie from a person of faith. The executive asked the young independent how much the movie cost to make. The independent inflated the budget. The executive walked, telling the independent that he made movies every day and knew exactly what the independent's movie cost, so who was the independent trying to fool?

Don't stoop to conquer.

The movies that do best at the box office are not those with sex and violence but rather movies with faith and values. One studio executive said that he was talking with a person who obviously came from the faith community but who pitched a movie with sex and violence. Evidently the young producer thought that he needed to put in sex and violence to sell his project. The executive walked, telling the young person to be true to himself.

Tell your story.

Every story has its own logic. A movie about faith triumphing over adversity must show that faith triumphs. If it waters down the faith element, the story will be diluted. While many people will tell you not to preach, which is true, the other side of that coin is that you must tell the story the way the premise demands or it will not make sense. Many movies by people of faith have been lackluster or mediocre not because the movie was preachy but because the movie did not deliver on its premise. One movie about a missionary gave no indication why the missionary would give his life to save the pagan natives who killed him. Thus, the movie made no sense whatsoever. The neophyte Christian producer was trying to hide his light and did it so well that no one understood the movie.

Hollywood and too often the church exhibit *schadenfreude*.

Schadenfreude is to take pleasure in someone else's misfortune. Often in Hollywood, people are happier about someone else's misfortune than about their own success. Beware this demon of envy.

On August 7, 2001, this article, "The Big Picture: Where They Root for Failure" by Patrick Goldstein, appeared in the *Los Angles Times:*

> The Germans have a word for it—*schadenfreude,* the pleasure one takes from the misfortune of others—and in Hollywood it's a way of life. If show business were a religion, its first commandment would be: Instead of enjoying your own success, take pleasure in others' failure. One producer I know used to go around his office chanting "OPMF." Translation: Other people must fail. As Ned Tanen, a former studio chief at Paramount and Universal, once put it: "The only words you need to know about Hollywood are negativity and illusion. Especially negativity.'"

> Why do so many people in Hollywood root for everyone else to fail? You could chalk it up to jealousy and insecurity. You could say it's a telling example of Hollywood's spiritual emptiness. You

could blame it on an insular culture that encourages cutthroat competition. Whatever the reason, schadenfreude is deeply imbedded in Hollywood culture. "This is a town filled with envy and jealousy," says *Tomb Raider* producer Larry Gordon, who's been a high-profile force in Hollywood for years. "You've got two kinds of people—the people who've made it who are angry that they're not more successful and the people who haven't made it who are angry because they think the other guy is a lucky [expletive]."

The equation is simple: Power + Success = Envy.

Hollywood is vulnerable.

Even with all the negatives of the Hollywood culture, it must be noted that the entertainment industry is vulnerable. Mel Gibson proved this with *The Passion of the Christ.* Pixar proved this with great animation. Quality, perseverance, and faithfulness will overcome.

Some are more than conquerors.

As Romans 8:37 in the King James Version tells us, "In all these things we are more than conquerors through him that loved us." Therefore, we do not need to be afraid of going into Hollywood or the lion's den. Pursue the vision God has given you with confidence in his grace, and do not be afraid.

Producer Penelope Foster's career provides some important insights into the entertainment industry. "A 12-year-old street kid . . . a three-ton killer whale . . . a friendship you could never imagine, and an adventure you'll never forget." Such is the tagline of the famous, memorable movie *Free Willy.* This 1993 family favorite was coproduced by Penelope Foster. Penelope has been in the film business for well over twenty years, producing movies for both television and theater release in a number of genres. What some audiences might not know about Penelope is that she is a woman of tremendous faith, a prayer warrior whose goal is to see quality, inspiring, life-changing films transform the silver screen. Please read her story in

MOVIEGUIDE® or in the "So You Want to Be in Pictures?" section of www.movieguide.org.

The key to theater release and to network television is your story. Not only movies, but according to George Heinemann, former vice president of NBC, television is also "a once-upon-a-time, storytelling medium." A strong story will help you convince strong talent with good track records—such as stars, a director, and perhaps a coproducer—to be part of your production. This talent in turn will help you convince foreign distributors, cable, and independent television to prepurchase your production, which in turn will help you convince a major movie studio to distribute your movie.

With a strong story you can go directly to one of the seven major distributors and have that movie studio finance and distribute your movie. The studio will want to oversee your production at every stage and will want talent who are successful at attracting people to the box office involved in your production. Even so, many producers have found that ultimately it is easier to work with a major studio that will often allow you to insert your faith and values as long as the faith and values are woven into the fabric of the story.

Normally, a major movie studio can only be approached through an agent, such as International Creative Management and the William Morris Agency, although there are exceptions where the studios are successfully approached directly because the story is extraordinarily strong. Even an agent will want a strong story, or your story will become a dust collector on the shelf. You must believe in your story for good reasons, which you can demonstrate to the agent in no uncertain terms.

Agents push what's hot because it is an easier sale to the studios. If you are an unknown commodity, you may have to team up with a known commodity, such as a producer or director with a track record, to break through the psychological barrier at the agency. On the other hand, agents are on the lookout for new talent and salable new ideas. The key is a salable story since agents work for money.

- If you are considering a television movie instead of approaching a network first, you can go to an advertiser like Hallmark and have that advertiser sponsor your program by buying the airtime and by paying for program production. The advertiser will want hot, bankable talent involved in your production and will want your story to enhance their image and/or promote the sale of their product. There are more advertisers to approach than networks.

- You can go to a cable movie channel, such as Home Box Office or Showtime, and have them prepay for the right to air your movie before, or after, it is released in theaters or airs on the network. You can use that prepayment to finance your production. Once the movie is produced, you can try to secure a distributor. Finished productions have the advantage of being known commodities; unfinished program concepts have the advantage of offering hope in a risk-oriented industry.

- You can go to foreign television or film companies and have them prebuy the right to air or distribute your movie in their countries. You can use that presale to finance your production; then, once produced, you will try to secure a distributor.

- You can involve a major, known producer in your production who will put the financing together, coproduce your movie with you, and try to secure a distributor.

- You can go to a stockbroker or investment banker and have your production underwritten. However, stockbrokers and investment bankers almost always want a major distributor attached.

- You can go to friends or acquaintances for private financing to finance all or part of your production.

- You can go to a church or denomination for underwriting to finance part of your production.

- You can go to the body of believers for donations to finance your production.

- Of course, you can involve any combination of the above sources of financing for part of the production moneys that will help you secure a major distributor for the remainder of the production moneys. This is a common approach that gives you some bargaining power and control.

- You can involve any combination of the above nonnetwork sources of financing to such a degree that you can use their money to finance your production and distribute your movie yourself, just as Mel Gibson did with *The Passion of the Christ.*

The story is the key. You can obtain a good story by writing one, hiring someone to write one, or by buying the rights to a book, play, life story, or event (from those who were involved). Here we run into another key: rights.

Rights

Jim Day, one of television's pioneers and a founder of WNET and educational television, boils network television down to rights: the legal right to produce a good story as a television program; of which a known star and/or director, and/or producer will want the right to a piece of future profits; which the networks will want the right to air to capture an audience to sell to advertisers; on which advertisers will want the right to advertise to sell their products; which foreign stations, cable systems, movie channels, and independents will want the right to play after network television; to which many companies will want the merchandising rights; and which the public will pay for the right to see by buying the advertiser's products.

Rights are the levels of ownership of the story, the pieces of the pie, or the shares of future profits that are bought and sold for money, time, energy, and commitment. Rights determine who owns what and what they can do with what they own.

An example of how rights secure financing and access to the networks is the story of the first television version of *The Lion, the Witch and the Wardrobe* in 1980, when I was president of the organization that owned the rights and produced the television movie:

The Episcopal Radio & Television Foundation[2] had C. S. Lewis record the Episcopal Series of the famous radio *Protestant Hour* that was broadcast on NBC radio in 1956. Lewis was delighted and gave the right to produce a television program and movie on all seven books of the *Chronicles of Narnia* to the ERTVF. The *Chronicles of Narnia* retold the story of the Bible from creation to Revelation in allegorical terms. *The Lion, the Witch and the Wardrobe* was the book in the series that retold the story of the death and resurrection of Jesus as an allegory.

After years of trying to make the movie, the Episcopal Radio & Television Foundation contacted the president of Kraft Foods through the church network of friends, who passed the idea of Kraft sponsoring a television program based on *The Lion, the Witch and the Wardrobe* on to Kraft's advertising agency. The agency suggested involving a coproducer with a track record, so the Episcopal Radio & Television Foundation joined forces with the Children's Television Workshop, who produced *Sesame Street*, by giving them a share of the television rights for producing the program.

After a year went by, Kraft decided to sponsor the program by financing the production and buying the right to air the program on CBS. The Children's Television Workshop brought Bill Melendez, who animated *Peanuts* for television, on board as the producer of the animation, and the production was underway. When completed, *The Lion, the Witch and the Wardrobe* aired two years in a row during Easter week on CBS.

Some rules of thumb[3] for dividing movie rights and future profits are:

- You may buy the movie rights from the author for a fee that should be around 2.5 percent of the production budget and no higher than 5 percent of the production budget. The author may share in 2.5 percent to 5 percent of your profits as producer. If you give the author a larger share, it will kill any deal in Hollywood.
- You may secure private financing for your production by giving up 50 percent of your profits.
- You may secure a big name screenwriter by giving up 2.5 percent to 5 percent of your profits plus a fee that should be no more

than 2.5 percent to 5 percent of your production budget. Many screenwriters require no percentage of your profits. Whether a screenwriter will take a percentage depends on how much you pay him or her and their reputation.

- You may secure a big name star by giving up 2.5 percent to 5 percent of your profits plus a fee. If you pay enough, you may avoid the percentage.

- You may secure a big name director by giving up 2.5 percent to 5 percent of your profits plus a fee. If you pay enough, you may avoid the percentage.

- You may secure a big name coproducer by giving up 5 percent to 25 percent of your profits plus a fee.

- You may presell a foreign territory, such as Italy, Germany, or France, by giving up all rights and profits in that territory for a period of time, such as two years or two airplays, whichever comes first. The entertainment industry magazine *Variety* publishes one or more issues every year giving the prices movies and television programs are getting in different territories. For instance, an A-level movie may get $1 million in Germany, while a B-level may get $500,000. These figures change every year, so you should consult *Variety* to get the going prices.

- You may presell a cable movie channel at $.30 to $.50 per subscriber for a period of time, such as two years or two plays, whichever comes first. If you have a very hot property or "cover," which will be featured on the cover of the movie channel's magazine, then you may receive as much as $7 million if you give the movie channel the exclusive rights to play your television movie two or three times. If your story demands only a "demey" or half a page in the channel's magazine, then you might expect $4 million if you give the channel two or three exclusive plays. Of course, by the time you read this, prices will have changed.

- If your property will be a movie before airing on television, then you could secure financing from a major motion picture distributor, such as Paramount or Universal, by agreeing to receive 10 percent to 30 percent of what that distributor receives from the theaters. The theaters often take 50 percent to 90 percent off the ticket price for their profit and overhead.

- If you go to an advertiser, he will want the right to sponsor your program for two to five airplays on television for the financing. After that, the program is yours.

- If you go to a network directly, you may receive nothing but a fee and some subsidiary rights to foreign, cable, or merchandising profits.

Remember that there is only 100 percent of producer's profits to give to talent and financing, but the theaters or cable channels take their percentage before the distributor or movie channel takes their percentage, with the producer's profits constituting the remainder. The box office receipts for a movie might end up being divided as follows:

$6.00 box office gross or ticket price (this is a national aver-

age, with most big cities charging $9)

- $3.00 or 50 percent for the theater

= $3.00 Distributor's gross

- $1.50 Prints and advertising

= $1.50 Distributor's net

- $1.20 or 80 percent for the distributor

= $0.30 Producer's gross, which he or she must divide with

the financing, talent, and author

You may end up giving up all your rights for a small fee that doesn't cover what you spend to buy and develop the property. In most cases you will not make money on your property/program until it is in its third rerun, or second sale, to the networks or to independents. To reach the third rerun, the movie must succeed at the box office and must capture a large audience in both of its previous airings.

If you are really dedicated to proclaiming the gospel of Jesus Christ, the amount of money you earn may not make a difference to you, although we are called to be good stewards of the resources he gives us. The most important thing to remember is to retain enough rights to control the production to the degree that it is true to your story given the changes required by the medium.

If you own the rights to a story you wrote or one that is not in itself famous, watch out that a similar story is not produced by a producer after you have shown them your story. You cannot copyright an idea, only the particular way you wrote up the idea. It is common to see the idea of a good but little known story copied in the entertainment industry with few changes, and there is practically nothing you can do about it.

The best remedy to this problem is to own the rights to a famous story that would attract such a large audience that that title, property, and story are valuable as such. The other remedy is to register your story with the Writers Guild. This gives you some leverage but not much. The best defense is a hot property. However, less than 10 percent of movies are based on books and true stories because both are hard to convert into viable dramatic scripts.

Accessing any other medium is easier than accessing the major movie studios and television networks, but you still have to understand the gatekeepers and persuade them that your communication will be a benefit to them and their audience. Research the medium, prepare your pitch, and then talk to them about your movie or television program.

Producer and former Columbia Pictures executive Bill Ewing provides us with important insights into the production process. You will want to read his advice in *MOVIEGUIDE*® and on www.movieguide.org.

CHAPTER 9

From Soup to Nuts— Preproduction

The next three chapters give you a recipe for producing your movie or television program.

In preproduction, your costs are limited to yourself and one or two others. In production, your costs will involve a large paid staff and lots of equipment. In planning your production, you will find ways to hold costs down by minimizing locations, using stock shots, cutting characters, and other devices. Time is money: if you have more time than money, invest it in cutting down your production and postproduction costs. The time you spend budgeting and planning your production will save you a great deal of money in actual production.

Preproduction is the critical phase that is often rushed in a low- to medium-budget movie. Often, as soon as the money (or even some money) is secured, the pressure mounts to rush into production without the detailed planning necessary to help your movie become a success. Therefore, right from the beginning, determine that comprehensive planning will be the hallmark of your production.

One of the greatest directors of all time, Alfred Hitchcock, was a stickler for planning every detail. This often frustrated those around him, but the results were many of the best movies ever made. Peter Jackson, the producer and director of the *Lord of the Rings* trilogy, is another filmmaker who plans, plans, and plans again. If you take the time to preproduce your movie properly, you will increase your odds of producing a hit.

As a rule of thumb, you will spend 50 percent of your time in preproduction, 20 percent in production, and 30 percent of your time in postproduction. As your skills improve, the time you spend in preproduction will decrease, and the time you spend in postproduction will increase until they are 30 percent preproduction, 20 percent in production, and 50 percent postproduction.

Before we look at the steps, you may want to consider the insights of a major Hollywood producer, Bill Fay. It is likely that we have all seen at least one Bill Fay movie in the last decade, though his projects cover a wide range of genres, from science fiction to historical epics. Most will remember two of his biggest box office hits, *Independence Day* and *The Patriot*, but many of us have also enjoyed some of the lesser known movies as well, including *Eight-Legged Freaks, Godzilla, The Hunted,* and *Jake Speed.* On our www.movieguide.org Web site and in *MOVIEGUIDE®*, Bill shares a bit of his adventure from film school to famous producer, and he imparts some heartfelt advice for those daring enough to join his fascinating but demanding industry.

Breakdown, Budget, Schedule, and Timetable for Your Production

As soon as you have a story, you should have your script broken down and start estimating the cost of producing your film. The distributor, the networks, and the financiers will ask you how much your motion picture or television program will cost to produce. Before you go to a movie studio/distributor, you should turn your story into a script and prepare a budget based on that script, unless you are seeking development funds to prepare a script, in which case you need to budget the development funds you need.

A budget generated before a breakdown and schedule is nothing more than an educated guess at best. The script breakdown isolates all the elements necessary for the production, from extras and wardrobe to set requirements and special effects (EFX). The schedule then lays out the most efficient way of shooting all the scenes. Without a schedule, you don't know how many days you will need a specific actor or, for that matter, how long it will realistically take to shoot the picture.

Therefore, prepare breakdown sheets showing the running orders of your filmings and/or videotapings.

TV MOVIE BREAKDOWN SHEET
(showing running order)

Page	Scene	Shots	Cameras/Audio	Day/Night	Cast
1	Painting	1	cam 1/sof	n	
5	Telly at table	6–8	1,2,3	n	Telly & bits
			recording break		
10	Car	18	1/dub	n	Telly & bits
13	Street	23	1	n	Chris & girl

FEATURE FILM BREAKDOWN SHEET

TITLE_____
BREAKDOWN PAGE NO _____

INT/EXT_____
SCENE #_____

SET # _____DAY/NIGHT_____PAGE CT_____LOC _____

DESCRIPTION _____

NOTES _____

NO. CAST	EXTRAS	ANIMALS/ VEHICLES	PROPS
			MAKEUP & HAIR

SPECIAL EQUIPMENT	ADDITIONAL PERSONNEL	SPECIAL EFXS	COSTUME

Also, prepare a shooting schedule showing when you are shooting what with what equipment, crew, and cast.

TV MOVIE SHOOTING SCHEDULE

Date	Sets	Scenes	Description	Cast	Location
1st day		Restaurant		Telly	Studio
		Scene:	Going away party	Chris	
		Props: Painting of Athens		Bits	
			Tables and chairs		
2nd day	Set:				
	Scene:				
	Props:				

If you are producing a movie, prepare a more detailed shooting schedule. Here is a classic shooting schedule.

IT'S A WONDERFUL LIFE   Page 1

Shooting Schedule

SHOOT DAY #1–Mon, Jul 06, 1992

Scene #24   **EXT – BAILEY BUILDINGS AND LOAN SIGN OVER ENTRANCE – DAY**   1/8 Pgs.
Establishing Bldg. & Loan sign.

Set Dressing
Bldg. & Loan Sign

Scene #18   **EXT–MAIN STREET – DAY**   1 4/8 Pgs.
George takes a cab ride.

Cast Members	**Props**	**Vehicles**
1. George	Bert's watch	Bert's motorcycle
7. Ernie	Large suitcase	Ernie's cab
8. Bert		Stunt car
11. Violet		

Extras

Elderly man

Stunts

Car screeches to a stop
Stunt driver

Scene #22   **EXT–FRONT PORCH OF HOUSE–NIGHT**   2/8 Pgs.
Grumpy old man watches George & Mary.

Cast Members	**Set Dressing**
37. Grumpy old man	Rocking chair

END OF DAY #1–1 7/8 Total Pages

SHOOT DAY #2–Tue, Jul 07, 1992

Scene #23 **EXT–STREET–NIGHT**   3 5/8 Pgs.
            George and Mary make a wish.

Cast Members	Props	Vehicles
1. George	Rocks	Bailey's car
2. Mary		
3. Harry	**Special Effects**	**Set Dressing**
4. Uncle Billy	Breaking glass	Rocking chair
37. Grumpy Old Man		
	Greenery	**Costumes**
	Hydrangea bush	Bathrobe
		Jersey & football pants
		Wet clothes

IT'S A WONDERFUL LIFE   Page 2

Shooting Schedule

END OF DAY #2–3 5/8 Total Pages

SHOOT DAY #3–Wed, Jul 08, 1992

Scene #21 **EXT–TREE-LINED RESIDENTIAL STREET–NIGHT**   3 5/8 Pgs.
            George and Mary's moonlight walk

Cast Members	Props	
1. George	Rocks	
2. Mary		
	Special Effects	**Costumes**
	Breaking glass	Bathrobe
		Jersey & football pants
		Wet clothes

END OF DAY #3–6 3/8 Total Pages

SHOOT DAY #4–Thur, Jul 09, 1992

Scene #25 **INT–BAILEY BUILDING AND LOAN OFFICE–DAY**   4 2/8 Pgs.
            B & L Directors meeting

Cast Members	Props	
1. George	Legal papers	
4. Uncle Billy	Wheelchair	
5. Mr. Potter		**Costumes**
21. Goon		George's coat
34. Dr. Campbell		
41. Lawyer		
42. Real Estate Salesman		
43. Insurance Agent		

END OF DAY #4–4 2/8 Total Pages

SHOOT DAY #5–Fri, Jul 10, 1992

Scene #19 **INT–BAILEY DINING ROOM–NIGHT**   6 3/8 Pgs.
            Dinner at the Baileys'

Cast Members	Props	Set Dressing
1. George	4 Pies	**Set Dressing**
3. Harry	Broom	Dining room set
12. Ma Bailey		Dishes
16. Annie		
17. Peter Bailey		

Here is a recent medium-budget movie shooting schedule:

Thu. Nov 27, 2003 Script Dated: Nov 16/03 PINK Shooting Based on: ****GOLDENROD One-Liner	*RIDING THE* ***BULLET***	**SHOOTING SCHEDULE** 1 ****GOLDENROD Revised

****GOLDENROD Revised: Thu. Nov 27, 2003 – 7:53 PM

Script Dated -> Nov 16/03 PINK Shooting (Yet to be Issued)

Day 14 -> Call: 0800 Wrap: 2100 Sun: 0739/1619

DAY 14–Fri, Nov 28, 2003

121	INT HOSPITAL/4TH FLOOR CORRIDOR	Night–2 7/8 Pgs	LOCATION:
	Alan finds his mom's room, enters.		St. Mary's, 4th Floor, 421

CAST MEMBERS	ART DEPT/CONSTRUCTION	GRIPS	SPECIAL EQUIPMENT
1. Alan Parker	Curtains to block windows at end of hall	Black south windows	40 x T8-3200
30. Nurse Annie Wilkes		Rig light in stairwell	85' Lift
EXTRAS	PROPS		
Hospital Staff (2)	Alan's Wrist Bandage and Duffle Bag	HAIR/MAKEUP	ADDITIONAL LABOR
		Spider bite	Daily Elec xt @
		Track hairline blood	

122	INT HOSPITAL/MOM'S ROOM	Night–2 2/8 Pgs	LOCATION:
	VISION. Mom points finger and screams.		St. Mary's, 4th Floor, 421

CAST MEMBERS			
1. Alan Parker	**PROPS**		
4. Jean Parker	Alan's Wrist Bandage & Duffle Bag	**HAIR/MAKEUP**	
30. Nurse Annie Wilkes		Spider bite	
		Track hairline blood	

123	INT HOSPITAL/MOM'S ROOM	Night–2 2 4/8 Pgs	LOCATION:
	Mom's really alive.		St. Mary's, 4th Floor, 421

CAST MEMBERS			NOTES
1. Alan Parker	**SET DRESSING**		Alan's bleeding from prior
4. Jean Parker	IVs & hospital equipment	**HAIR/MAKEUP**	head wound
30. Nurse Annie Wilkes	**PROPS**	Alan subtle bleeding from behind ear	
	Alan's Wrist Bandage & Duffle Bag	Spider Bite	

30	INT HOSPITAL HALL/MOM'S ROOM	Night–2 4/8 Pgs	LOCATION:
	VISION. POV moves down corridor into room. Mom has no face!		St. Mary's, 4th Floor, 421

EXTRAS			SPECIAL MAKEUP FX
Hospital Staff (2)	**SET DRESSING**		Jean Parker Photo DBL
Jean Parker Photo DBL	Heart monitor	**COSTUMES**	Mom face removal
	PROPS	Jean Parker Photo DBL	
	Hospital bracelet	**HAIR/MAKEUP**	ADDITIONAL LABOR
	Medicine tray for BG	Jean Parker Photo DBL	KNB Makeup FX Supervisor
	Push trolley for BG w/sheets & pillows 7		
			NOTES
			Video sync for heart monitor?

41	INT HOSPITAL/MOM'S ROOM	Night–2 5/8 Pgs	LOCATION:
	VISION. Mom just starts screaming. "Your mother needs you now."		St. Mary's, 4th Floor, 421

CAST MEMBERS			NOTES
1. Alan Parker	**SET DRESSING**	**ELECTRICS**	Rain?
4. Jean Parker	Radio	"Flashboard" Effect	
21. Doctor in Mom's	**PROPS**		
room	Dr.'s stethoscope		

107-8	INT HOSPITAL/MOM'S ROOM	Night–2 1/8 Pgs	LOCATION:
	MONTAGE. Mom near death.		St. Mary's, 4th Floor, 421

CAST MEMBERS			NOTES
4. Jean Parker	**SET DRESSING**		Shoot 8mm?
	IVs & hospital equipment	**HAIR/MAKEUP**	
		Jean is near death	

End of Day 14–Total Pages–4 7/8

Day 15 -> Call: 0900 Wrap: 2200 Sun: 0740/1619

DAY 15–Sat, Nov 29, 2003

Next to your script your budget is the most important tool you have in a production and helps you determine where you are going and how to get there.

Most budgets are broken down into above-the-line costs and below-the-line costs. Above-the-line costs are the variable and negotiable costs that relate to writing, performing, and the production team, such as the scriptwriter, the star, and the director. These are generally the primary creative elements and the financing elements (i.e., executive producers). Below-the-line costs are the various fixed costs, back-up services, and physical elements involved in a production, such as equipment, transportation, and operations personnel, including the cameraperson, soundperson, and technical director. However, in the arcane world of the mass media of entertainment, these are not all fixed costs. The rates of director of photography, composer, editor, production designer, and other HODs (heads of departments) are generally negotiated.

Budgets are also divided into a summary, a top sheet, and then many pages of details that break down every element of the top sheet. Budget forms are available from many sources, including equipment rental houses. Budgets can range from a sparse million dollars to the Hollywood heavyweights of around $200 million, with the average Hollywood movie budget running around $80 million. The range of the budget depends on the scope of the project, from talent cost, length of production, complexity, number of locations, setups, stunts, grip and electrical requirements, action/adventure versus drama, stunts and obviously visual special effects.

Of course, there are movies that do more with much less. Robert Rodriguez of *Spy Kids* fame made his first big splash in the talent pool with his movie *El Mariachi*, an entertaining movie that was produced for $7,000. Hard to believe, since this is the budget for catering tea and crumpets on most Hollywood productions.

Below is a sample top sheet for an $18,731,642.83 medium-budget movie:

	TOP SHEET OF BUDGET DETAIL		

B. PRODUCTIONS Inc. Presents

"MOVIE TITLE"

Producers:
Director:
Schedule: 57 Days Principal Photography
Unions Budgeted: WGA, Canadian ACTRA, Canadian I.A.T.S.E.
Assumptions: 20 Days Location; 37 Stage

Screenplay:
Script Version: Writer's Third Draft
Budgeted for: Canada

British Director, Cameraman and 3 Crew

Budget Dated: 00/00/2000
Initial Pass Budget

Budget Prepared by: Claude Lawrence

Acct#	Category Title	Page	Total
11-00	STORY & SCENARIO	1	$711,838
12-00	PRODUCERS UNIT	2	$877,815
13-00	DIRECTION	2	$634,391
14-00	CAST	3	$3,370,505
15-00	A/B/L TRAVEL & LIVING	5	$562,357
	TOTAL ABOVE-THE-LINE		**$6,156,906**
20-00	PRODUCTION STAFF	7	$1,017,218
21-00	ATMOSPHERE (EXTRAS)	10	$225,275
22-00	ART DIRECTION	12	$313,032
23-00	SET CONSTRUCTION	13	$910,402
24-00	SET OPERATIONS	18	$318,744
25-00	SPECIAL EFFECTS	19	$215,848
26-00	SET DRESSING	21	$303,844
27-00	PROPERTY	24	$153,222
28-00	ANIMALS & PICTURE VEHICLE	24	$108,373
28-50	ANIMATRONICS & PUPPETS	25	$55,350
29-00	WARDROBE	25	$284,248
30-00	MAKEUP & HARDRESSING	28	$211,80
32-00	LIGHTING	29	$374,364
33-00	CAMERA	30	$571,503
34-00	PRODUCTION SOUND	32	$94,036
35-00	TRANSPORTATION	33	$517,301
36-00	LOCATION	37	$517,082
37-00	STAGES & FACILITIES	39	$407,160
38-00	FILM (PRODUCTION)	40	$387,762
41-00	SECOND UNIT	41	$32,500
	PRODUCTION PERIOD TOTAL		**$7,019,243**
45-00	EDITORIAL	41	$496,958
46-00	MUSIC	42	$423,609
47-00	POSTPRODUCTION SOUND	42	$264,050
48-00	POST-FILM & LAB	43	$111,240
49-00	TITLES & OPTICALS	44	$67,000
50-00	COMPUTER GENERATED IMAGES	44	$2,331,254
51-00	GREEN SCREEN	47	$130,000
52-00	MINATURES	47	$217,750
	TOTAL POSTPRODUCTION		**$4,041,861**

65-00	PUBLICITY	47	$47,050
66-00	LEGAL & ACCOUNTING	47	$190,250
67-00	INSURANCE	48	$228,488
68-00	GENERAL EXPENSE	48	$502,263
	TOTAL OTHER COSTS		**$968,051**
70-00	FINANCE FEES & MARKETING ALLOWANCE	49	$0
	FINANCE/MARKETING FEES AND COSTS		**$0**
	Contingency: 0.00%		$0
	Completion Bond: 3%		$545,581.83
	FINANCE INTEREST & POINTS NOT BUDGETED 0.00%		$0
	TOTAL ABOVE-THE-LINE		$6,156,906
	TOTAL BELOW-THE-LINE		$12,574,736.83
	TOTAL ABOVE & BELOW-THE-LINE		$18,731642.83
	GRAND TOTAL		$18,731642.83

Often, the producer uses the 3, 4, 5 percent formula: 3 percent of budget for story unit, 4 percent for directors unit, 5 percent for producers unit. This varies a great deal but is a reasonable standard.

Here is how a detail of one account in your top sheet might look.

```
Project:_____
Date Prepared:_____


Acct. Description      Rate   Total  Totals   Totals____
20 / Costumes & Makeup_____
   /  _____
   / A. Wardrobe Dept_____
   /  _____
   / 1. Wardrobe Designer 1,400/wk 5wks   7,000.00_____
   / 2. 1st Wardrobe Person    2wks    1,788.00_____
   / 3. 2nd Wardrobe Person    16days   2,063.00_____
   / 4. Tailor_____
   / 5. Seamstress                500.00_____
   / 6. Extra Help_____
   /  _____
   /  _____ Subtotal 11,351.00_____

   / B. Makeup & Hairdressing_____
   /_____
   / 1. Head Makeup Person 1200/wk 5wks  6000.00_____
   / 2. 2nd Makeup Person_____
   / 3. Head Hairdresser    1000/week—4wks 4000.00_____
   / 4. Body Makeup Person_____
   / 5. Extra Help_____
   /  _____
   /  _____ Subtotal  10,000.00_____

              Total      $21,351.00
```

Most accounts on your budget will be broken down into even greater detail than "Costumes & Makeup." Many costs will be negotiable or can be lowered through substitution.

At the same time you prepare your budget, you will prepare a production timetable. Your master production timetable will be an overview of the entire production and help you to establish the deadlines that will keep your production on course. You will also want to prepare detailed timetables relating to each element in your production, such as personnel. Here is a sample of a master production timetable.

```
PRODUCTION TIMETABLE

Task_____ Month_____
                    1  / 2  /  3/  4/  5/  6/  7/ 8/  9/  10/  11 /  12
Scripting           xxxxxxxxxxxxxxxxxxxxxxxxxx
Staffing                xx        xxx        xxxxxxxx  xx    xx
Preproduction       xxxxxxxxxxxxxxxxxxxxxxxxxxxxx
Production                                  xxxxxx
Postproduction                                        xxxxxxxxxxxxxxxx
Distribution or Broadcast                                         xxxxx
```

Storyboard and Plan Your Production

Many experienced directors don't bother with storyboards except for the action sequences, which often require a storyboard to get the action right. Even so, a first-time director should storyboard his movie, and many of the great directors do just that. The producer may require a storyboard so he knows where the director is going.

Preparing a storyboard is essential to helping you and your director and producer picture exactly how you want each shot to look and to flow together. When I brought the Christian theological advisors in to help advise on *The Prince of Egypt*, many of the walls of the DreamWorks animation facility were covered floor to ceiling with storyboards. Extensive storyboarding makes the actual shooting of the movie much easier. Preparing your storyboards will help you to make many of the artistic decisions so that your movie just has to be shot and edited together.

Storyboards help you and the director think visually about your story. You do not need to use realistic drawings in your storyboards. Stick figures for the people are fine as long as your storyboard gives you an idea of how each shot will look.

As you prepare your storyboard, think about:

- Composition—the positioning of people and things in each shot.
- Lighting—from above, below, or from the side.
- Point of view or POV—from whose point of view—the hero? a third person?

You can find many examples of storyboards on the Internet, some from famous movies. Here is an example of a storyboard for the James Bond movie *Live and Let Die*.

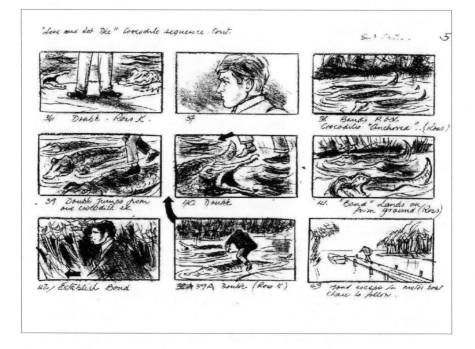

So that you can accurately plan your production, turn your script into a rough storyboard that you will want to revise and perfect as you proceed. Here are two different types of storyboard forms.

I

STORY BOARD FORM

II

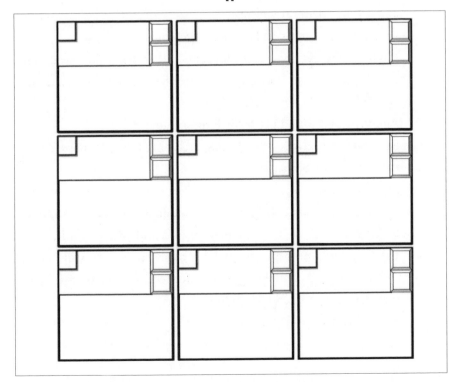

You may want to sketch important scenes and difficult shots from different angles to show required camera treatment.

Another approach is used by Robert Rodriguez, who scouts the locations with a video camera and uses stand-ins to approximate the blocking of the scenes to be shot so that when the crew arrives, the key folks know exactly where to place equipment.

Study your script, storyboard, and sketches. From discussions with your key talent, determine how you are going to produce every aspect of your production. Remember to consider:

- Cast, including costume and makeup requirements.
- Preproduction publicity.
- Sets and staging designs, including sketches showing lighting, directions, action, and camera shots. Make sure you have enough studio or location space for shots, moves, cable routing, and equipment, such as booms. Therefore, you must predetermine the facilities, both studio and location, that you will use and what permissions and arrangements are needed.
- All on-camera props and other set dressing.
- Photography, filming, stock shots, and all material that needs special arrangements, clearances, fees, permissions, permits, insurance, scheduling, and extra staffing.
- All music and sound needs, including sound effects.
- Special effects, graphics, and titles, including artwork, maps, charts, models, and displays.
- Equipment.
- All other necessary and special equipment, including teleprompter, telecine, slide chain, film chain, monitors, and cuing facilities.
- Lighting and atmosphere, making sure that shots will match. Analyze any special lighting that is needed in terms of cost, manpower, equipment, and feasibility.
- Film, videotape and audiotape.
- Editing needs.

- Publicity.
- Distribution.

Keep in mind throughout your production that every effect (including a camera move, special effects, insert, action, and a technical move, such as a wipe, fade, or dissolve) acts as a blinking neon light to attract the attention of the viewer. Too many effects, like a busy neon sign, are annoying. Too few and you may lose your audience.

Every effect and action must flow organically from the story and not intrude on the story unless there is a compelling artistic reason to do so. The technical effects should affect viewers, but at no time should viewers be aware of any specific effect unless you are engaging the viewer as an active character in the action of the story or you are exposing the mechanism of the story for stylistic reasons.

Bring Your Key Above-the-Line Talent on Board

Your above-the-line talent will be determined to a degree by whom you need to bring on board to make your production bankable. What big names, or talent with track records, will cause a major movie studio or private capital to finance your production?

Sometimes all you need is one star, such as Pierce Brosnan or Julia Roberts. Sometimes a director, such as Stephen Spielberg, will make your production bankable. Often, you will have to join forces with a coproducer, who may end up with the credit, such as George Lucas. Of course, getting any of these renowned megatalents is close to impossible, but look for available talent who appreciate the type of movie that you are producing.

Besides making your story bankable, the above-the-line talent will affect: your budget, because of the size of their fees and percentages; your story, because most of them will want a voice in the final script, or you will want to adapt the final script to fit them; and your production, which they will help you plan and interpret. Be open to their input and their genius. You will probably pay them a great deal of money, unless they are giving you their time for charitable reasons, so get as much out of them as possible. They can help your production succeed.

There are many qualified Christians in Hollywood, and there are many qualified Christians in the Christian movie world. They may make a better fit with your project than someone who is not a believer, although great movies with strong Christian themes, such as *Chariots of Fire,* have been made by unbelievers.

Make sure you hire the right person for the right job. One production hired a top-notch cameraperson to be the producer, something he was incapable of handling. Furthermore, avoid using your friends just because they are your friends or they invested money in your production.

As you team up with these entertainment industry notables, please note:

- The *producer* is the chief executive and operating officer. He is in charge of the production and the production personnel. He controls the budget and is ultimately responsible for the success or failure of the production.

- An *executive producer* role may be placed above the producer in the chain of command. If so, the executive producer is either responsible for financing the production or for interfacing with the network or studio, or both. He will assume the role of chief executive officer, but he will delegate budget responsibility to the producer or an associate producer.

  The executive producer credit given in most long-form television is the equivalent of a producer credit on a film. The executive producer in TV is directly involved with the creative and physical production. The executive producer in film is generally only concerned with the financing of the project.

- The *director* is responsible for directing the actors and crew. He stages the production. He is responsible for the visual and audio treatment of the production. He became the *auteur* of the production in the 1960s as a result of the French New Wave movement. Before that, and even now in many instances, he was the conductor for hire but not the auteur—that is, he was and is part of a collaborative team, not the sole author of the movie.

The director is usually responsible for the entire production up to a completed movie. He defines his vision for the movie and helps to determine the schedule and create the storyboards.

The director often selects the locations or must approve them if you have a location scout. He helps plan the shots with the cinematographer and works with the editor to edit the movie.

- The *assistant directors* (AD) are responsible for organizing scheduling and managing the daily set operations. The ADs are the ones responsible for the schedule and tracking the daily production report that translates into a daily hot cost for the studio or financier. Often there are three ADs.

- A *director of photography* (DP) helps the director set the visual treatment of the film. Thus, the creative aspect of the shot is set with the director, and the DP supervises the crew elements to achieve that shot, freeing the director to direct the actors, crew, and stage action.

Finalize Your Script and Organize Everything that Needs to Be in Your Production

(This applies mostly to television production.)

With the input from your key talent, finalize your script. Then working from your final script, obtain or arrange for graphics, photography, film, stock shots, film clips, properties, and everything that needs to be in your production.

Cast and Staff

Casting is critical. Be selective. Be careful. Cast the right person for the role, someone who can play himself or herself, at least.

Movies are a larger-than-life medium that lends itself to spectacle and close-ups. Make sure your cast will emote naturally in a close-up. Your characters become the cast; therefore, make sure that the actors you choose are your characters. Television is a smaller window on the world. In movies you can have a cast of thousands; in television a small group will suggest a large crowd.

The actors work closely with the director to find out how their characters can best be played. They must go beyond memorizing their lines to think about how their character would say his lines by paying attention to what that character wants in the scene. The actors should work with the director to determine their character's goals, desires, or needs.

On page 189 of this chapter is another important document: the "Actor Day Out of Days." This document tells the producer and casting director exactly how many days during the production an actor will be working, which is instrumental in determining what an actor will cost you.

The following staff is typical in a production:

- The *line producer/unit production manager* keeps track of the budget.
- The *assistant director* lines up all the elements of the production for the director and manages the daily running of the set. The first AD runs all the extras on big Hollywood films.
- The *script person* checks the production against the script and keeps track of time.
- The *set designer* designs the sets.
- The *production designer* determines the look of the production by designing and preparing all graphics and visuals. The art director works under the production designer.
- The *makeup person.*
- The *hair stylist.*
- The *costume designer.*
- The *gaffer/chief lighting technician.* The more you know about movies and television, the more you will realize how important and difficult lighting is. Achieving the right level of lighting on camera is difficult, even if it is a low-light camera. Achieving good, attractive, atmospheric, uniform lighting for multiple television cameras is an art.
- The *postproduction sound mixer* controls audio quality and mixes the sound. Good sound quality demands great care and marks the difference between a poor production and a good one.
- The *camera operator and camera assistants* operate the camera(s) with the help of the camera crew.

- The *soundperson* or sound people operate the sound booms, microphones, and audio equipment.
- The *grips* are responsible for changing the camera positions by building platforms, operating dollies, rigging camera mounts, building stands, and securing lights or mounting the camera equipment and personnel in unimaginable places.
- The *gaffer and electricians* are responsible for all electrical wiring and for rigging lights and measuring light in order to expose the film properly. Never use a first-time gaffer who does not have a well-established mentor available as a lifeline by phone.
- The *special effects person* creates and produces all special effects.
- The *production assistant* who goes for this and that.
- The *visual EFX supervisor* helps determine and execute the necessary digital and optical visual effects, 2 and 3D animation, etc. This is different from special EFX, which is all practical.

With the new lightweight, compact equipment, some documentary producers have cut the number of personnel down to just themselves and their camcorder. However, to be sure you get your shot, the minimum staff needed for a small production is:

- Producer/Director
- Assistant Director
- Production Assistant
- Cameraperson
- Soundperson
- Lighting
- Talent
- Writer

Organizing Artistic and Technical Services and Facilities

- Reserve all facilities, studios, and locations.
- Prepare for the rental and purchase of all equipment. Each department develops a list and initiates conversations with vendors. The

unit production manager/line producer finalizes the deals. The production coordinator organizes the pickup and delivery of the equipment according to the schedule prepared by the ADs.

- Prepare for all artistic services and technical services so that everything is ready and available when you need it.

- Prepare all artwork, graphics, special effects, audio effects, music, costumes, and props.

- Prepare for all location filming. The location manager initiates all conversations and negotiates with property owners as well as files location permits. Once upon a time, my wife was serving as a location manager for an Italian production company filming in New York City. They kept changing their minds about locations and started filming a shootout in a new location. Needless to say, the New York City police were not amused.

- Begin the construction of all sets and scenery.

- Reserve all facilities, studios, and locations.

The chain of command and delegation are crucial to the success of any shoot, so there is a specific person attached to each of these tasks. Thus, a movie production is similar to a complex military campaign in its need for organization, command, and delegation.

Producers Are Coaches

Over the last fifteen years, worldwide audiences have been thrilled by the stunning, memorable family movies *Who Framed Roger Rabbit?*, *The Hunchback of Notre Dame*, and *Beauty and the Beast*. These movies boasted several firsts in the areas of animation technology advances, digital enhancements, and colorization.

The producer of these movies, as well as other beloved classics such as *The Lion King*, *The Emperor's New Groove*, and *Atlantis*, is the talented Don Hahn, of the Walt Disney Company. Go to our Web site at www.movie guide.org to read an interview with Don.

Obviously, Don Hahn does a great job as he continues to entertain the world with his colorful, well-produced Disney animated classics.

"IT'S A WONDERFUL LIFE"

Report created Mon, May 24, 2004 Page 1

July
Month: ......Day of
Week: ......Day of
Days: ......Shooting

Character	6 Mon 1	7 Tue 2	8 Wed 3	9 Thu 4	10 Fri 5	11 Sat	12 Sun	13 Mon 6	14 Tue 7	15 Wed 8	16 Thu 9	17 Fri 10	18 Sat	19 Sun	20 Mon 11	21 Tue 12	22 Wed 13	23 Thu 14
1. George	SW	SW	W	W	W				W	W	W	W			W	W	W	W
2. Mary		SW	W	W	W				W	W	W	W			H	H	W	W
3. Harry		SW	W	H	H			H	W	H	H	H			W	H	H	H
4. Uncle Billy			H	H	W			H	H	H	H	W			H	W	H	W
5. Mr. Potter			H	W	H							W					H	W
6. Mr. Gower				SWD				SWD										
7. Ernie	SW	H	H	H	H			H	H	H	W	H			H	W	H	H
8. Bert	SWD															PW	W	H
9. Joe										SWF								
10. Clarence	SW	H	H	H	H			H	W	H	H	H			H	W	H	H
11. Violet					SW			H	H	H	H	W			W	W	H	H
12. Ma Bailey				SWD														
13. Mrs. Hatch																		
14. Mr. Martini																		
15. Cousin Tilly					SWD			H	H	H						PW	H	H
16. Annie	S				W						SW	WD						
17. Peter Bailey																		
18. Cousin Eustace																		
19. Ruth																		
20. Peter Bailey				SW	H			H			H	WD			W	H	H	W
21. Goon											SW	WD						
22. Carter												SW						
23. Marty									SWD									
24. Sam Wainwright		WF							SWD									
25. Maria Martini																		
26. Ed									SWF									
27. Freddie																		
28. Nick																		
29. Tommy Bailey																		
30. Janie Bailey																		
31. Charlie																		
32. Tom																		
33. Zuzu Bailey																		
34. Dr. Campbell								H	H	H	WD							
35. Mr. Carter																		
36. Principal	SW			SW					SWD									
37. Grumpy Old Man																		
38. Jane Wainwright																		
39. Tollkeeper																		
40. Mickey				SWF														
41. Lawyer				SWF														
42. Real Estate Salesman				SWF					SWF									
43. Insurance Agent																		
44. Suitor #1																		

CHAPTER 10

Lights, Camera, Action— Production

P roduction is where all your planning pays off. This is where you finally get to tell your story through the medium of film or television.

Before getting to the step-by-step instructions, you may want to look in *MOVIEGUIDE®* or in the "So You Want to Be in Pictures?" section of www.movieguide.org for inspiration from expert producer Ralph Winter. Ralph has been involved in the making of *X-Men I, II,* and *III, Star Trek II, IV, V,* and *VI,* and *Mighty Joe Young,* among many other movies.

Rehearsals

This applies mostly for television although top movie producers have said that there should be more rehearsing in film production.

At this point, if you are producing for television, you will start rehearsing your cast and crew. Run through your script to begin the process of blocking out all movements of cast, cameras, sound equipment, and crew. Have your performers practice their lines, actions, and performances. Make sure that the timing is what you want.

The sequence of "recorded live" TV rehearsals may include:
- A walk-through or dry run
- A stagger-through to coordinate technical services

- A predress run-through to polish
- A dress rehearsal
- Production

For movies, however, there may not be a rehearsal. Often there is just a walk-through because time is money on a film production. Stars are paid big bucks, so the producer will want to film them and dismiss them as fast as possible. However, many top producers have said that ideally you will want to rehearse to potentially save time and money.

Here is a possible order for movie production:

- A walk-through or dry run for technical people
- A rehearsal, which often means that the actors go off the set and work on the scene
- Production

Note that you will want to rehearse each type many times to achieve a quality production.

Camera and Other Scripts

In the last chapter we looked at a shooting schedule. From that you may want to prepare a shot list showing what each camera is doing when and how, especially if you are producing a television movie.

It is important to lock a script prior to shooting. Locking the script means that this is the script you are filming. However, even under the best of circumstances, there may be changes, which are inserted in the script as pink, yellow, red, or other colored pages in place of the pages being replaced.

TV MOVIE CAMERA SHOT LIST

Camera:_____

Shot	Position	Lens Angle	Scene
1	B	13	Restaurant CU of painting
2	A	35	PULL BACK to LS of Telly in front of painting.
6	C	20	MCU of Telly at table

Keep in mind the distance a camera needs for a shot and what camera angles give you or your director an ECU (extra close-up), a CU (close-up), an MCU (medium close-up), a BCU (big close-up), a 2-S (two shot), a 3-S (three shot), an MS (medium shot), or a LS (long shot).

In television you will want to prepare a script for every member of your team who needs to know what they are doing when and how.

You may want to familiarize yourself with the working of the respective equipment and with standard abbreviations to prepare these scripts. Books on production will take you only so far. You must have some working knowledge of basic equipment and what it can do to adequately prepare your production, even when you have hired the best talent.

Sound Stages and Locations

Most movies are filmed on sound stages that are usually rented unless you own a major studio. In the rush to the sound stage to produce the program, the producer and director often find that the studio is not prepared to do the type of production work that is required.

You, your producer, and your director should meet with the sound stage to confirm the availability of everything that is essential to your production—the space, the equipment, the back-up facilities, the crew, the storage space, the time to set up, the technical equipment, the electrical facilities, the dressing rooms, the green room, etc.

Be careful not to be overcharged for electrical power. This is a high cost item that many times defeats a budget.

Every production is different, so many sound stages rent the special equipment they will need for each production from an equipment house. You need to prepare them to have online, in the system, everything you need before the big day of the production when you will be spending money by the minute on cast and crew.

Before the day of production, know your way around your studio, know the key personnel, know the equipment, and be prepared for emergencies. Also, have insurance to cover your losses.

Make sure you have filed the proper work orders, forms, or requisitions depending on the facility, and prepare contracts for everything. You know what you need at the studio and on location; spell it out in writing.

Unlike movie sound stages, most television studios have equipment, but you have to rent each piece of gear separately.

As your production becomes more complex, you will add more equipment. Be aware of how that equipment works and how it interfaces with other equipment.

Line up transportation for your staff and cast. Also line up catering so you have the food and beverages in the studio or on location that will keep your personnel happy.

The art director works with the set director to convey the essence of the story you are trying to tell in that scene. It can be a preexisting place, like a church, or a place that is constructed to look like a church. The art director helps to design the set and looks at every single scene that is going to be shot to figure out how to make each scene look right.

The art director or property manager secures and places the props. The props include all the items on a set. Props help the audience understand what is happening in the movie and who the characters are.

The grip is responsible for the adjustment and maintenance of production equipment on the set. Typical duties include laying dolly tracks and erecting scaffolding.

Camera Blocking and Equipment Preparation

Before your production starts, you need to know what you want your camera, sound, and other equipment to do; when you need it; and how it will be used. Since the camera is a critical piece of equipment, you should be familiar with operating a camera and know the different ways video and film cameras are used to tell a story.

There are three key people on the camera staff:

1. The cinematographer or director of photography is in charge of the camera staff, lighting the set, and making all the important decisions.

2. The camera operator films the scene.

3. The gaffer or chief electrician works with the cinematographer to light the set.

There are three basic camera positions:

1. A *stationary* camera is in the same place for an entire shot, although it may swivel, and is usually mounted on a tripod to keep it steady.

2. A *hand-held* is held by cameraman and moves with him. Often the image looks shaky.

3. A *moving* moves during the shoot by some means, such as a dolly or a hand-held.

Your cameraperson has to compose a good picture. He or she must keep in mind the subject and the lights at all times. Help him or her by planning each shot.

Plan your shot so that:

1. It shows what you want it to show and no more.

2. It accomplishes your purpose. Every camera move has an effect on your audience. You should know what those effects are and use them to tell your story.

3. It emphasizes what you want it to emphasize. Simplify the elements in a picture. Note that with a zoom there is no parallactic movement; there is only a compression or stretching of perspective. It is not a natural movement. When we move through a space, such as down a city block, there is parallactic movement so that the parallel lines of the buildings increase in size as we approach them and then decrease as we pass them by. A dolly is better to convey the feeling of parallactic movement because it actually moves through a scene. The movie *2001: A Space Odyssey* was applauded in contrast to many earlier films because the dollying through the star field created a feeling of actual movement. Zooms in and out on a flat star field, while cheaper, do not create the feeling of movement. However, zooms have the advantage of creating other emotional reactions. So the best rule at first is to use zooms sparingly and where appropriate.

4. It is neither too close nor too distant.

5. Attention is focused and not diffused or distracted by extraneous objects or lines in the shot. Vertical or horizontal lines in the scenery or background should never divide a scene or the subject in two halves. A change in camera position will solve this problem. You can focus attention by:

   - Exclusion
   - A visual or audio clue
   - Color
   - Camera angle
   - Composition
   - Contrast
   - Movement
   - Performance

6. The main subject is framed properly. This is easier said than done. Do not compose your picture for perfect symmetry because symmetry will take away from visual interest. For an interesting perspective, shoot from a slight angle.

7. You know when action will enter and leave the shot. Movements away and toward a camera are more dramatic than lateral movements across the field of vision.

8. The shot establishes the effect you want by revealing, concealing, misleading, or focusing on the central subject. Low shots, looking up, make subjects look stronger. High shots, looking down, make subjects look weaker. Normal viewpoint is chest high.

9. The camera avoids lateral reversal effects that occur because the human eye tends to wander toward frame right. Frame left can support more people, more weight, and more darkness without looking shut in or crowded.

In my Communicate Workshops, each student videotapes a scene to demonstrate how the medium affects communication. When we review those scenes, many evidence a lateral reversal effect, which the student producer didn't expect and which distorted what they wanted to communicate.

Lateral reversal effects are perceptual tricks played by our eyes and minds that cause subjects to look heavier on screen right, diagonals to suggest up or down depending on the direction of their slope, and pictures to look static composed one way and dynamic the other way. Such effects will often change the meaning of a scene by affecting the audience's perception.

With regard to diagonals and slope, the following illustration is instructive:

These lines are the same in every respect except the direction of their slope. Our left-to-right perceptual orientation causes us to perceive the one on the left as having a downward slope and the one on the right as having an upward slope. In fact, neither line goes up or down. Every environment is made up of lines. Filming or videotaping an environment without regard for the lateral reversal effects that could be lurking therein can cause interesting perceptual consequences that will alter to some degree the meaning of the intended communication.

- Your composition is what you want. Rectangular or square compositions should be avoided. Triangular compositions are pleasing. The right angle suggests opposition and contrast. An S curve is slow and restful. A Z curve is fast and exciting. A cross expresses a merging of interests. A circle represents continuity.
- The color is appropriate. Green backgrounds will upset your audience. Blue backgrounds are pleasing. Pink backgrounds establish

warmth and love. Be aware of how colors affect people and how to use them properly. In Japan they tend to use more yellow tints in their pictures; in Hollywood, they tend to use more blue; and in New York photographers tend to use more gray and green.

- Your picture has unity, variety, harmony, balance, rhythm, pacing, proportion, and continuity with everything before and after.
- You will use unusual angles or moves only where appropriate.
- The camera will not intrude on your story.

There are three basic camera moves:

1. Pan—where the camera moves from side to side.
2. Tilt—where the camera moves up and down.
3. Zoom—where the camera moves in from a wider shot to a closer shot or out.

Here are four of the most common shots:

1. Long shot (LS)—where the main subject appears small among its surroundings
2. Medium shot (MS)—where you see the person from the waist up
3. Close-up (CU)—where you see details only, such as a face, etc.
4. Extreme close-up (ECU)—where you see extreme detail, such as an earring

Whenever the camera moves, remember that the camera is shaking even more than it looks to be through the viewfinder.

Always shoot the shot several times in several ways, which is known as coverage, to use in editing.

If the movie looks great, it may be because the director of photography/cinematographer is the highly experienced, faith-filled J. Michael (Jim) Muro. Jim has worked on a number of music videos and independent films, including his own, as well as grand epics such as *Open Range* with Kevin Costner and *Titanic* with James Cameron. Jim jokingly points out that it wasn't just *Titanic*'s captain that went down with the ship; it was also he and his Arriflex camera! Check out his article in *MOVIEGUIDE®* and on our Web site at www.movieguide.org.

Plan Your Lighting

Lighting can be realistic or atmospheric. Lighting may reveal, hide, enhance, texture, shade, modify, and enlighten. Soft broad light illuminates without casting shadows. Hard light focuses attention, creates modeling, and casts shadows.

Plan your lighting to help establish mood and atmosphere as well as focus attention. Lighting influences your audience by changing their perception of a scene.

- Often you will have a direct fill light to light your subject with a back light to cut down on modeling and harsh shadows and a key light within ten to twenty degrees of a person's nose to give form to your subject. Note that your fill light will reduce wrinkles and unwanted features, and your key light will enhance desirable features.
- Have the subject of your key light look toward the light.
- Avoid steep lighting. A steep backlight will spill over onto the face of your subject. A steep front light will cause harsh modeling, giving black eyes, long nose, neck shadows, and a haggard appearance. It will also emphasize baldness.
- Avoid shallow lighting. A shallow backlight will flare into the picture. A shallow front light will make the subject look flat.
- Avoid lighting that is too far off the camera axis. Such lighting will create hot spots and strange shadows.
- By careful balance of back and front lighting, you will give your subject the appropriate three-dimensional look.
- You can create realism by imitation or simulation. For example, if you wanted to create the look of a church by imitation, you could shine a light at an angle through a stained-glass window on the set. If you wanted to create the same look by simulation, you could use several lights with gels,[1] or use a slide. You can also use stencils, flicker wheels, and patterns to create atmospheric effects.
- Your lighting must be planned with the type of camera you will use

in mind. Every camera has different light sensitivity for which your lighting has to adjust.

- Analyze your subject to see which features you want to minimize and which features you which to emphasize.
- Make sure any graphics are evenly lit.
- Determine how movement will affect your lighting.

With respect to the lighting, the gaffer is the chief lighting electrician. The gaffer is in charge of all the electrical wiring and equipment.

Graphics

In television, plan your graphics so that they will compose properly within the future proof 16x9 while being safe for the standard 4:3 proportions of television. Always provide an adequate border. Make sure that there are no wrinkles or imperfections because television will magnify any imperfection. Plan your colors and tones to be pleasing or to achieve the effect that you want. Clear tonal and color separation is advisable if you want your graphics to be clear. Keep detail to a minimum and simplify structural forms. Maps should have no more than the essential blocks necessary to indicate the main features. One graphic is better than a succession of graphics; therefore, simplify and combine information.

Audio

The audio may control the picture's impact, or the picture may control the audio's impact, or the impact may be the cumulative effect of both. Plan the relationship between the audio and the visual.

- Contrast—a loud sound in the midst of a peaceful picture.
- Uniqueness—your sound can establish that the same picture has a different meaning than it had before.
- Suspense.
- Humor.
- Emphasis.
- Repetition.
- Surreality.

- Comparison.
- Foreshadowing.
- Revelation.
- Incongruity.

Remember to check the microphone boom and all the microphones so that there is no sign of them in the picture. Make sure there are no unwanted shadows and cables in the shot.

Microphones are designed with different listening or pickup patterns and with different ways of mounting. The audio person chooses the right microphone and puts it as close as possible to the source of sound in order to get the most audio and the least unwanted noise.

Note that in low-budget productions, the video-camera-mounted microphone is usually too far from the source so that the voice gets mixed with too much noise. However, the camera microphone is good for getting ambient or natural sounds of crowds, traffic, rustling leaves, etc.

Try to record ambient or natural sound for each location. In editing, the natural sound mixed with program audio will help create smooth audio transitions.

Audio is just as important as the picture; therefore, always test your sound equipment before you use it.

Run-Through and Final Rehearsal

(This is primarily for television.)

In television production, you will want to run through your script to remove any kinks and timing problems. The last run-through is sometimes called a "giggle-through" because it gives the performers and the personnel a chance to let off any unwanted emotions or feelings prior to production.

You may want one uninterrupted rehearsal prior to production, although this is very rare.

Pay close attention to continuity.

The director will make sure that the performers know who they are in terms of the script, that props are being used properly, and that the performers hit their marks. The director will not let one performer cover another and won't let them be too far apart. On camera the performers will look further apart than they are, so the director will bring them in closer than you would normally imagine. He will make sure that one performer does not upstage another.

The director will think in terms of shots and how the shot will look. You may want to use a viewfinder if it helps you to think in terms of shots.

The director will make sure the performers are framed properly and the audience can see who they are supposed to see. He will get rid of excess detail. With the help of the director of photography, he will make sure your camera is not shooting off set and there are no unwanted subjects in the shot.

Check the boom and microphones so that there is no sign of that technology in the picture. Keep an eye out for unwanted shadows and cables in the shot. Make sure everything is straight, level, and the way you want it to look. Check for any distracting set elements or blemishes.

The first assistant dirctor will check costumes. The director may have the cast stay away from satins or any reflective materials unless he intends that effect.

Light tones make people look bigger and formless. Dark tones minimize size but also decrease modeling.

In television, colors that are too strong will saturate the picture. Noisy patterns can cause a strobe, flicker, or moiré effect that can be annoying for your audience.

Noisy costumes and jewelry can create sound problems.

Stay away from colors that will look like skin tones, giving your performers a naked appearance.

The makeup person will help your performers look natural under the lights. Less is more. He or she will choose a base that is slightly lighter than the skin tone of the performer and use powder to prevent shine. They will not choose colors that will read blue or orange on camera unless that is your intent. Highlights and shading will correct for facial faults and define features. Encourage the director to check the makeup on camera to make sure it works.

Costumes, makeup, and hairstyling help tell your story by giving the audience visual details about the characters.

The hair, makeup, and costume people *visually* transform the actors into the characters they are playing. They help the actor look the part while he acts the part.

The makeup artist should write down the cosmetics used for every actor and, if possible, should take photos of the actor to help ensure continuity between scenes and shots.

Plan your production so that your story is told and none of the technical aspects of the production intrude on and detract from the visual dramatic telling of the story. If you have decided to pursue a symbolist approach to your material by revealing the technical aspects of your production to your audience, do so; however, make sure that such revelation is part of the fabric of your program and not an obstacle to the audience's enjoyment of your film. The French playwright Maeterlinck, the father of symbolist theater, revealed the stage to his audience by making them a part of the play, not by having effects intrude on the perceptions of his audience.

Remember the cardinal rule of production: Do not break the suspension of disbelief!

Location Production

If you have planned carefully for shooting on location, things should go well. Beware of extraneous noise, weather, crowds, and traffic. Bring everything you need. Double-check all connections, lighting, sound equipment, video equipment, and continuity to make sure you get what you want. Continuity can be a large problem when you are shooting on location.

- Make sure color, brightness, contrast, tones, light direction, shots, perspective, and picture quality match from shot to shot.
- Make sure weather conditions match from shot to shot.
- Don't let your camera cross the line of axis on reverse shots.
- Make sure costumes match makeup and hair. These are all continuity issues.

- Make sure performances match.
- Make sure action matches.
- Make sure props match and time passes uniformly. Don't jump from a half-full glass to a full one.
- Make sure sound matches.

Sound Stage Production

Come in as early as possible. If you can, set up your sets the day before or even before that. Check and double-check all equipment to make sure it works the way you want it to work. Warm up all equipment. Test every part of your equipment. Clear out all unnecessary cables and all obstacles. Make sure all equipment is clean. Check quality. Relax. Pray. Enjoy yourself; you are paying for this production. Shoot.

Cast Party

Establish a good rapport with your cast. Plan to work together again. Be supportive.

Snapshots: The Director and the Actors

The Director

The director is the storyteller. He turns the story into a film. He decides where and how the images are filmed and edited, how the actors portray their characters, and what the audience experiences. The director's vision for the story determines how the audience feels about the story: sad, amused, bored, scared, or humble. The director translates the story into a movie by using the techniques of filmmaking, such as character development, camera angles, and editing.

The director has to deal with limitations of a movie, such as actors, locations, weather, time, and, of course, money. Being prepared for all eventualities is one of the most important keys to success for a director. The director should try to anticipate all of the things that could go wrong on any individual shoot and have a backup plan.

Go to www.movieguide.org to check out some important advice from the award-winning director of *Gettysburg* and *Gods and Generals*, Ron Maxwell.

The Actor

There are several approaches to acting. The classical approach to acting holds that the actor's job is to become the character and leave his or her own emotions behind. The classical approach believes that you learn your lines, show up prepared, and act the way you and the director think the character would act.

In the twentieth century "the method" came into vogue. I studied at the renowned Lee Strasberg Studio (now known as Lee Strasberg Theater Institute) while Lee was still teaching. Lee brought "the method," developed by the Russian Constantin Sergeyevich Stanislavsky, to the United States. Born in Moscow in 1863, Stanislavsky asserted that if the theater was going to be meaningful, it needed to move beyond the external representation that acting had primarily been. Over forty years he created an approach that was the forefront of the psychological and emotional aspects of acting. The Stanislavsky System—or "the method," as it has become known—holds that an actor's main responsibility is to be believed (rather than recognized or understood).

To reach this "believable truth," Stanislavsky first employed methods such as "emotional memory." To prepare for a role that involves fear, the actor must remember something frightening and attempt to act the part in the emotional space of that fear he or she once felt. Stanislavsky believed that an actor needs to take his or her own personality onto the stage when playing a character. This was a clear break from previous modes of acting.

To understand acting, you should ask yourself how often have you said your peace, stated your argument, given detailed instructions, or tried to communicate an intensely felt emotion only to find that your audience had not understood what you were communicating? All of us who have communicated to an audience have experienced that sinking moment when we find out that our audience has not understood the most basic point of our communication. What we communicate is frequently not what we want to communicate.

Performing a scene in an acting class is an excellent way to discover communication problems. Our clothes, our posture, our grooming, our state of mind, our self-control, our objectivity, and our environment interact to determine what we are communicating. Knowing our lines, knowing what we want to communicate, is only the first step toward communicating exactly what we want to communicate.

For an actor or actress, the other steps involve getting in touch with his or her feelings, being relaxed, putting on makeup, getting into costume, going on stage, pacing his or her delivery, reading the audience, and physically expressing the appropriate feelings within the context of the play. For other communicators, the other steps involve applying the answers to the pertinent ascertainment questions and constructing a logical communication with reference to the medium of choice.

When Richard Burton performed in his first movie scene with Liz Taylor in *Cleopatra*, he thought she couldn't act because she was so low-key. However, when the film rushes came back from the laboratory that night, he noted that her acting was powerful while his acting was too exaggerated and unnatural. Watching the rushes, he realized that he was accustomed to theatrical acting where he had to project his emotions to the back of the theater, but the film medium magnified everything he did. Underplaying the part, as Liz was doing, was necessary to achieve a natural yet powerful effect on screen.

Translating a communication from one medium to another can drastically alter the message. In her review of the BBC television program *The Jewel in the Crown,* adapted from the novel by Paul Scott, Martha Bayles notes: "The trouble is, the obsessive reconstruction of events which occurs in Mr. Scott's fiction is hard to bring off in the relatively literal medium of film. When we see something happen on film, we assume it really happened that way. Granted, this is a pretty obtuse reaction, but film makers usually have to respect it. There is no real cinematic equivalent to the novelist's device of having characters ruminate in different voices about an event they can neither fathom nor forget."[2]

Not only does the medium affect our message, but our delivery can also make a difference in the way the audience perceives our communication. Even a slight mispronunciation can make the difference between life and death, as in the Old Testament book of Judges where the revengeful Gileadites slaughtered the fugitive Ephraimites because they could not pronounce the password *shibboleth*.[3]

Most professional actors spend many years studying acting by taking classes, studying movies, plays, and television programs, and reading a lot of books.

An actor should read and reread the script, meditate on the character's history and daily activities, and ask:

- Who is my character?
- What does my character want and why?
- What motivates my character?
- What does he think?
- Is he happy?
- What does he do in his spare time?
- What kind of mass media of entertainment does he use?

Acting is doing and reacting. Actors react to what other actors do, using body language as much as dialogue.

In *MOVIEGUIDE®* magazine and in the "So You Want to Be in Pictures?" section of www.movieguide.org are some enlightening reflections by some wonderful actors: John Ratzenberger, Morgan Brittany, Stephen Collins (who plays Reverend Eric Camden on WB TV's hit television series *7th Heaven*), and superstar Jane Russell.

CHAPTER 11

Cut—Postproduction and Beyond

N o matter how well everything went in production, postproduction brings it all together in a way that will not only make sense but also captivate your audience. Postproduction is the key to making a good movie great.

As of the time of this writing, Pixar is the only movie company in history that has hit a home run with every one of their movies: *Toy Story, Toy Story II, A Bug's Life, Monsters Inc.*, and *Finding Nemo*. Each one of their movies has been a blockbuster because they cared enough to strive for excellence. I was asked to screen *Toy Story* a few months before it opened. Then I was asked to screen it again about a month before it opened, and I was surprised to see that significant changes had been made. Finally, I screened it just before it opened, and even more changes had been made in editing, music, and sound. The same thing happened with *Finding Nemo*. Talking with the producers, director, and other key people at Pixar, I found that they wanted excellence and were not satisfied until they achieved it.

Music and Sound

Music and sound effects will make or break a movie or television production. The right music and the right sound can propel a movie into fame and fortune. Sound helps set a mood. With animated movies, sound is even more important in capturing the audience and making them believe.

The postproduction sound mixer figures out what kind of sound effects and/or music can be used to enhance the movie. He often creates those sound effects. He is in charge of making sure the overall sound of the movie is correct, including the dialogue.

Sound effects (EFX) and sweetening are crucial for filling out a production's sound design, setting mood and atmosphere. Good sound effects (SFX for short) not only make a movie a lot more interesting, they help tell the story as well. The sound of footsteps offscreen will set up suspense or foreshadow mood. Great sound and music stir the audience's imagination.

When you use music, be aware of the impact of music and SFX on your movie. Choose your music and sound carefully to reflect the feeling and pace of your shoot.

There are different types of music, such as an original score and licensed songs. A score can come from library music or may be composed specifically for the production.

How important is music? Watch the same scene from a movie with and without sound. It is essential for creating tension, suspense, and many of the other emotional flavors necessary for an effective production.

The Poseidon Adventure was a hit to a large degree because of its great Academy Award-winning music. In *MOVIEGUIDE®* and in the "So You Want to Be in Pictures?" section of www.movieguide.org, the renowned Al Kasha gives an important insight into music and wanting to be in pictures.

Editing

Some of the best directors, such as Alfred Hitchcock, teamed up with great editors throughout their careers. Some of the most talented directors fall short of greatness because they cannot cut out surplusage, which, as they say, vitiates.

The editor takes all the raw film or video and sound that is shot for a movie and shapes it into a finished movie. The editor, working with the director, decides:

- What shots to use
- How to put the shots together
- How long to hold each shot before cutting to the next one

Good editing involves selecting shots and combining them to convey the director's vision. Poor editing makes the movie seem labored and boring.

Before you edit, you will want to spend a great deal of time off line[1] reviewing your production. Plan your cuts precisely so that you will save as much money as possible during online editing. Keep track of all your edit points so that you can go online and make your edits without searching for your edit points.

Avoid mismatched cutting. Watch for continuity and make sure your transitions are so smooth that they are invisible, unless your story demands otherwise.

Add titles, music, audio effects, graphics, film clips, and whatever you need to make your production work. Take your time.

Be free to improve on what you have filmed even if the improvements lead you away from the strict letter of your script. An editor can make or destroy a production. Good editing requires as much creativity as a good script. Good editing potentially alters the structure of the movie. The ending might become the beginning; the beginning could become the end. You might want to add a voice-over narration, write entirely new lines of dialogue to explain unclear plot points, and play scenes in slow motion or fast motion or backward or whatever might seem appropriate. Ironically, the simplest, least complex form of storytelling is generally the way to go, but sometimes an editor will have to use every trick in the book to make the best possible film.

Think in visual terms. Advancing your story through pictures is more important than advancing it through words, although both must be there in harmony to fully tell a story through movies and television.

A movie is like a puzzle with individual scenes, music, sound effects, and perhaps some visual effects. All these elements need to be put together to make a complete movie. The audience often does not notice good editing, but the story moves along quickly with plenty of surprises. When the editing is poor, the movie tends to be boring or confusing. The final cut is the finished movie.

When editors create a scene, they often talk about it as "building" a scene because they are building it by adding layers of picture, natural sound, music, and special effects.

There are different types of edits, which are simply changes, from one shot to another.

- A cut is when you go immediately from one shot to another.
- A fade is when a scene slowly goes black for a moment before another scene comes up.
- A dissolve is where one scene fades in while another is fading out.

Review everything that has been said up to this point to make sure you are on target and have used the medium to its maximum effectiveness.

Pray.

Review

Does your program work? Reedit if necessary.

Distribution/Sales

You are ready to be distributed in movie theaters or to air on network television or other avenues of distribution that you have set up, such as PBS, foreign, and cable. Keep track of where your program is going. Make copies, distribute, and keep records.

Your movie or program may have a long life if you keep on top of it. Every new sale is financing for your next production.

The Life of a Movie

Here is a chart of the life of a theatrical motion picture. Walt Disney established the golden cycle where he rereleased a movie every five years or so to a new generation of children. Most movies, however, will not stand up to rerelease. Furthermore, television movies generally do not have the life span of theatrical films, but yours could be the exception:

THE LIFE OF A MOVIE

YEAR	1	2	3	4	5	6	7	8	9	10	11	12	13	14
Theaters	x													
Pay-per-view Cable	x													
Pay Cable & STV	xx	xx			x									
Network TV		x	x	x										
Independent TV						xx	xx	xx	xx		xx	x		
Home Video			xxxxxxxxxxxxxxxxxx											
Foreign			xxxxxxxxxxxxxxxxxxxxxxxxxxxxxxxxxxxxxxxxxx											

Now that you have gotten this far in your production, you should be aware that the work has not yet even begun. Distribution is so time-consuming, arcane, and convoluted that major movie stars and moguls have given up on it. The success of *The Passion of the Christ* offers great hope, but the behind-the-scenes word is that the distributor and Mel Gibson's company collected much less of the box office receipts than they should have.

For many years people have come to me to discuss distribution, and I have introduced them to some of the best on both sides of the equation: the distributors and the theater companies. One group wanted to distribute a well-made movie with strong Christian values, so I introduced them to one of the biggest theater companies. The person in charge spent an hour talking about all the different ways producers lose money in theaters, from the local theater that hides ticket sales to delayed payment for independents who have no clout. In brief, the theaters need to be monitored continually.

In the beginning, Woody Allen hired a New York accountant (a friend of mine) who hired young men and women to monitor each theater where Woody's movie played so that he could contest the box office receipts if there were any discrepancies. The Christian producer mentioned above tried to do the same thing and was overwhelmed by the extent of the coordination and work involved.

Even if the theater gives a real accounting of the box office, they often delay payments to independent distributors because those distributors have so few movies coming down the pipeline. Without an in-demand movie, the independent has no clout to demand payment backed by the threat that the independent won't give the theater their next big movie if the theater does not pay immediately. Major distributors, on the other hand, get paid and often squeeze the theaters because they do have the clout.

To find out more about the arcane world of theatrical release and distribution, read *Fatal Subtraction* by Pierce O'Donnell and Dennis McDougal about Art Buchwald's 1988 lawsuit against Paramount Pictures. The authors expose the major Hollywood studio's questionable accounting practices that have enabled them to deprive creative talent of millions of dollars in royalties by claiming that top-grossing films earned zero net profits. The book details Hollywood's net-profits clause, allowing a studio to deduct its overall losses from its hits' earnings so that through creative accounting, small-time creators are denied rewards despite a film's massive returns.

The entire process of distribution is tough as nails. A March 3, 2002 *Los Angeles Times* article by Claudia Eller entitled "The Mild-Mannered Superman of Disney" details a battle between Disney and two of the biggest theater chains. In 1989, Disney took on two of the country's most powerful theater chains: United Artists and Cineplex Odeon. To increase Disney's percentage of box office receipts, Disney said that it

> abandoned the customary practice of negotiating "the split" with exhibitors across the country. [Disney] told them they had to bid against each other to show Disney films. UA and Cineplex, feeling squeezed, retaliated. They refused to screen Disney movies in any of their theaters, including those in 20 cities where one or the other had a lock on the market. But [Disney] struck back. In those cities where Disney was shut out, [they] made deals to play the company's new releases in high school auditoriums, community halls, churches, and at Rotary Clubs. "In a couple of towns, we exhibited films on bedsheets," [Disney's representative] said. In Baton Rouge, La., [Disney] rented the civic auditorium for an entire summer. "We never did more business in that city, before

or since." According to [Disney], the battle continued for about a year, until UA and Cineplex relented.

One of the great distributors of all time is Barry Reardon, the former president of distribution of Warner Bros. Most people over the age of thirty will likely remember the thrill and amazement of sitting in the theatre in 1981 and watching *Chariots of Fire,* a beautifully produced, directed, and acted film that clearly showed an admirable protagonist living his life to glorify God through his skills and talents: "When I run, I feel God's pleasure." Had Hollywood really produced such a God-honoring, inspirational movie for secular audiences? And what about the film that followed closely behind it, *The Mission?* Who could forget the opening scene of a missionary strapped to a cross, cascading over a waterfall?

Fans may not realize that these inspiring productions, which opened the door to modern faith-based movies, were almost not released. Believing that their market was too limited, major studios passed on *Chariots,* but the foresight and vision of one distributor, Barry Reardon, rescued it from its demise. Go to www.movieguide.org and read where Barry shares some of his journey in the world of moviemaking and gives insight into a process that involves divine appointments, seizing opportunities, and persistence through challenges.

Follow Up

Check the ratings, promotion, advertising, and any payments and billings that are due. Artists will receive payments every time your program plays. Know when and what you have to pay.

Also you will receive moneys according to the distribution deals that you have set up. Know when and how you are to be paid. Trust God and not man.

Survey the reaction to your production so that you can do better next time.

To produce a movie or a television program, you have to be creative, self-disciplined, organized, unstructured, persistent, flexible, imaginative, and practical. As a rule of thumb, 50 percent of your energy will be expended doing the work of producing your movie; another 50 percent will be expended fighting for your production. If this seems overwhelming to you, trust God, and you will succeed in producing a powerful program telling the story he has given you to tell.

This overview of the techniques and principles that apply to producing a movie is also applicable to your television production no matter what size; however, smaller productions will require less of everything.

If you are embarking on producing a video on your church, review the steps and select those principles and techniques that are relevant to your production. By familiarizing yourself with the most complex form of production, you will excel in simpler productions, including productions in other audiovisual media.

An excellent exercise is to assemble a group from your church and produce a movie in miniature with amateur equipment. If you take care to follow all the appropriate steps, you will be proud of your production. If not, you will know it because of the glaring flaws in your final product. These flaws will help you learn what to do and not do the next time you produce something. Therefore, try it. Have fun and apply yourself to achieving excellence in God's service.

Movers and Shakers

Finally, every movie and television production involves a constellation of talents. Key roles need to be addressed, such as the studio executives, important variations on roles that provide different insights such as an animation or television producer, and the little known but crucial role of the film buyer for the theater company.

Check out www.movieguide.org and *MOVIEGUIDE®* to read some excellent advice from some of these important behind-the-scenes people in the world of entertainment, including major movie studio CEOs such as Dick Cook, chairman of the Disney Studios, and Frank Yablans, former president of Paramount Pictures; TV network owners such as Bud Paxson;

animation studio chairmen such as Phil Roman; major movie studio distributors such as Chuck Viane, president of Disney's Buena Vista Film Distribution Group; major corporate advertising executives such as Rob Hudnut, executive producer for Mattel Toys; television executives such as Peter Engel of *Last Comic Standing, All About Us, One World Malibu, CA, City Guys, USA High, Hang Time,* and *Saved by the Bell* fame; producers such as Brenda Hampton, producer of *7th Heaven*; marketing mavens; script doctors; theater owners; film buyers; and much more.

CHAPTER 12

Further In and Further Up

S o *You Want to Be in Pictures?* is just the beginning. The interesting articles from some of the top people in the entertainment industry on www.movieguide.org will give you profound insights and practical guidance in how to produce a movie, including how to finance and distribute your movie. Therein, some of the most successful people in Hollywood will give you guidance about every stage of movie production and distribution.

God Is Still in Control

Too many moral Americans believe we are facing overwhelming odds and unassailable power.

Paul Klein, former vice president of NBC, said, "Television is the most powerful force in the world today."

Not even close. Television, nuclear power, communism, capitalism, the United States, sin, Satan, man, and all other powers combined pale in importance and potency—fading to shadowy insignificance—when compared to the power of God: "Through him all things were made; without him nothing was made that has been made" (John 1:3 NIV).

Do not despair. God is in control. Trust in him at all times.

The Answer

Jesus, of course, is the answer. He alone can deliver us from sin and death. Only the sword of his Spirit, his written Word, can give us victory over the evil influences of this age.

216

Jesus was the master of communications. His dramatic parable word pictures are as pertinent today as they were two thousand years ago. He understood the power of communications and how ideas shape civilizations. His Word toppled one of the most powerful civilizations in history, the Roman Empire, and continues to transform the world today.

We must care enough for him and for our neighbor to communicate his gospel with power and love throughout the world and to take every thought captive for him. We must learn the principles of powerful communication so that we can communicate the gospel through the mass media of entertainment to reach every man, woman, and child with his truth.

Furthermore, we must redeem the mass media of communications so that the good, the true, and the beautiful—not vain, false, and evil imaginations—are proclaimed through the mass media of entertainment throughout the world.

In obedience to his written Word, Christians need to reclaim the media for Christ by advancing on several fronts:

- We need to raise the consciousness of Christians to impact the industry.
- We need to lobby the television and motion picture companies to observe a code of decency so they can be inclusive, not exclusive, of the Christian audience.
- We need to witness to and disciple those in the mass media.
- We need to produce quality programming and motion pictures.

Help Stop Christophobia

One reason there is so little evangelism and so much ignorance about the biblical worldview is the rampant growth of Christophobia in our society. *Christophobia* is a term coined here to refer to those who have an irrational fear of and hostility toward Jesus Christ and anything Christian.

The symptoms are simple and insidious. Some of the symptoms of this aberrant phobia include:

- An unhealthy fear of using the name of Jesus as anything but a profanity in public

- A dread of discussing biblical principles in public
- A horror that someone, including politicians and government officials, would expose or discuss his or her Christianity in public, much less put Christian principles into action
- An aversion to using biblical standards to make decisions and to determine right and wrong in any given situation
- A perverse fear of the Bible

There are many more symptoms of this dysfunctional condition and many other situations where Christophobia is evident in our society. Christophobia rears its ugly bias all too frequently in our schools, media, and government institutions. For example:

- Christmas is now called winter holidays.
- Easter vacation is avoided by school systems, even if it means skewing school calendars to create unbalanced terms.
- Newspapers, radio stations, and television executives ask Christians to edit out any biblical references, while those who do edit are mocked and humiliated in print and on the public airwaves.
- Courts refuse to consider the biblical point of view.

This destructive phobia has spread throughout our culture to the extent that Christians are often the most Christophobic members of our society. These Christophobic Christians get livid when someone brings up a biblical perspective, apologize when the name of Jesus is used in reverence, complain when Christians stand together, and worry that some Christians may be wearing their Christianity on their sleeves.

Often these fearful Christophobic Christians fret about using biblical standards to determine right and wrong. They are horrified that these standards might be applied to common "problems" such as murder, adultery, lying, sodomy, homosexuality, and the other evils condemned by the Word of God.

If this phobia continues at its current pace, it will become the most debilitating psychological aberration of our age. Christophobia causes many to hide their Christianity, others to deny it, and still others to lash out at Christians. It may even inaugurate a widespread persecution of Christians and a denial of the Christian roots of our society. History will be revised to blame Christians for all the problems in the world, and the immorality condemned by the Bible will be acclaimed as the solution to our problems.

This abnormal psychological condition must be routed out of our national psyche before it is too late. Christians must help others understand the dysfunctional aspects of this disease. We must deliver those who suffer from it by introducing them to Jesus Christ and instructing them in the wholesome benefits of the biblical worldview.

Deliverance

There is a war raging around us, but not the one on the news. Rather, the war is a spiritual war being fought for the heart and soul of each human being. The victory in this war is only to be found in Jesus Christ.

In Christ, protection from powerful negative spirits begins with the awareness of the subtle effect that other individuals, groups, and even the media often exert on us. Following such awareness, we need to recognize that he wants to, and will, deliver us from the demons of our age.

In addition, if we discover compromise in our lives, we need to repent, turn away from it, and seek the Lord with all our hearts. We also need to break off any associations not of God and renounce any ungodly spirits. Then we must avoid any further spiritual oppression by staying in the Word of God daily, walking in the Spirit of God, and using the spiritual armor God has given us through Jesus Christ. Thus we can enjoy the provision Christ has made for us to walk in him and not give way to the evil that surrounds us, for "greater is he that is in you, than he that is in the world" (1 John 4:4 KJV).

Delivered from the judgment they deserve, those who know his salvation cannot keep on sinning, for "no one who continues to sin has either seen him or known him" (1 John 3:6 NIV).

Cast Your Vote

Once we are saved, redeemed, and delivered, we need to exercise discernment in order to know the difference between good and evil. Discernment comes from seeking knowledge of God and understanding of God's Word, the Bible. However, there is more than discernment. As one young caller said to the author on a radio program, "I have discernment; that's why I can see these vile movies." What this individual lacked was the next step after discernment—wisdom, which means choosing the good and rejecting the bad.

This choice at the box office is known as patron sovereignty. Patron sovereignty has traditionally been commended by Hollywood as the right of movie patrons to determine what they want to see, or avoid, by their activity at the box office. In our free society we can again exercise our freedom to influence the motion picture industry to produce moral, uplifting movies. Despite widespread preferences that favor sex, violence, and anti-Christian messages, the producers in Hollywood are ultimately concerned about the bottom line—how much money they can make at the box office. If Christians attend good films and avoid immoral films, our impact will be quickly felt in Hollywood.

The adversary often convinces us that we are powerless, that there is not much we can do except complain, escape, or avoid. The truth is that we have great power. We can change the nature of television and films.

Tools

We publish *MOVIEGUIDE®: A Biblical Guide to Movies and Entertainment* every month. The publication gives you a detailed review of each movie so you can choose the movies to see and those to avoid. Each review provides a biblical perspective, enabling you to decide whether to go based on your biblical worldview.

MOVIEGUIDE® also equips you to confront ungodly communications and take every thought captive for Jesus Christ.

While some Christians choose not to watch any movies, more than two-thirds of born-again, evangelical, and/or charismatic Christians watch what non-Christians watch. And many parents have written us saying they had no idea what their sons and daughters were watching until they subscribed to *MOVIEGUIDE®*. Now they talk about movies with their teenagers and discuss why they should not watch specific movies and videos. Other people thank us for making them aware of things they missed in a movie or video, which helped them be more discerning.

MOVIEGUIDE® is available on the Internet at www.movieguide.org for those who want immediate information on movies and videotapes. It is reprinted in many Christian publications and is broadcast over the USA Radio Network. In addition, the MOVIEGUIDE® television program is broadcast by more than three hundred television stations, networks, and cable/satellite systems throughout the United States and in more than 215 other countries.

Many teenagers have told us they did not notice the evil in many movies until they started reading *MOVIEGUIDE*®. Many say they turned from those films toward the Bible. Others say they gave up movies entirely.

The Media-Wise Family is a book that teaches you how movies, television, and other entertainment media influence your children. It helps you understand the way your children learn and what is appropriate viewing at different age levels. It also gives you skills and tools, fun exercises you can do as a family to evaluate what you view and to help you use discernment in your media choices.

Beverly LaHaye describes it as "practical ways for parents to protect their children from inappropriate entertainment. . . . One of the best resources a parent can own."

"A Godsend to parents," adds Cal Thomas, nationally syndicated columnist.

Dean Jones says, "Required reading for anyone negotiating the mine fields of today's movies and television . . . an encouraging revelation. . . . Four Stars!"

The Media-Wise Family Tool Kit is a two-DVD set of a four-part series teaching media wisdom that will help you understand what effect the media has on your child at different stages of growth and what you can do to help them develop discernment.

Frodo & Harry: Understanding Visual Media and Its Impact on Our Lives, a comparison of *The Lord of the Rings* with *Harry Potter*, contrasts the fictional "real world" in *The Lord of the Rings* with the occult world of *Harry Potter* and gives guidelines on protecting your children against negative influences.

What Can We Watch Tonight? is a comprehensive family guide to acceptable movies released in the last decade, from a Christian worldview.

Good News

Good News Communications, Inc., and the Christian Film & Television Commission™ have undertaken to reestablish the church's presence in Hollywood, and by God's grace, we are making a difference. In fact, we have seen great breakthroughs visible in the movies being released at the box office. Undergirded by the grace of God, the reasons we have had such success in Hollywood are fivefold:

1. We have been able to demonstrate through our extensive research to Hollywood executives that family films and clean mature-audience films do better at the box office.

2. As the audience gets older, which it will continue to do until the year 2009, it will move to more family fare in movies and television programs.

3. Many of the Hollywood executives and talent now have families and want to produce movies and programs their families can watch.

4. Many Hollywood executives and talent are now involved in their own causes and find it difficult to deny the influence of the media with regard to violence and sexual mores when they claim it influences people politically or environmentally.

5. Many Hollywood executives and talent are coming to know Jesus Christ as Lord and Savior and are going or returning to the church.

Some of the signs of success include:

- A major movie studio passed on two anti-Christian movie projects.
- Several television and movie producers have consulted with us on their scripts and, following our advice, rewrote them to appeal to a broader audience.

- A television network and several top Hollywood producers and talent have met to strategize producing more family films.
- Several top executives and producers met with us to learn more about broad audience movies and programs.
- To help encourage more godly movies and television programs, philanthropist Sir John Templeton appointed MOVIEGUIDE® and Christian Film & Television Commission™ to present a cash Epiphany Prize for the "Most Inspiring Movie" and the "Most Inspiring Television Program."
- Doors to the most important offices in Hollywood have been opened, and evidence mounts that a powerful sea change is occurring in the entertainment industry at the very highest levels.

Though pessimistic voices say the golden age of Christianity is over and suggest the Christian faith is being replaced by Islam and other beliefs, Christianity is the world's fastest-growing religion. It is growing faster than the world's population.

The Lausanne Statistics Task Force reports the ratio of non-Christians to Bible-believing Christians now stands 6.8 to 1, the lowest ratio in history. The evangelical movement, worldwide, is growing three times faster than the world's population.[1]

While the mass media of entertainment tries to associate Christians with rednecks and rubes, the Barna Research Group says church attendance increases with education.

What Will Happen?

We will continue to make an impact on the entertainment industry, encouraging production of positive, morally uplifting films and television programs. We will continue to help the heads of the entertainment companies understand the issues involved. And we will help more Christians develop discernment.

Despite those who rail against biblical values, the work of MOVIEGUIDE® and Christian Film & Television Commission™ will have a lasting effect on the mass media of entertainment. It has already caused many of those who fashion the popular culture to shift their perspective and reevaluate their relationships.

The bottom line is that through this proven strategy, the United States truly may become a kinder, gentler nation.

Communicate with Power

Another key to winning the culture wars is to equip Christians to produce successful mass media products. Throughout history the church has used drama to communicate the gospel. We need to reclaim the power of dramatic communications by producing quality television programs, films, and radio programs. To do so we need to learn and apply the principles of powerful communication.

To produce these good movies and television programs, Christians are going to have to take up scriptwriting and learn that craft much better than the hacks in Hollywood. That means not only learning the principles of powerful communication but also refining the craft, paying one's dues, and going the extra mile.

Christians often want to short-circuit the process of learning how to communicate with power by appealing to their friends with money on the basis of shared ideological goals. The result is a mediocre, embarrassing film because the scriptwriter, director, or producer has cut short the refinement process necessary to perfecting a script, or they aim the film at their backers instead of the audience.

Be Approved

The greatest communicators of the gospel of our age have learned the principles of powerful communication. You can do the same if not better. However, it takes work. You must master the principles of powerful communication.

God is more concerned with our character than our accomplishments. He will patiently work on us until we are ready to fulfill the mission he has given us.

The great missionary/explorer David Livingstone left England for Africa at a young age to take the gospel to the Dark Continent and to deliver the people of Africa from the slave trade. He preached every day for years with little success. He suffered malaria attacks more than sixty times and lost the use of one of his arms to a lion while rescuing a black friend. Then he disappeared into the uncharted jungle.

A brash *New York Herald* reporter named Stanley was sent to find Dr. Livingstone. After one year, by the grace of God, he found Livingstone being cared for by the slave traders he had come to destroy. While on his deathbed, Livingstone introduced the reporter to Jesus Christ.

Stanley's articles opened up Africa to the missionaries, and within three years the king of Portugal signed an edict abolishing the slave trade. All Livingstone had set out to do was accomplished, but first he had to become the humble man of character who could serve as a vessel for the pure gospel of Jesus Christ. In a similar manner you must first submit to Christ before you can reach the world with the good news of his salvation.

Are You on God's Side?

In the midst of the worst fighting of the Civil War, Abraham Lincoln was approached by a minister who said, "Mr. President, I hope that the Lord is on your side."

Lincoln replied, "I hope not."

The minister was shocked.

Lincoln explained, "I pray that I am on the Lord's side."

Let us all pray that we are on God's side and that he does his will in and through us to the honor and glory of his holy name.

For more information, call or write:

MOVIEGUIDE®

Christian Film & Television Commission™

P.O. Box 190010

Atlanta, GA 31119

(800) 899-6684

MOVIEGUIDE® exists in five formats:

1. *MOVIEGUIDE®* TV Program—Featured on E.T.C.: Entertainment That Counts on Paxson Communications and many other networks and TV stations, *MOVIEGUIDE®* is broadcast around the world. The program is also broadcast on SKY ANGEL.

2. *MOVIEGUIDE®* Online at www.movieguide.org is available on the Internet.

3. *MOVIEGUIDE®* Radio Program—The program features capsule summaries and critiques of the latest movies and occasionally news and notes. It is available in two- and five-minute versions. The program is produced every two weeks on CD and mailed to participating radio stations first-class and free of charge.

4. *MOVIEGUIDE®* Early Edition for Publishers—Allows other publications to reprint its reviews in exchange for running a *MOVIEGUIDE®* advertisement or by paying a fee based on the size of readership. This version is produced every two weeks and is now available on the Internet. Those who do not have Internet access can still receive a printed version of our publisher's edition.

5. *MOVIEGUIDE®: A Family Guide to Movies and Entertainment*—The magazine is published at least every four weeks. Subscription cost is $40 per year (26 issues) or $100 for three years.

What You Can Do

- Become informed about what is happening in Hollywood and the media by subscribing to *MOVIEGUIDE®* and other publications that give you information from a biblical perspective,

- Spend your entertainment dollars wisely. Every time you buy a movie ticket, it is a vote to the producer to make more of the same. Cast an informed vote.

- Voice your concerns to those responsible. Write to producers, distributors, and sponsors. The only way they will know your objections is if you tell them. (*MOVIEGUIDE®* gives you those names and addresses.)

- Actively participate in boycotts and pickets of companies who act contrary to our biblical beliefs.
- Support with your time, talent, and money the ministries and organizations that are involved in this vital mission field.
- Become a member of the Christian Film & Television Commission™ by sending us your name, address, and e-mail address, so that we can increase our clout in Hollywood and the mass media.
- Sign the Concerned Americans for Moral Entertainment Pledge and send a copy to:

> Concerned Americans for Moral Entertainment
> P.O. Box 190010
> Atlanta, GA 31119
> (800) 899-6684

Epilogue

The one who believes in the Son of God has the testimony in himself. The one who does not believe God has made Him a liar, because he has not believed in the testimony that God has given about His Son. And this is the testimony: God has given us eternal life, and this life is in His Son. The one who has the Son has life. The one who doesn't have the Son of God does not have life.

1 John 5:10–12

Notes

Preface, Stories and Parables

1. Jim Ware, "'The Lord of the Rings'?! Isn't That a Pretty Pagan Book?" *Wireless Age,* October–December 2001.

Chapter 1, There's No Business like Show Business

1. George Barna, Barna Research Group, "Americans Draw Theological Beliefs from Diverse Points of View," *The Barna Update,* 8 October 2002.

2. Ibid.

3. H. Richard Niebuhr, *Christ and Culture* (London: Faber and Faber, 1952).

4. Copyright 1986, The Coalition on Revival, Inc. All rights reserved. The Coalition on Revival, Inc., P. O. Box 1139, Murphys, California 95247.

5. Noam Chomsky, *Language and Responsibility* (New York: Pantheon Books, 1979).

6. Also note that each medium is composed of one or more tools, from pencil and paper, that compose a note, to the sophisticated cameras, recorders, editing machines, satellites, and other hardware and software that are necessary to produce and broadcast a television program.

7. Years later I found out that there was an excellent film at the Protestant exhibit; but at the time of the New York Fair, the existence of that film was hidden from some of the visitors by the solemn atmosphere of the primary room, which was the first room a visitor entered.

8. Including animators, architects, artists, audio engineers, builders, choir, composers, computer programmers, contractor, director, electrical contractor, exhibit designers, engineers, film producers, lighting designers, music producers, photographers, production assistants, sensory effect producers, sound producers, video producers, and writers.

9. The African Methodist Episcopal Church; The African Methodist Episcopal Zion Church; The Christian Church (Disciples of Christ); The Christian Methodist Episcopal Church; The Church of the Brethren; The Church of God, Cleveland, Tennessee; The Church of God, Mountain Assembly; The Cumberland Presbyterian Church; The Episcopal Church; The Greek Orthodox Archdiocese of North and South America; The Lutheran Church in America; Presbyterian Church in the U.S.; The Roman Catholic Church; The United Methodist Church; and The United Presbyterian Church.

10. The solipsist is incapable of knowing anything except him or herself. He or she believes that he or she is all there is and everything else is a part of him or her. This belief is unconscious and intrinsic to the nature of the solipsist as opposed to someone who is consciously self-centered or egocentric. According to the famous child psychologist Piaget, the process of maturing from a child to an adult involves cognitively growing from a solipsistic state of mind to a state of awareness of the reality of the outside world and the other people who inhabit it.

11. I was nominated for an Emmy Award for hosting a program on "War and Peace."

12. In fact, PBS carries a great deal of religious programming, and Christians should use PBS more often. On the other hand, some member stations do not carry religious programming.

13. In telecommunications, radio and television, the gatekeeper is the individual or corporation who controls access to the use of the channel or medium of communication.

Chapter 2, In the Beginning

1. John Donne, *Devotions*.

2. William Wordsworth, "My Heart Leaps Up."

3. David Puttnam, "Chariots Begins at Home," *Hard Cash: How to Finance Independent Feature Films* (Los Angeles: Independent Feature Project, 1982), appendix, 1.

4. Johannes Heinrichs, "Theory of Practical Communication: A Christian Approach," *Journal of the World Association for Christian Communication*, 28 (1981), 6.

5. Pasolini, a well-known Italian film director and committed Communist, did not give an ideological interpretation of the life of Christ in this film but adhered closely to the spirit and the facts of the gospel.

6. Abraham Maslow, *Motivation and Personality* (New York: Harper, 1954).

Chapter 3, Places Please

1. Henrik Ibsen, quoted by Lajos Egri, *The Art of Dramatic Writing*, rev. ed. (New York: Simon & Schuster, 1960), 32.

2. Bernard Haldane, one of the pioneers in career counseling, in his book *Career Satisfaction and Success: A Guide to Job Freedom* (New York: Amacom, 1974), and Richard Bolles in his book *What Color Is Your Parachute?* (Berkeley, Calif.: Ten Speed Press, 1981; reprinted October 2003) have set forth some simple do-it-yourself guides, charts, and other tools to help you discern your motivational talents. I highly recommend these books if you are interested in in-depth career counseling or self-discovery.

3. Richard Bolles, *What Color Is Your Parachute?*, 83.

4. Hal Lancaster, "Hey Fans! It Was Some Kinda Action, a Real Barnburner!" *The Wall Street Journal*, 3 December 1984, 1, 24.

Chapter 4, If It's Not on the Page

1. Kathryn Morton, "The Story-Telling Animal," *The New York Times Book Review*, 23 December 1984, 2.

2. Gary Smalley and John Trent, *The Language of Love* (Pomona, Calif.: Focus on the Family, 1988), 20.

3. Ted Bundy, an infamous serial killer, granted an interview to psychologist James Dobson just before he was executed on January 24, 1989. The Dobson interview was on January 23. It is in a Focus on the Family video called *Fatal Addiction: Ted Bundy's Final Story* by Ted Bundy and Dr. James Dobson.

4. Stewart M. Hoover, "Television and Viewer Attitudes about Work," *The Annenberg School of Communications*, 10 April 1981.

5. Paul Johnson, *Modern Times: The World from the Twenties to the Nineties*, rev. ed. (New York: HarperPerennial, 1992), 130.

6. Gerhard Rempel, *Hitler's Children: The Hitler Youth and the SS* (Chapel Hill and London: The University of North Carolina Press, 1989), 76.

7. Lajos Egri, *The Art of Dramatic Writing* (Carmichael, Calif.: 1972, reprint), 263.

8. Ibid., 6.

9. See Northrop Frye, *Anatomy of Criticism* (New York: Atheneum, 1968). From one point of view, our civilization's stories have gone from mythic to demonic.

10. George Gerbner, "Television as Religion," *Media & Values,* Fall 1981.

11. See Rene Wellek and Austin Warren, *Theory of Literature* (New York: Harcourt, Brace & World, 1956), 226–37.

12. Quoted by Rudolf Flesch in *The Art of Readable Writing* (New York: Harper & Row, 1949), 46.

13. Note, for commercials a rough correlation between number of words in a script and length is: 10 seconds = about 25 words; 30 seconds = about 65 words; 1 minute = about 125 words. Of course, there may be fewer words in the script depending on music, visuals, and action content.

14. This commercial was produced for the Episcopal Church. The actual script is much longer.

15. V.O. indicates an unseen speaker whose voice is heard over the picture.

16. A great introduction to scripting for television is Robert L. Hilliard's book, *Writing for Television and Radio* (New York: Hastings House, Publishers, 1976).

17. Directors Guild of America: The Artists Rights Foundation, *Making Movies: A Guide for Young Filmmakers* (Los Angeles: DGA, 2001), 26.

18. *My Palikari,* starring Telly Savalis and produced by The Center for Television in the Humanities, played on PBS, HBO, SHOWTIME, and The Disney Channel.

19. B.g. is an abbreviation for background.

20. Mario Vargas Llosa, "Is Fiction the Art of Lying?" *The New York Times Book Review,* 7 October 1984, 1, 40.

Chapter 6, Understanding Your Audience

1. James Scott Bell is a writer and novelist in Los Angeles. This article originally ran as an op-ed piece in the *Los Angeles Times* on October 19, 2002. It is reprinted with the permission of the author. His Web site is www.jamesscottbell.com.

2. Ibid.

3. Jim Impoco, "TV's Frisky Family Values," *U.S. News & World Report,* 15 April 1996, 58–62.

4. Ibid.

5. Michael Medved, "Hollywood's 3 Big Lies," *MOVIEGUIDE*® vol. XI, no. 1: 960101, January A, reprinted from *Reader's Digest,* October 1995.

6. Teenage Research Institute, Wheaton, Illinois, as reported in *MOVIEGUIDE*® vol. IX, no. 3 and 4: 940207.

7. See Jean Piaget, *The Origins of Intelligence in Children,* Margaret Cook, translator (New York: W. W. Norton Co., 1963), and David Elkind, *Children and Adolescents: Interpretive Essays on Jean Piaget* (Oxford: Oxford University Press, 1970).

8. Baehr, *supra,* pp. 115–17.

9. Piaget called this the sensorimotor period.

10. Piaget called this the preoperational period.

11. Barbara J. Wilson, Daniel Lynn, and Barbara Randall, "Applying Social Science Research to Film Ratings: A Shift from Offensiveness to Harmful Effects," *Journal of Broadcasting & Electronic Media,* vol. 34, no. 4 (1990): 443–68. Reprinted by permission in *MOVIEGUIDE*® vol. VII, no. 14 and 15: 920724.

12. Ibid., citing C. Hoffner and J. Cantor, "Developmental Differences in Responses to a Television Character's Appearance and Behavior," *Developmental Psychology* (1985) 21:1065–1074.

13. Ibid., citing P. Morison and H. Gardner, "Dragons and Dinosaurs: The Child's Capacity to Differentiate Fantasy from Reality," *Child Development* (1978) 49:642–48.

14. Ibid., citing G. G. Sparks, "Developmental Differences in Children's Reports of Fear Induced by Mass Media," *Child Study Journal* (1986) 16:55–66.

15. Ibid., citing W. A. Collins, "Interpretation and Inference in Children's Television Viewing," in J. Bryant and D. R. Anderson, eds., *Children's Understanding of Television: Research on Attention and Comprehension* (New York: Academic Press, 1983), 125–50.

16. Ibid., citing G. Comstock and H. J. Paik, *Television and Children: A Review of Recent Research* (Report No. XX) (Syracuse, N.Y.: Syracuse University, 1987) (ERIC Document Reproduction Service No XX).

17. Ibid.

18. Ibid., citing A. Bandura, "Influence of Models' Reinforcement Contingencies on the Acquisition of Imitative Responses," *Journal of Personality and Social Psychology* (1965) 1:589–95; A. Bandura, D. Ross, and S. A. Ross, "Vicarious Reinforcement and Imitative Learning," *Journal of Abnormal and Social Psychology* (1963) 67:601–7; M. A. Rosenkrans and W. W. Hartup, "Imitative Influences of Consistent and Inconsistent Response Consequences to a Model on Aggressive Behavior in Children," *Journal of Personality and Social Psychology* (1967) 7:429–34.

19. Ibid., citing A. Bandura, "Influence of Models' Reinforcement Contingencies on the Acquisition of Imitative Responses" (1965) 1:589–95.

20. Ibid., citing Potter and Ware, 1987.

21. Ibid., citing A. Bandura, "Influence of Models' Reinforcement Contingencies on the Acquisition of Imitative Responses" (1965) 1:589–95.

22. Ibid., citing W. A. Collins, "Interpretation and Inference in Children's Television Viewing," 125–50.

23. Ibid., citing C. K. Atkin, "Effects of Realistic TV Violence vs. Fictional Violence on Aggression," *Journalism Quarterly* (1983) 60:615–21; S. Feshbach, "The Role of Fantasy in the Response to Television," *Journal of Social Issues* (1976) 32:71–85.

24. Ibid., citing A. Bandura, *Social Foundations of Thought and Action: A Social Cognitive Theory* (Englewood Cliffs, N.J.: Prentice-Hall, 1986).

25. Ibid., citing L. R. Huesmann, K. Lagerspetz, and L. D. Eron, "Intervening Variables in the TV Violence-Aggression Relation: Evidence from Two Countries," *Developmental Psychology* (1984) 20:746–75.

26. Ibid., citing W. A. Collins, "Interpretation and Inference in Children's Television Viewing," 125–50.

27. Ibid., citing L. Berkowitz, "Some Aspects of Observed Aggression," *Journal of Personality and Social Psychology* (1965) 2:359–69; T. P. Meyer, "Effects of Viewing Justified and Unjustified Real Film Violence on Aggressive Behavior," *Journal of Personality and Social Psychology* (1972) 23:21–29.

28. Ibid., citing M. A. Liss, L. C. Reinhardt, and S. Fredricksen, "TV Heroes: The Impact of Rhetoric and Deeds," *Journal of Applied Developmental Psychology* (1983) 4:175–87.

29. Ibid.

30. Ibid., citing A. Bandura, *Social Foundations of Thought and Action: A Social Cognitive Theory* (Englewood Cliffs, N.J.: Prentice-Hall, 1986).

31. Ibid.

32. Ibid.

33. V. B. Cline, R. G. Croft, and S. Courrier, "Desensitization of Children to Television Violence," *Journal of Personality and Social Psychology* (1973), cited by The UCLA Television Violence Monitoring Report, UCLA Center for Communication Policy, September 1995.

34. William J. Bennett, "Quantifying America's Decline," *The Wall Street Journal,* 15 March 1993.

35. Source cited in *MOVIEGUIDE®* vol. VII, no. 3: 920214.

36. According to a 1994 UCLA Center for Communication Policy/*U.S. News & World Report* survey mailed to sixty-three hundred decision-makers in the entertainment industry, receiving a 13.76 percent response.

37. See chapter 2.

38. Several studies done in this regard are cited in chapter 4.

39. *The New York Guardian,* December 1993.

40. MOVIEGUIDE® vol. VII, no. 10: 920522.

41. John Grisham, "Unnatural Killers," *MOVIEGUIDE®* vol. XI, no. 18: 960826.

42. *MOVIEGUIDE®* vol. XVI, no. 10: 010516 = May B and vol. XVI, no. 11: 010530 = May C. Michael E. O'Keeffe is assistant professor of religious studies at Saint Xavier University in Chicago, Illinois. Dr. O'Keeffe teaches a variety of courses in the area of Catholic studies. He received his doctorate in systematic theology from the University of Notre Dame, where he specialized in Christology, Trinitarian theology, and pneumatology. Kathleen Waller is associate professor of religious studies at Saint Xavier University in Chicago, Illinois. Dr. Waller teaches courses in Christianity and culture, systematic theology, Christian ethics, women's studies, and in the honor's program. A graduate of the University of Chicago Divinity School, Dr. Waller's doctoral dissertation was on the authority of Scripture for Christian theology. Dr. O'Keeffe and Dr. Waller team-teach the popular Religion and Film course at Saint Xavier University that explores several of the

themes examined in this article. They lecture widely on the impact of the mass media on American Christianity and are currently writing a college-level text on religion and film.

43. Paul Tillich, *Christianity and the Encounter of the World Religions* (New York: Columbia University Press, 1963), ch. 1.

44. J. M. Barrie, spoken by Kate in *The Twelve-Pound Look,* 1910.

Chapter 7: The Producers

1. Off-line time is time reviewing the videotape on a less expensive VTR, and any time where you are not on the line of full production with its heavy expense.

Chapter 8: The Art of the Deal

1. 1934 Communications Act.

2. Prior to my presidency thereof.

3. Note that these rules of thumb are very rough guidelines that may vary a great deal from the actual rights and percentage of profits a producer gives up depending on track record, negotiating strength, the nature of the program, time, and the state of the television industry.

Chapter 10: Lights, Camera, Action

1. Gels are transparent, colored sheets that go in front of your lights to adjust color temperature and create mood.

2. Martha Bayles, "A Passage through India," *The Wall Street Journal,* 17 December 1984, 32.

3. Judges 12:5–6.

Chapter 11: Cut

1. See note for chapter 7.

Chapter 12: Further In and Further UP

1. The Lausanne Statistics Task Force of 1989, cited in *Final Warning* by Grant R. Jeffrey (Eugene, Oregon: Harvest House Publishers, 1996), 251–54.

Glossary

Ambient sound: background sounds

Audio: any kind of sound in a film or video

Base light: the existing amount of light in a room

Cast: the actors in a film

Close-up (CU): a very close shot of something, usually a person's face or some other object

Composition: the positioning of people and objects in the frame

Continuity: the art of maintaining consistency from shot to shot and scene to scene, even when scenes are shot out of sequence

Coverage: a shot used by the editor to break up the action

Crew: the technical people working on a movie

Cutaway: an abrupt cut from the scene to something else or to a new scene

Dailies/rushes: the film shot during one day of shooting

Dialogue: a conversation between actors

Dissolve: when the end of one shot fades into the next one

Edit: to assemble a film by cutting and repositioning the shots

Establishing shot: shows the audience a wide shot of the setting

Extreme close-up (XCU): a really close shot

Extreme long shot: taken from a great distance

Eye-level angle shot: shot at eye level

Fade: when the end of a shot darkens into a black screen and then fades up

Final cut: the final edited film

High-angle shot: higher than subject

High contrast: when the tones of color, or black-and-white, are more extreme

Hook: an enticing beginning of a movie that sets the tone

Illumination: the amount and quality of light on a subject

Lamp: a special light used for photography or cinematography

Lighting: the method of illuminating a shot

Long shot: taken from a longer distance, giving slightly more detail than the extreme

Low-angle shot: subject is above the camera

Lyricists: people who write the words (the lyrics) to songs

Medium close-up: a shot of a person from the waist up

Montage: editing many images rapidly together

Narration: the offscreen voice of the observer-commentator

Object: things in a shot that are not people

Pan: moving the camera from side to side

Pickup shot/scene: a shot that is added after the editing phase

Props: objects in a scene that decorate the set or objects that an actor uses (short for *properties*)

Real time: a shot or scene filmed in actual time

Score: adding music to the movie

Sequence: number of scenes taken together

Set: the place, created or preexisting, where a scene is shot

Setup: each time the camera position is changed

SFX/sound effects: sounds created to mimic objects or subjects in a film

Shot: the smallest unit of film taken in one uninterrupted process of the camera

Sound glitch: unwanted sound on the film footage

Storyboard: a shot-by-shot layout drawn before shooting or editing the scene

Subject: a person in a shot

Superimposition: when two images are shown one on top of the other

Tilt: moving the camera up or down

Voice-over: when the invisible narrator speaks

Zoom: moving in on an object from a wider shot to a closer one